ANDOVER to REDBRIDGE

'The Sprat and Winkle Line'

Nigel Bray

ANDOVER to REDBRIDGE

'The Sprat and Winkle Line'

Nigel Bray

©KRB Publications and Nigel Bray, 2004.

KRB Publications
P.O. Box 269
SOUTHAMPTON
SO30 4XR

www.krbpublications.co.uk

All rights reserved.

No part of this publication may be reproduced, stored in a retrieval system, transmitted in any form or by any means, electronic, mechanical or photo-copied, recorded or otherwise, without the consent of the publisher in writing.

Printed by The Cromwell Press

ISBN 0954485947

Front cover: 30287 near Kimbridge in June 1957.
(SC Townroe/Colour Rail)

Title page: 'Hampshire' 3-car DeMU unit No 1103 on an Andover Junction service at Fullerton, 19th April 1963.
(R. Joanes)

Contents

Introduction and Acknowledgements		vii
Chapter 1	From Canal to Railway	1
Chapter 2	A Line on a Shoestring	9
Chapter 3	Wider Horizons	13
Chapter 4	The Southern Railway Era	27
Chapter 5	Late Southern to Early BR	41
Chapter 6	The Dawn of the Diesels	53
Chapter 7	A Hostile Climate	63
Chapter 8	Killed by Whitehall	69
Chapter 9	The Line Described	81
Appendix A	Signalling Diagrams	113
Appendix B	Track and Building Plans	119
Appendix C	Andover Line Traffic	127
Bibliography		136

Stockbridge, July 1964. *(Rod Hoyle)*

The 6.40pm Andover Junction to Romsey local service near Stockbridge on 21st June 1955. Eastleigh based T9s were regular performers on the 'Sprat and Winkle' line right up to the time of the introduction of diesel units. The carriage stock used dates from LSWR days, and comprises three vehicles of what would once have been a four-coach set. This would have changed little over the preceding decades. In the 'six-foot', between the up and down lines, engineers have installed a number of gauging posts, which were provided where 'creep' was suspected. In this way, the position of the running lines could be measured against a known datum, and action taken when necessary to slew the running lines back to their set position.

(E.W. Fry)

INTRODUCTION

My interest in this line arose as a result of my mother's decision to take a part-time job with Heelas (now John Lewis Reading) in 1972. Through her membership of the John Lewis Partnership, our family has been able to stay at its recreational centres including Leckford, Hampshire. My acquaintance with Leckford began long after the railway between Andover and Romsey had closed, and indeed after much of the trackbed had been converted to a footpath forming part of the Test Way. During holidays at Leckford I have come to appreciate how such glorious countryside was once accessible by rail and how both Andover and the Test Valley are the poorer for the loss of the line.

This area of Hampshire has lost an inter-regional, rather than a purely local, railway. In the 1890s the Andover & Redbridge line, by then part of the London & South Western Railway, became part of a north-south trunk route, originally proposed in the 1840s, linking Southampton with the Midlands and North. As such, it was intensively used as a supply route during both World Wars and retained some strategic importance while express freight trains continued to use the former Midland & South Western Junction route from Cheltenham to Andover. Unfortunately, this role was killed off in the late 1950s when British Railways drastically reduced services north of Andover in a spirit of panic-driven cost cutting.

The A&R itself had gained a regular interval diesel service in 1957 which boosted passenger numbers but, without the through freight traffic, its double track was not being used to anything like full capacity north of Romsey. Ironically, this section was closed a few years before Andover's population was set to triple and the port of Southampton was due to expand. Rather than wait a few years for the natural growth of business, BR in 1964 was more interested in wiping out some of its earlier achievements for the sake of getting a little closer to financial viability.

Not only did the closure cause a great deal of hardship locally, but it was a thoroughly bad business decision as well.

Happily, the A&R is still very much alive south of Romsey as part of the Wessex Trains Cardiff–Portsmouth route, continuing a tradition begun by the Great Western and L.S.W. Railways in 1896. It is also part of the main route for freight between Southampton, the West of England and South Wales.

One mystery I have not been able to solve is how the A&R came to be nicknamed the "Sprat & Winkle". This puzzled John Moreton, writing about the line in 1910 and it has baffled my contributors also. Possibly it was a derogatory, if affectionate, term coined in the early years to imply that users should not have any great expectations about train service quality.

In my research I have consulted documents that were cleared out from the BRB Archives at Paddington in the 1980s, notably correspondence from the 1860s. Thanks are due to the staff of the National Archives (formerly the Public Record Office) at Kew; the Hampshire Record Office, Winchester; and to Mr Charles Rudd, keeper of the Clinker Collection at Brunel University.

I am most grateful for the contributions and guidance from Adrian Banfield, Alan Butcher, Haydn Cridland, Larry Crosier, Denis Cullum, Peter Cupper, Doug Stevenson, Dai Evans, Ron Grace, Graham Hatton, Mick Hutson, Roger Joanes, David Lindsell, Roger Merry-Price, Brian Morris, Jack Morris, John Nicholas, Carl Nowell, Peter Noyce, Mike Pain, Norman Pattenden, Kevin Robertson, Tony Sedgwick, Roger Simmonds, Paul Strong, Denis Tillman, Peter Waller and George Woodward.

Nigel Bray.
March 2004.

ANDOVER to REDBRIDGE

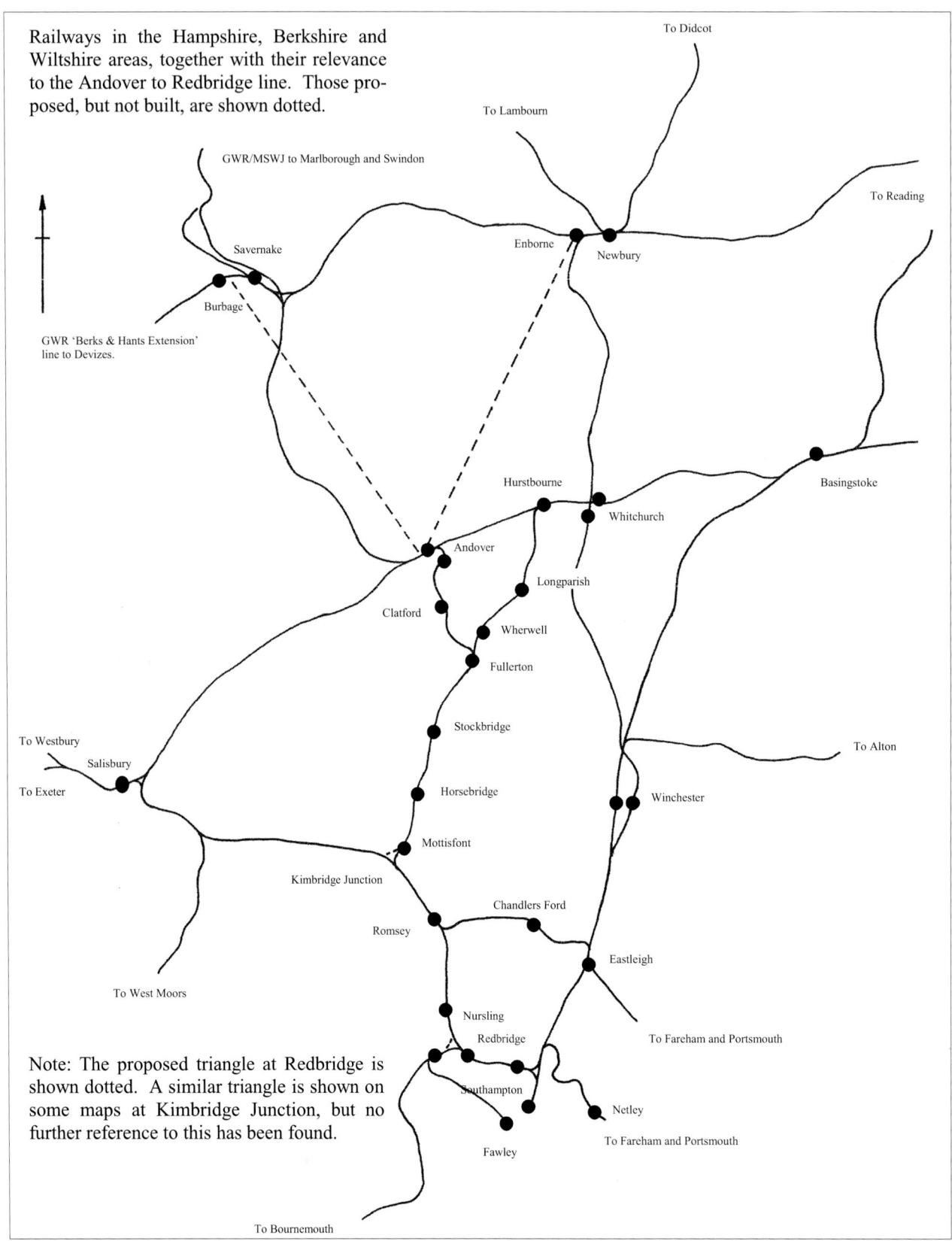

Chapter 1

FROM CANAL TO RAILWAY

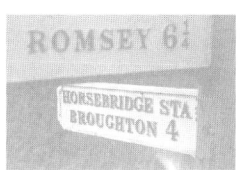

Andover developed as a market town in Saxon times, when its proximity to the royal hunting ground of Harewood Forest placed it within easy reach of Winchester, the capital of Wessex and later of England. Its situation on the River Anton a tributary of the Test, provided a water supply for local industry, although the chalky soil of its catchment area favoured sheep rearing rather than dairy or arable farming. When London became the capital, Andover was still in a good position for substantial growth because it lay on the main road from London to Salisbury and Exeter, the old A30, now in part the B3400 via Whitchurch. Five coaching inns were already established in Andover by the late 18th century, when leading citizens felt that the town needed better north-south communications.

Andover's natural outlet for international trade was through Southampton, 25 miles by road to its south, but the main road via the Test Valley was (and still is) narrow and winding. The Industrial Revolution created rapid population growth at ports such as Southampton and in regions with easier access to raw materials, placing inland market towns at a disadvantage. The industrially developing regions were often in coastal areas able to receive minerals by sea, but several inland conurbations grew rapidly in the 18th and early 19th centuries, partly because they invested in canals. By the 1780s, leading Andoverians were convinced that the town needed a canal to overcome its comparative isolation from heavy industry and world trade.

Following a survey by Robert Whitworth in 1788, the Andover Canal was sanctioned by Act of Parliament in 1789 and had opened by 1796, extending 22 miles from the town centre in Bridge Street to Redbridge on the western outskirts of Southampton. Wharves were provided at Andover, Clatford, Fullerton, Stockbridge, Mottisfont, Timsbury, Romsey and Redbridge. It was built with 24 locks for 65ft by 8ft 6in barges and its main cargoes were farm produce and coal. At Kimbridge, west of Romsey, it linked with the Salisbury & Southampton Canal, authorised by Parliament in 1792 but which never reached Salisbury and ceased trading in 1808 with substantial debts.

By the early 1840s, the pace of canal building had greatly diminished in favour of railways. The Andover Canal was now at a disadvantage because it did not connect directly into any other inland waterway, and it was in a natural corridor for projected railways. In 1845, a proposal was launched for a Manchester & Southampton Railway, with a route from near Cheltenham to Andover similar to that eventually taken by the Midland & South Western Junction Railway; south of Andover it would have followed the Test Valley via Stockbridge and Romsey to Southampton. The M&SR Bill attracted much support in Southampton, where business interests welcomed the proposal for another railway that might compete with London & South Western Railway from London to Southampton and its projected branches. Naturally, the LSWR opposed the Bill, as did the Great Western Railway, whose own territorial ambitions towards the South Coast in the form of the Wilts, Somerset & Weymouth Railway Bill had received the Royal Assent the same year.

The M&SR proposals involved conversion of the Andover Canal into a railway, which would have the virtue of minimising the scale of earthworks, at the cost of some severe curves in the proposed line north of Fullerton. The Andover Canal Sale Bill was passed in 1846 but the M&SR Bill itself aroused opposition from both LSWR and GWR interests, the latter Company regarding the scheme as a direct threat to the expansion of its broad (7ft ¼in) gauge and the Bill was defeated. Another attempt in the 1847 session was rejected because levels surveyed by Robert Stephenson were claimed to be inaccurate.

Meanwhile, the LSWR saw an opportunity to expand its territory by promoting the Andover & Southampton Junction Railway Bill. In this scheme, the Andover Canal would be converted southwards from Rooksbury Mill (between Andover and Upper Clatford) to Redbridge, now served by the Southampton & Dorchester Railway, which had opened on 1st June. At Romsey, the proposed line would cross another newly opened railway, the LSWR's branch from Salisbury to Bishopstoke (later Eastleigh), which had opened for traffic on 27th January 1847.

Although the Bill was passed, the powers to build the Andover & Redbridge Railway lapsed after the collapse of confidence in railway schemes that followed the "Railway Mania" of the mid to late 1840s. The LSWR could not now afford to build more lines in thinly populated areas such as the Test Valley when it was struggling to make ends meet on an existing network, which had developed too rapidly to produce an adequate return on expenditure. Its rival, the Great Western Railway, was facing the same difficulties with its own scheme for lines towards the South. Its Wilts, Somerset & Weymouth Railway, authorised by Parliament in 1845, had opened no further than Westbury by 1848 when further progress was stalled by shortage of capital.

Financial viability, and with it business optimism, had revived sufficiently by the mid 1850s for railway schemes to be energetically promoted again. The opening of the Salisbury & Basingstoke Extension on 3rd July 1854 put Andover on a line to London and, with the existing LSWR lines, meant that no part of the Test Valley was

ANDOVER to REDBRIDGE

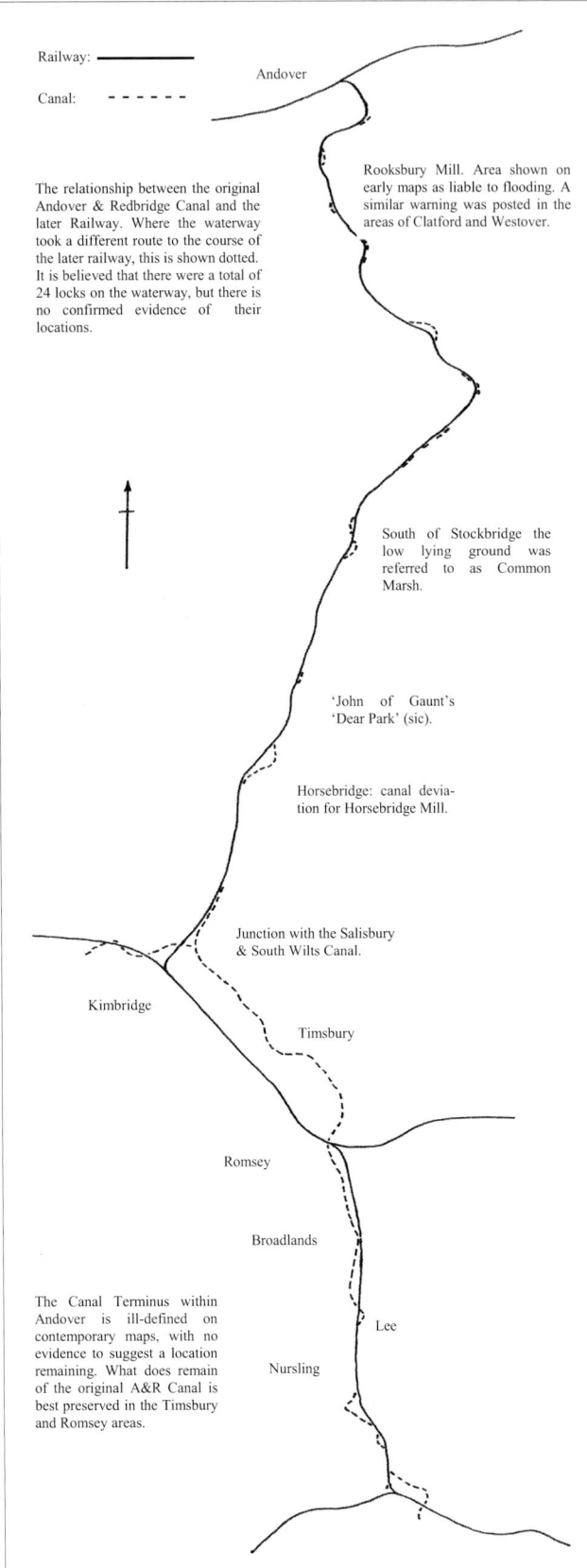

now more than seven miles or so from a railway. The Great Western also reached Salisbury in 1857, where its broad (7ft ¼in) gauge terminus was alongside the standard (4ft 8½in) gauge LSWR branch from Bishopstoke. In the same year, the GWR opened its branch from Holt Junction, on the Chippenham–Westbury line, to Devizes, about 25 miles north-west from Andover. If the Great Western was to strike into LSWR territory and reach Southampton, its best chance lay in promoting a line to Andover, either from the Newbury direction as a branch from its existing Reading–Hungerford line, or as an offshoot from the proposed Berks & Hants Extension Railway from Devizes to Hungerford.

Accordingly a representative selection of the great and the good from both London and local area perceived the idea of a railway through the Test Valley to be worthy of pursuit, and accordingly the inaugural meeting of provisional Directors for the Andover & Redbridge Railway Bill was held at the offices of Messrs Deacon, Stead and Tyler, Solicitors, in Southampton on 28th December 1857 with George Hunt in the Chair. The first entry in the Minute Book was headed "Andover Canal Railway".

Although the A&R was a notionally independent company, the Great Western backed the Bill, which estimated the cost of construction and working capital at £130,000, to be raised in £10 shares. The line would commence at the canal basin in Andover and utilise most of the canal formation as far as a terminus in the parish of Millbrook, "at or near the occupation bridge of the said Canal at the First Lock, near Redbridge". The difficulty facing the GWR was how to get into Southampton itself, where all existing railways were "narrow" (standard) gauge. The Bill therefore proposed a connecting line from the lock into the LSWR Redbridge station, despite the obvious need that would have arisen for the transhipment of goods and passengers between broad and narrow gauge services. The whole line would also have proven to be a broad gauge anomaly, being totally isolated from any other line of similar gauge.

Surprising to recount then that the Andover Canal Railway Bill became law on 12th July 1858, this despite strenuous LSWR opposition. The Great Western also lost little time in supporting bills for further broad gauge lines both into Southampton and north of Andover. The Andover & Redbridge Extension Railway Bill of 1859 proposed an independent route from Redbridge to Southampton, south of the existing LSWR Southampton and Dorchester line, terminating near the Royal Pier; while an extension from Andover to Burbage, near Pewsey, on the Berks & Hants Extension Railway was proposed on 13th August. Interestingly, this junction with the B&HER would face Devizes and so provide for through running between Southampton, Bristol, South Wales and Plymouth.

FROM CANAL TO RAILWAY

Burbage was then an important wharf on the Kennet & Avon Canal, where coal brought by barge from Somerset was currently transferred to carts for a 19-mile journey to Tasker's Waterloo Iron Works. These works had opened in 1815 at Upper Clatford, about a mile south of Andover, on what would later become the route of the A&R. A west-facing junction at Burbage would enable the Great Western to transport the coal directly from the pits served by its Radstock branch, opened on 14th November 1854, by way of Frome, Devizes, the already authorised B&HER, and the projected A&R Extension Railway. Perhaps not surprisingly, William Tasker was among 29 provisional Directors listed in a Prospectus for the scheme.

On 9th August 1858, the A&R Chairman, Ralph Etwall (the fate of George Hunt is not recorded) had reported to his fellow Directors on the success of the Bill. Referring to LSWR opposition, he said the South Western had made "very strenuous efforts to impress upon your Directors the obligation to construct the line on the narrow gauge….but the importance of having complete independence of action induced your Directors to contend for unfettled powers, so as to adopt such gauge or gauges and such policy as (they)…..deem most suitable to your interests". The Act had not specified the gauge of the line, but it was evidently late 1860 before Etwall arranged an inspection of the works with John Fowler, by then the Consulting Engineer, to determine whether the levels and sleepers would be suitable for a broad gauge line.

In the early summer of 1859, the A&R Directors were predicting traffic forecasts on the basis of the goods traffic already handled at Andover's existing station. They claimed that this greatly exceed the total carryings of the canal, which had lost traffic to existing LSWR stations at Andover, Dunbridge, Micheldever, Redbridge and Romsey. Another reason for their optimism was the claim that some of the existing 45 mills and factories along the Canal were already sending and collecting their goods "some miles to and from the Rail by wagons to take the train to Southampton and other places". The Directors even predicted that the Test Valley "would become suburban to Southampton".

On 16th June, the Directors gave three months notice of their intention to close and stop up the Canal, and it was closed on 18th September. Two days later, the first sod for the A&R was cut by the Prime Minister, Lord Palmerston, at Ashfield Bridge, near his country estate of Broadlands, south of Romsey. The Company Minutes record that his positive opinions expressed on the occasion were taken as a good omen for the venture.

But the A&R needed more than moral support because the Company's essential difficulty was that its desire to remain independent of the LSWR committed it to promoting costly extensions at the same time as financing the work authorised by the 1858 Act. This left little margin for contingencies such as engineering difficulties, or problems with contractors on the line under construction. Naturally, the Prospectus for the Extension Railway Bill described works for the A&R being in progress, and claimed "they will be far advanced by the period when Parliamentary sanction for the proposed extension can be obtained". The extensions were said to require no bridges or tunnels, nor to pose any engineering difficulties. Dividends of at least 7% on the capital were predicted, even on a conservative estimate of revenue! Those buying shares in the Extension scheme were promised to become shareholders in the existing A&R project under the title of "The Southampton, Andover and Wiltshire Railway Company" when the Extension Railway Bill became law.

Early in 1860, the Extension Railway Bill received a setback when the Admiralty, although not opposing the Andover–Burbage extension in principle, objected to the proposed four-mile line from Redbridge to Southampton Royal Pier because it might prejudice future development of the docks. A worse blow in 1861 was the insolvency of the A&R Company itself while work on its line was in progress.

This hiatus was to give the South Western its lucky break, although not before the A&R and GWR had jointly promoted a Bill on 19th December 1861 to lease the whole project to the Great Western. The Bill provided for the GWR to acquire up to £50,000 in shares in the A&R Company. More significantly, the Great Western would be empowered to lay additional rails to provide a mixed gauge line.

South Western Counter-Proposals

With the A&R moving towards the adoption of standard, or at least mixed, gauge, the LSWR Board was developing its options, and in August had accepted a report from its Directors that it was now too late for the Company to argue that the A&R should not have been sanctioned by Parliament, or should not now be built largely as authorised. The same report added: "it would be equally unwise for its (the A&R's) proprietors to continue their contentions in favour of extensions, in hostility to this Company. Parliament has decided both these points and both Companies would do well frankly to accept its decisions and make arrangements in the spirit of them."

Aware that the A&R scheme had been widely supported in Southampton as a desirable competitor to its own local monopoly of rail communications, the LSWR Directors were anxious to project themselves as potential saviours of a railway project that had run into difficulties. Company Secretary L. Crombie therefore wrote to the *Hampshire Independent* on 29th August, offering explanations for the South Western's opposition to the 1858 Bill and cooperation, in principle, with completion of the project.

He said the LSWR had opposed the 1858 scheme as unnecessary, unremunerative, and likely to become "the stepping-stone for more extended and competing measures". Parliament had decided otherwise, although at Committee stage in the House of Lords the Chairman had "distinctly intimated" that he hoped arrangements would be made for the line to be made and worked in connection with the London & South Western.

Crombie added that his Directors had "always been willing to do their share towards effecting these objects" but claimed that no formal approach had ever been made by the A&R, despite support from individual members of the latter. On the contrary, the A&R had twice applied to Parliament for extensions "with the avowed intention of introducing a competing system of railways to the district and they have on each occasion failed to satisfy Parliament that there was any public necessity for such a measure".

Asking, rhetorically, why his Company was said by supporters of the (GWR-backed) Extension schemes to be opposing the efforts of Southampton people to bring new railway lines to the town, Crombie leapt to a spirited panegyric of his masters' investment:

> "The answer simply is: because the South Western Company has spent an enormous capital by which Southampton has acquired railway connections with the north, the east, the west and the south-west; because this Company has worked and co-operated with others in working these railways fairly; has directly added to the shipping conveniences of the port, by furnishing and running superior steam-packets of its own; and has…given every encouragement to the great Ship Companies, the Docks and other commercial interests of the port and town. This is not the answer of the South Western Board alone but is the verdict of three successive Committees of Parliament."

He then emphasised that the LSWR would offer "liberal arrangements" with the A&R if the latter would approach it "in a spirit of conciliation and with a view to working it in harmony with this Company's system".

Crombie referred to his Company's desire for "proper connections between (the A&R) and the South Western Lines at Andover and Romsey", adding that "if the new line be executed as at present authorised" (that is, broad gauge)….. "there must be shifting and cartage from one system to the other at both these points". The LSWR was, he said, willing to enter into "proper leasing and working arrangements, by which the fair and efficient working of the Andover & Redbridge undertaking by this Company, in connection with its existing railways shall be properly secured".

He concluded that if these terms were agreed, the line, "as yet not more than half finished, might be completed and at work in little more than a year's time". In another move to win public support in Southampton, the LSWR Directors accepted a request at their meeting on 12th September to provide a station at Millbrook, which opened on 1st November.

Following a correspondence with William Cubitt, now the A&R Chairman, Crombie wrote on 26th September asking permission for Wyndham Portal, an LSWR Director who was also an A&R shareholder, to attend the A&R's half-yearly meeting expressing the readiness of the South Western to "assist in the completion of the line as originally projected, but on the narrow gauge, with proper junctions at Redbridge and Romsey, and to work it afterwards on fair and mutually advantageous terms." He added that his Company was willing to meet a deputation of the A&R Directors to arrange terms, with any differences to be referred to the Board of Trade.

This meeting was convened on 21st October at the Mansion House, the official residence of the Lord Mayor of London. No agreement was reached and, despite an offer by the South Western delegation to consult its Board with a view to getting a mandate for terms more favourable to the A&R, it was later intimated by the Lord Mayor that the A&R had already concluded an arrangement with the Great Western.

Undeterred, Crombie wrote to Cubitt on 3rd January 1862 outlining the South Western's latest offer. It was now promising to provide all the necessary capital required to construct the junctions at Andover, Romsey and Redbridge and also to take up all unallocated shares in the A&R venture. Additionally, the LSWR offered to work the A&R as if it were part of the LSW system, to take out a perpetual lease of the line, and guarantee a dividend of 4% for the first three years on shares already allocated by the A&R Company. This would rise to 4.5% for the fourth and subsequent years. Crombie concluded that these terms would ensure early completion of the line and harmonious working with existing lines in the district (which happened to be LSWR ones), and avoid the expense of "another Parliamentary contest".

Cubitt replied on the same date "I cannot do more than say it shall be brought before our Board on Tuesday (7th January) and an answer sent to you". In the event, the A&R Secretary Augustus Browne replied merely that the Directors had declined to consider Crombie's letter, "having already, as I believe you have for some time been aware, a sealed agreement with the Great Western Company for leasing and working the Andover and Redbridge Line".

Despite this rebuff, the LSWR Directors stuck to their guns. Crombie replied on 11th January that he had not been aware, prior to Browne's letter, that an agreement between the A&R and GWR was absolute fact, adding:

> "I believe I am right in assuming that any such agreement has not been submitted to the shareholders of the Andover and Redbridge Company, and that without their sanction it cannot be considered the act of your Company. The Directors of this Company, therefore, trust that your Board will not fail to bring the offer of this Board under the notice of your proprietors, at the same time that they submit the provisional agreement which appears to have been entered into by your Board and that of the Great Western Company."

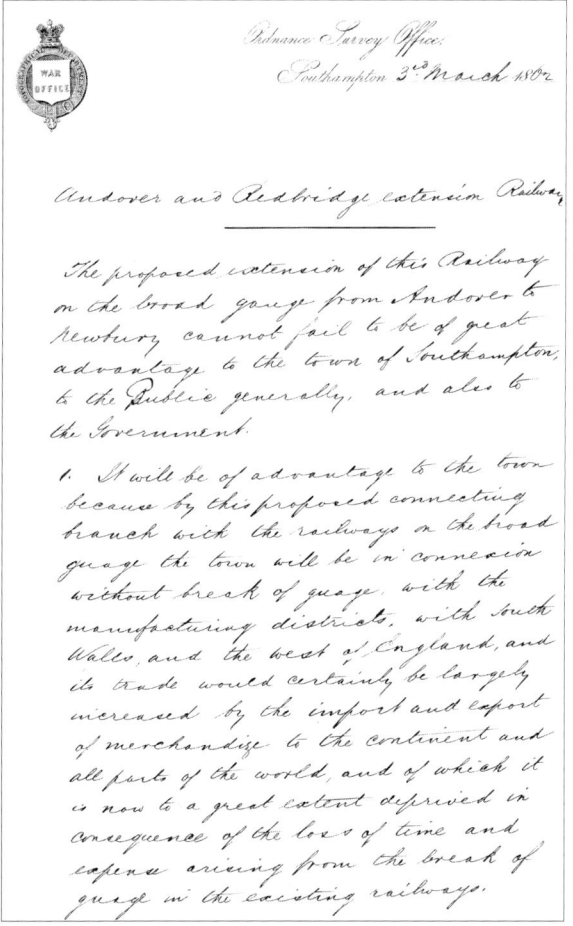

Part of the supporting letter of 3rd March 1862 from the Ordnance Survey Office, referring specifically to the broad gauge. It was signed by Colonel Henry James.

The South Western's persistence was sustained by its realisation that, unless the proposed extensions north from Andover and from Redbridge into Southampton were sanctioned by Parliament, a broad gauge railway would be isolated from both the Great Western system and the port of Southampton, and as such probably doomed to failure. In this context, the local support for a broad gauge line between Southampton and points north is remarkable, and must have been due to deep dissatisfaction with the service provided by the LSWR.

Meanwhile, a new course for a line north of Andover was promoted in the Andover & Great Western Railway Bill of 1862, which proposed a single extension of 15 miles 30 chains from "near Andover" to Enborne, just west of Newbury. The junction here would face London, but through running to the Midlands would be possible via the Reading West curve. Strong support for this came from the Ordnance Survey, based in Southampton and at that time a division of the War Office. Writing to the Town Clerk of Southampton, Colonel Henry James of the OS welcomed the prospect that the Bill offered the port in terms of "direct communication.....without break of gauge with the manufacturing districts", adding that a large increase in its ocean-going trade was a certainty.

Col James also displayed an almost manic enthusiasm for the Great Western scheme in parts of his letter, with repeated use of the phrases "without break of gauge" and "import and export of merchandise....to all parts of the world". He omitted to say that there would still be break of gauge at Redbridge, as the independent route to the Royal Pier had been left out, possibly to secure an easier passage through Parliament. The Board of Trade had already noted that the Bill did not specify the gauge for the A&R but as it was required to join the LSWR at Redbridge, the connection would have to be "narrow" whereas the GWR itself was broad gauge. To get round this dilemma, the GWR and its supporters had promoted an Andover, Redbridge and Southampton Railway Bill in the same Parliamentary session, proposing a 4 mile 12 chains line from "a junction near Redbridge" to near Royal Pier, very similar to that in the 1859 Bill. The BoT remained concerned, however, that in both of the 1862 Bills, the powers to carry out and raise capital for the construction of the lines rested largely with the Great Western rather than the A&R Company itself.

The Admiralty again raised objections to AR&S Bill, arguing that the projected new route into Southampton would cut off access to waterfront land eminently suitable for enlarging the port. Their Lordships noted "there is already a railway from Redbridge to the Custom House at Southampton" and made it clear that their assent to the proposed broad gauge line would be conditional on the Railway Company providing and maintaining a walled public road, at least 100 feet wide and raised three feet above the high-water mark, to give access to the shore. Nor would they tolerate any deviation seaward of the proposed route as shown on the deposited plans.

Determined that the Great Western should not capture a foothold in Southampton, the South Western now set its sights on its rival's heartland by proposing a Bristol & South Western Joint Railway, to run from Buckhorn Weston near Gillingham by way of Wincanton and Shepton Mallet. Parliament enforced a compromise by which both Companies agreed not to promote new lines in each others' territories but instead to afford each other facilities for through traffic, particularly between the Midlands and South Coast. The GWR therefore had to surrender its interest in the A&R, although by a twist of fate it would gain running powers over it 60 years later.

An enabling Act of 29th July 1862 authorised the A&R to raise an additional £20,000 capital and extended the deadline for completion of works to 1st January 1864. That deadline was put back another year by a further Act of 29th June 1863 authorising amalgamation of the A&R with the LSWR and confirming the gauge as 4ft 8½in. The LSWR thereby assumed responsibility for the liabilities of the A&R, including claims from contractors involved in the early phases of construction, but was empowered to extend the line to its own Andover station, and to make deviations to join the Salisbury–Bishopstoke line at Kimbridge, west of Romsey.

Construction Gathers Pace

Applications to tender were sent to Messrs Peto & Betts, Thomas Brassey, George Wythes, Messrs Watson, Rowland Brotherwood, and J.R. Allen. Quotes were then received from J.R. Allen at £51,905, Peto & Betts at £59,629, Watson at £59,964, and Rowland Brotherwood at £60,004 although this was later amended to £56,379. The actual work was carried out by a succession of organisations including George Furness, Richard Hattersley, Henry Jackson and Company, Rowland Brotherwood, and the LSWR. The areas of responsibility of each are not reported, nor are the identities of the inevitable array of sub-contractors and suppliers that would have been involved. The Engineer to the scheme had initially been John S. Burke, but he was replaced by John Collister from 1861 onwards.

Andover was now assured of a railway to Southampton, although the defeat of the GWR schemes delayed the creation of a north-south route via Andover to the Midlands until the Swindon, Marlborough & Andover Railway opened in 1883.

Construction involved draining the canal bed and filling it with chalk from the downs on the eastern side of the route. The series of excavated chalk pits became one of the salient features of the line, and have been described as "the tombstones of the Andover Canal, standing white, high and prominent amidst their background of lush green grass and woodland, alongside the railway from Fullerton to Mottisfont". Of about 20½ miles of new line built, 14½ were on the old canal bed.

Chalk extraction at Mottisfont also provided the impetus for the Mottisfont Paint, Colour, Putty & Whiting Company founded by William Prince of Romsey.

South of Bridge Street, Andover, where there had been canal wharves, to Mottisfont, the railway was for the most part originally laid on the old canal formation, but a number of deviations were made. These included a stretch of about half a mile in the parish of Wherwell, between Clatford and Fullerton Bridge stations. Here the railway took a shorter course at this point, through a cutting on the west side of a small copse, to avoid the flood plain of the River Anton and the canal which ran east of the copse. The 1858 Act provided for this unused portion of canal to revert to Sir William Heathcote, Bt. of Hursley Park who claimed to be the original owner of the land.

South of Stockbridge, construction was slower because of the difficult terrain. For the first mile and a half below the town, the line crossed the waterlogged Common Marsh. At Horsebridge, the railway took a much straighter course west of the canal, which had looped to the east of Horsebridge Mill before converging just south of Horsebridge Farm. This placed the station slightly further from Kings Somborne, the largest village in its catchment area, but avoided creating a reverse curve. Between Horsebridge and Mottisfont the railway made numerous crossings of the River Test, which there divides into several channels in an area prone to flooding.

At Stonymarsh, just north of Mottisfont, the line struck in a south-westerly direction to join the LSWR Bishopstoke & Salisbury line at Kimbridge Junction whereas the canal veered south-east and did not meet any railway again before Romsey. Just south of Mottisfont station, the line crossed the derelict Salisbury & Southampton Canal.

The junction at Kimbridge was only half a mile from Mottisfont station, but for the next three miles to Romsey, trains would use existing LSWR metals. The Andover Canal passed under Romsey station and the A&R diverged from the Bishopstoke (Eastleigh) line shortly afterwards, keeping slightly east of the canal for about two miles until Lee, north of Nursling. This latter deviation was the result of a clever manoeuvre by Lord Palmerston, who had arranged for the Romsey–Southampton turnpike road (the present A27) to be diverted alongside the canal away from his estate, increasing his privacy but conveniently providing a better railway alignment into the bargain! South of Nursling, most of the canal formation was converted as far as its first lock near the Anchor Hotel at Redbridge. This enabled a junction with the Southampton & Dorchester line to be made west of Redbridge station but east of the River Test.

By converting the canal, the A&R had avoided building any tunnels or major viaducts, and had reduced the number of river bridges that might otherwise have been necessary. Crossing the marshy ground south of Stockbridge would have added greatly to the expense of construction, if the canal bed had not been used. Use of the canal wharf in Andover to site the Town station committed the LSWR to a steeply graded route to its existing station, ¾ mile away at a significantly higher altitude.

The 1863 Act had extended the deadline for completion of works to 1st January 1865 but the line was still far from complete on 12th August 1864, when the *Andover Advertiser* remarked:

> "Month after month goes on and there are at times vague reports floating about that in a few months the line will be opened. Then it is reported that eight miles of the line have been condemned by the Government Inspector and will have to be taken up again, the opening day being postponed 'a few months'."

The editorial went on to say that had the canal bed not "offered an opportunity for making a cheap line, the Andover & Redbridge Company would probably never have started". It claimed that the delay might be a ploy to persuade shareholders to sell their holdings back to the LSWR. It also claimed that the A&R might already be open if it had remained an independent Company and "kept quiet" about its potential to carry merchandise from the industrial North. The latter assertion is hardly credible because the A&R, as authorised in 1858, was useless as a through route without the support of one or other larger companies to provide extensions to link it with their own systems.

The contractors must have made rapid progress that autumn, because in early December, the *Advertiser* was able to report there was now "a clear way from Redbridge nearly up to (the existing station at) Andover and the works near the latter are being pushed forward with greater earnestness than ever before....men are working night and day to complete the connection to the Exeter line" (the LSWR having reached Exeter via Salisbury and Yeovil Junction in 1860). It added that the signal posts were "ready for fixing and the stations nearly all complete", noting that the one at Stockbridge was the most behind, yet, "very conveniently arranged

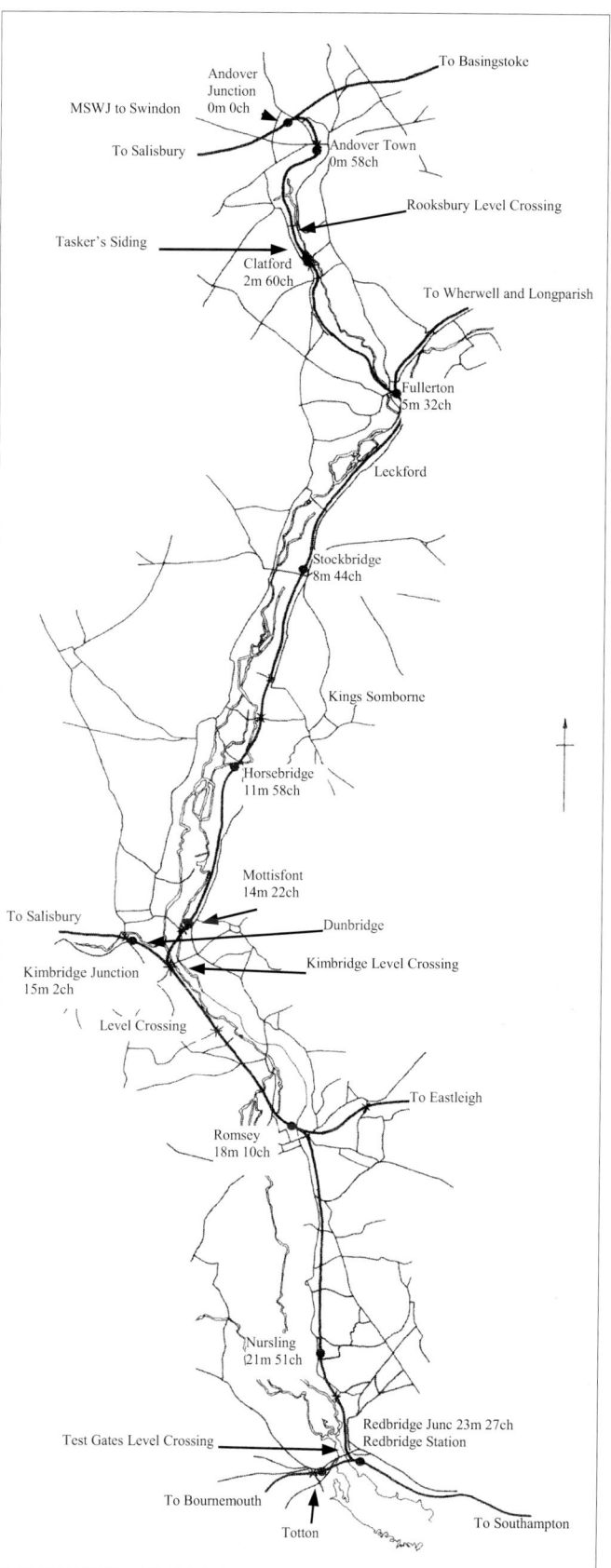

for passengers, goods and racehorses, in which there will be considerable traffic".

On 19th December, according to the *Advertiser*, "a large South Western engine…weighing 38 tons" arrived at Stockbridge with an army of 50 men "and will put the rails and bridges to their trials….it is the heaviest and most powerful we have had yet". This was probably a 2-2-2 Single of the Etna class, built between 1850 and 1853. Reference was also made to a dispute with a subcontractor that had held up the delivery of some iron components (possibly lintels for the road overbridge or columns for the station canopy). "There is yet much to be done", said the *Advertiser*, which considered that "the haste shown by the contractors as the time draws near" was to make up for wasting summer daylight.

Its Andover reporter noted "for some months work has been going on night as well as day and even on Sunday (18th December)", when a large iron girder bridge across Charlton Road, south of the existing LSWR station, had been laid. The reporter added "the telegraph posts and all the apparatus had arrived at the Wharf station and with them upwards of 50 men" and expressed pleasure that the work was "so near completion" when it had appeared a week or so earlier that it might be stopped by frost. The South Western was taking no chances however, and was reported on 30th December as having given its contractors "about 12 days grace" to complete the work, the local press claiming that 12th January was "the day now named for starting the first train". Before this could happen, the LSWR had to notify the Board of Trade to request an official inspection.

As originally built, the line was single track, consisting of single-headed flat-bottomed rail, weighing 65lbs per linear yard, in lengths of about 24 feet. Ballast was entirely gravel on some stretches, but between Andover and Kimbridge Junction it consisted of a foot thickness of gravel resting on nine inches of hard chalk. A major limitation of using the canal bed for the greater part of the route was that doubling the track at a later date would require further land acquisition, except on the stretches such as Mottisfont–Kimbridge Junction and Romsey–Redbridge, or between the two Andover stations. Some of the 15 overbridges and 3 underbridges crossing roads had been built for a single line only.

Stockbridge High Street looking east, probably in late Victorian times. The incline that carried the road over the railway by means of a bridge can be seen in the distance, while the wide thoroughfare with its varied architecture is still recognisable over a century later. It was at Stockbridge that the Prince of Wales, later King Edward VII, would join his mistress, the actress Lillie Langtry, and would also enjoy horse racing at the nearby course until this ceased at the end of 1898.

(Commercial postcard)

Chapter 2

A LINE ON A SHOESTRING

When Colonel Yolland inspected the line on 31st January 1865, he was conveyed from Andover Junction (the name now applied to the LSWR station already open) to Redbridge in a two-coach train hauled by two locomotives. The *Andover Advertiser* reported that the journey to Stockbridge passed off without difficulty and that the party, probably including LSWR officials, then detrained for "a hasty dinner" at the Grosvenor Arms Hotel. "Although the day was wet and cold, the natives turned out in large numbers to view the engines and welcome the Directors." Referring to the actual inspection, the newspaper assured readers that "some trifling alterations are ordered which will take only a few days to complete".

This was classic British understatement. When the Colonel reported on his inspection of the new line on 2nd February, he expressed grave reservations about its readiness for traffic. He noted that the workmanship on an underbridge "might have been better", and that several of the river bridges required additional joists to support the rails. He asked for an additional platform at Andover Town, Fullerton and Horsebridge stations, because these were crossing places, adding that the platform at Fullerton was too narrow where the signal box stood on it. One or two platforms (unspecified) were said to lack ramps.

However, the most glaring deficiencies concerned the state of the track between the two Andover stations, and inoperative signals:

> "The line between Andover Junction and Andover Town station is unfinished and not in good order. Gravel ballast is required for the whole of this distance…and as the Basingstoke and Salisbury branch is mostly a single line, it is desirable that the double junction at Andover should be lengthened on the eastern side."

> "The signals and distant signals at several of the stations and junctions were not in working order, and at some the distant signals could not be seen for intervening trees. In several cases the facing points at the ends of the loops or passing places were weighted to stand open for the wrong road."

Col. Yolland also considered that the sleepers, placed at intervals of three feet, were too far apart for the class of rail, identical to that used on the London, Chatham & Dover Railway between Strood and Beckenham, on which the sleepers were at 2ft 6in intervals. He would insist on additional sleepers with spikes unless the LSWR were prepared to use engines of no more than 20 tons weight.

Anticipating that special trains might be run for Stockbridge races, he asked the LSWR to give an undertaking that it would not terminate any trains at Stockbridge until a turntable had been installed there and was in working order. Finally, he asked for clocks to be provided at all stations, visible from the platforms, and in the junction signal boxes.

His report concluded that he had not received any undertaking as to the mode in which the LSWR proposed to work the line, that is, time interval, staff and ticket, electric telegraph, "I have now therefore to report that by manner of the incompleteness of the works the opening of the Andover and Redbridge Railway for traffic cannot be sanctioned without danger to the public using the line."

The effect on the LSWR was electric because the Colonel passed the line fit for traffic when he made his second inspection on 27th February.

An LSWR internal notice advised of the imminent opening of the line and detailed the instructions for working it. The existing Andover station would henceforth be known as Andover Junction, although the physical link with the Salisbury & Basingstoke line was merely a connection from the down main line to a new bay, an arrangement that would make through running difficult, if not impossible:

> "There is no junction at Andover Junction station; the trains on the New Line all starting from and arriving upon a siding behind the Down Main Line platform. The points leading from the New Line on to the Main Down Line must be kept locked to prevent anything getting upon the Main Line without the signalman's permission."

The need for careful driving over the section from Andover Junction to Andover Town, which had a falling gradient of 1 in 78, was emphasised in one of the first paragraphs:

> "Trains must go down that incline cautiously and slowly, with steam shut off, as there is a public level crossing at the foot of the incline, just before Andover Town station. Gates will as a rule be kept closed across the railway, unless opened for a train to pass."

ANDOVER to REDBRIDGE

The line as opened was single throughout, apart from junction loops at Kimbridge, Romsey and Redbridge Junctions. The three miles of double track between Kimbridge Junction and Romsey already existed as part of the Salisbury & Bishopstoke branch. All the stations on the A&R itself had crossing loops with the exception of Clatford and Mottisfont, the latter being only 60 chains north of Kimbridge Junction. The longest single-track sections were Andover Town to Fullerton Bridge (four and a half miles) and Romsey Junction to Redbridge Junction (over five miles).

In the opening timetable, the only booked crossing of trains on the A&R proper was at Fullerton Bridge, most trains being timed to meet at Romsey or Redbridge stations. In the event of abnormal working, "Mr. Worsley, who will be stationed at Stockbridge, will be the sole party entrusted with the duty of changing meeting places."

Drivers were instructed to slow down for curves of 15 chains radius, of which there were several between Andover Town and Fullerton Bridge, and also for the sharp curve at Andover Junction. Level crossings were a major feature of the line from the beginning:

> "There are numerous occupation crossings along the line, chiefly used for the passage of sheep and cattle. There are two public level crossings, one close to Andover Town, the other near to Redbridge Junction; also level crossings close to Clatford and Mottisfont; and one about ¾ mile south of Andover Town…and these crossings must be approached cautiously."

Several of these crossings would become a major source of frustration to road and farm users in the 20th Century, when three would experience accidents, fortunately without loss of human life.

Signalling on the Line

The line was provided with semaphore signals, all with the arms on the left side of the posts, (this reference to the obvious was specifically included) as at stations and approaches to junctions. Andover Town and Stockbridge had pairs of distant signals on both their approaches, Fullerton Bridge had two from the Andover direction, while Clatford and Horsebridge had two each from the direction of Redbridge only.

At Kimbridge, Romsey and Redbridge Junctions, main line trains would always have preference over those on the A&R. If trains were approaching from both routes, the signalman had to keep all his signals at danger until he became aware that one of the trains had come to a stand. The normal position for all stop and distant signals at all three junctions was 'On', except when a train was due to pass. An A&R train held at any of these junctions was required to draw forward so as to be within the protection of the distant signal but clear of the junction points.

The special instruction for Kimbridge Junction required the level-crossing keeper to go to the loop points in good time for an approaching train from Andover so that he could set them for that train to run onto the up Salisbury line. Before leaving his gates he had to lock them across the road, although the Signalman was allowed to exercise discretion to open them in cases of urgent necessity, provided that he maintained all signals at danger.

Down trains approaching Romsey Junction from Redbridge had to pass loop points provided with an indicator before reaching the junction. The Romsey Junction pointsman had to set the points so that trains heading for Andover would run onto the down Salisbury line.

A&R trains approaching Kimbridge and Romsey Junctions were required to sound two long whistles. No discs were to be displayed on the locomotive during daylight, but two head lamps showing white lights had to be displayed during darkness. Salisbury line trains were required to give one long whistle when approaching these junctions and to display two white discs by day and two headlamps (one with a white light, the other with green) at night.

The safe and efficient working of Redbridge Junction depended on gong and disc communication with Test Bridge level-crossing box just to its north on the A&R. This was because the gateman here worked the points (by levers inside his box) for the junction loop on which a train from the Andover direction would stand before it could be accepted onto the main line. The normal position for all signals worked by the Test Bridge gateman and the Redbridge Junction pointsman was at danger, the discs displaying red. The level crossing would normally be closed across the railway.

Before a down A&R train could leave Redbridge station, the Junction pointsman would sound his gong once and the Test Bridge gateman had to acknowledge this by one sound of his own gong. The gateman would then close his gates to road traffic and, when satisfied that it was safe for the train to proceed, would set the disc in Redbridge Junction box to Off. The pointsman would then authorise the train to pass over the Junction.

When the gateman saw, or heard, an up train approaching the level crossing, he first had to close the gates across the road, and then sound his gong twice. The Junction pointsman would acknowledge this in the same way. If it was safe to admit this train into Redbridge station, the pointsman would clear the lower arm on the Test

A LINE ON A SHOESTRING

Bridge signal post, an action which also turned the gateman's disc to the Off position. The gateman would then clear his own signals to permit the train from Romsey to pass over the junction.

The Line Opens

When the opening date of 6th March was confirmed, the *Andover Advertiser* predicted that "the opening ..... cannot fail to increase the magnitude of Stockbridge races", which it suggested would span a whole week and soon come to rival Newmarket in importance. It was less convinced about the financial prospects for the line itself, bearing in mind the sparse service to be provided and the abandonment of proposed extensions to the GWR and B&HER. "Whether the branch in its present state will ever pay its way is doubtful.....(but) there is every reason to believe a vigorous prosecution of some extension will be attempted."

Prior to the first public trains, a special train conveying Archibald Scott, General Manager of the LSWR, and other railway officials ran from Andover Junction on Saturday 4th March, calling at all six new stations to deliver furniture. On opening day, the weather and the gradient from Andover Town to Junction proved very taxing for the first train, the 6.30am Mixed Passenger and Goods from Southampton Docks, due in Andover Junction at 8.36:

"The morning was damp and the rails consequently greasy, so that in ascending the hill to the Junction, the train twice came to a standstill. It was said that the Driver had no sandbox."

Rail adhesion problems are clearly nothing new!

The *Andover Advertiser* reported that several passengers with luggage transferred from the first down train from Waterloo into the first up service over the A&R, the 9.25 from Andover Junction to Southampton, but that staff at the Junction seemed to regard the new line as a non-event. By contrast, many people lined the route to the Town station, where hundreds assembled, many of them boarding. The intermediate stations were "all more or less attended by a crowd of sightseers, while at every farmhouse and cottage a number of eager faces might be seen".

Two areas of concern were raised by the *Advertiser*. It considered that attention was needed to the management of level crossings, claiming that one gatekeeper had kept road users waiting while he went shopping, and that public roads had been "virtually closed, our informant stating Mr. Scott's orders to keep the line clear at all times". The newspaper argued that railways had no right to obstruct public highways!

Its other contention concerned the deficiencies of the timetable, which it claimed did not cater for visitors to Andover market "as the first available train arrives after 1pm". The newspaper also criticised the lack of a return train to Andover on Sundays, the one service being a round trip from Southampton in the morning and back from Andover at lunchtime.

The inaugural timetable did provide a 9.45am Southampton–Romsey on Tuesdays only (Romsey mar-

Test Bridge level crossing signal box, seen from the south, probably circa 1895. The structure here is of Signalling Record Society classification '1A' and is of similar type to the signal boxes provided at Stockbridge, Horsebridge, and Mottisfont. It is possible that these structures dated from the time of opening, but this is doubtful and 1871 (at the earliest) is more likely. The box closed on 18th November 1930 when a new road flyover was provided.

(BRB Central Photographic Unit)

ket day). Within a month this was extended to Andover, reaching the Town station at 11.26 and Junction at 11.31. A further revision amended the new train to run six days a week, but another was withdrawn to keep the basic service at four trains each way.

Romsey had thus gained a second route to Southampton but all Salisbury–Southampton services continued to run via Chandlers Ford and Bishopstoke because the A&R itself was single track.

By January 1866, the first down train was starting 40 minutes later (7.15am Southampton) as a passenger service, crossing at Horsebridge with a much earlier first up train (6.40 Andover Junction), which was Mixed and allowed 2hr 36min for the journey, about double the schedule of the fastest passenger train over the line.

The South Western soon came to the conclusion that not much money was to be made from the A&R and, in September, reduced the service to three trains each way, with none on Sundays. The first up, as well as the first down, trains of the day were now both Mixed, but taking (only!) two hours to complete the 28-mile journey between Southampton Terminus and Andover Junction.

This meagre service was still on offer at the beginning of 1871, except that the Mixed trains had been superseded by a Goods train starting from Southampton Docks at 9.30am and reaching Andover Junction at noon, whence it returned at 12.45, five minutes behind the 12.40 Andover Junction passenger train, which drew steadily further ahead as the up Goods shunted the yards at all stations. The first down passenger train was now 10.28 from Southampton Docks, which reached Andover Junction at 11.49, the down Goods being shunted at Town for it to overtake.

Nearly four years later, in December 1874, the basic service remained at three passenger trains each way, but supplemented by a Mixed Train departing Southampton at 9.55am, 10 minutes after the first down passenger. The Mixed train had long dwell times at stations, including 25 minutes at Romsey although not for crossing other trains. A footnote in the working timetable advised that "the 10.15am Goods train from Southampton will convey passengers between Romsey and Andover". There were no Mixed trains from Andover, the up Goods now departing the Junction at 1pm, with allowances of five to eight minutes at stations (ten at Andover Town) to reach Southampton Docks nearly three hours later. A light engine was booked to leave Andover Junction at 4.15pm to collect wagons from the Town, whence it returned at 4.30. Andover could now be reached by 11am, while the final departure from Southampton at 7.55pm was more convenient for long distance travellers. These enhancements suggest a growing local economy, and perhaps that the LSWR was beginning to understand the business needs of Andover and the Test Valley.

There is anecdotal evidence that passenger comfort was compromised by the economies made in constructing the line, particularly the sharp curves resulting from use of the canal formation. Writing almost 45 years after the line opened, John Moreton recalled many journeys over it in its early years "when a journey on this railway by anything in the nature of a fast train was fraught with considerable excitement and not a small amount of danger….and sticking to one's seat was a matter of considerable difficulty and the luggage placed on the racks frequently provided a minute bombardment to those seated beneath".

Unconnected with the course of the line and its effect on the traveller was a derailment that occurred on 25th January 1878, which also had nothing to do with skimped construction of the line, but a great deal to do with LSWR carriage maintenance. The 2.35pm Southampton Docks–Andover Junction, consisting of a tender loco, two third, one second and one first class coach, brake van and cattle truck had just passed Kimbridge Junction at no more than 10mph, a speed which the crew later described as usual on account of the sharp curve (15½ chains radius) as the A&R diverged. The train passed through the junction loop onto the single line and was crossing an underbridge when the axle of the leading (third class) vehicle broke, causing it, and the other third class coach, to derail.

Thanks to careful driving, damage to the train and permanent way was slight, being confined instead to the leading carriage, the loop point rodding, and timbers of the underbridge. Two passengers complained on arrival at Mottisfont station of being shaken but otherwise there were no casualties. Driver James Turton, on seeing the front coach jerking, had whistled to the Guard to apply the brake while he applied his own brake and put the engine into reverse. Guard William Laker found the broken axle in the four foot and Driver Turton noticed a flaw extending around the circumference for a depth of about an inch. He told the inquiry that the flaw was just inside the back of the left-hand wheel, and could not easily have been detected without removing that wheel. These technical comments were copied almost verbatim in the Report by Major Marindin of the Board of Trade.

Major Marindin noted that the axle had been manufactured in 1863, and fitted to the carriage in August 1877. He added that there was no record kept of the number of miles the vehicle had run, despite regular reminders by Inspecting Officers to railway companies. The difficulty of detecting the flaw because of its location pointed "to the inadvisability of…fitting an old axle from stock to any carriage, as the flaw must have developed long before August 1877".

Chapter 3

WIDER HORIZONS

Twenty years after its difficult birth, the A&R was well on the way to becoming an important north-south route as the Manchester & Southampton scheme of 1845 had envisaged. The transformation came about because two connecting railways were opened locally; the Swindon, Marlborough & Andover in 1883 and the South Western's own Longparish branch, formerly known as 'Northern and Southern Junction Railway', in 1885.

The latter was planned and built by the LSWR as a double track route, this despite traversing the sparsely populated upper Test Valley. It was intended to thwart the fledgling Didcot, Newbury & Southampton Railway Company's (DNS) north-south line; they had recently altered their intentions by promoting an independent route to Southampton instead of sharing the LSWR main line from near Micheldever. By building what was the 'Northern and Southern Junction Railway' (the grandiose title for a six mile line from Hurstbourne to Fullerton) and offering the DNS running powers from Whitchurch west as far as Hurstbourne and thence over the new line and the section of the A&R south from Fullerton to Southampton, the LSWR hoped to curtail the ambitions of the DNS. Somewhat obstinately as it transpired, the DNS refused to cooperate, and instead continued their thrust for Southampton although, in the event, the monies ran out at Winchester where a terminus existed from 1885 to 1891. There never was any connection between the DNS and LSWR at Whitchurch and, in consequence, the LSWR was left with what was in effect an irrelevant double-track railway serving one of the most sparsely populated areas of Hampshire. It was understandably destined to become an early casualty to closure.

Publicly at least, the LSWR put on a brave face, the Hurstbourne–Fullerton line referred to in the local press as "intended to expedite the journey time between London and Bournemouth" although to avoid a reversal at Redbridge, a west facing curve would have been necessary.

More important than the line from Hurstbourne, as

Nineteenth century views of the A&R route, particularly before doubling appear to be conspicuous by their absence. This view of Horsebridge, which was probably taken around 1900 (judging from the ballast over the sleepers), is one of the earliest known. *(Lens of Sutton collection)*

it transpired, was the Swindon, Marlborough & Andover Company's line, which arrived at Andover from the north-west in 1883. This particular concern (later to become part of the Midland & South Western Junction Railway) had been authorised as far back as 1873, but the scheme had lain moribund due to lack of finance for some years. With the SM&A eventually able to proceed, that company entered into an agreement in 1882 with the LSWR over a number of issues that would effect the Andover Redbridge line and which committed the South Western to upgrading the A&R to double track, together with some realignments to flatten out sharp curves inherited from the old canal formation. These improvements were legislated by the LSWR (Various Powers) Act of the same year. Running Powers Agreements between the SM&A and the LSWR via the A&R were signed on 28th June and 15th August.

Upgrading the Line

Upgrading of the A&R was considered necessary in anticipation of heavy through traffic from both the SM&A and the Hurstbourne–Fullerton line, although the latter was possibly only likely if the west curve at Redbridge were ever built. This would have involved a chord from the A&R just north of Redbridge Junction, which would bypass Redbridge station to join the Southampton–Bournemouth main line. It had been authorised in the SM&A Act of 1882, along with a proposed branch from Totton to Stone Point, opposite Cowes. The SM&A had envisaged this as a new route to the Isle of Wight, but the LSWR evidently had other ideas.

At a meeting on 27th February 1882, Archibald Scott, General Manager of the LSWR, declined to offer running powers into Southampton to either the SM&A or DNS Companies unless the latter abandoned its proposed independent line as he could not be sure into whose hands that line might eventually fall. This drew a protest from James Shopland, Resident Engineer of the SM&A, that his Company's shareholders would not have supported the SM&A scheme had there been no prospect of its trains reaching Southampton. Mr Scott then promised "every possible assistance for the transmission of through traffic" on to the LSWR system at Andover Junction, and also expressed doubt that the current DNS Bill would be passed.

The SM&A opened from Swindon to Andover Junction on 5th February 1883, providing through carriages (though not yet through trains) to and from Southampton Docks station. A siding was installed at the south end of Romsey station in May in order to accommodate engineers' trains for the doubling of the line. That same month, the section between the two Andover stations became the first stretch of the A&R to operate as a double line.

Even before these improvements began, train services over the A&R had significantly improved. By January 1883, there were five passenger trains each way on weekdays (although still none on Sundays) plus a very slow Goods in each direction. The first down train, 7.50am Southampton Docks, was Mixed and overtaken at Fullerton by the 9.30, which reached Andover Junction in just 1hr 12mins. Serious commuting to Southampton was now an attractive proposition, with a return train from the Docks station at 5.55pm, due in Andover Junction at 7.14. Two trains each way were now booked to cross at Horsebridge.

Naturally, there was a major revision when the SM&A reached Andover Junction. The A&R weekday passenger service now comprised six trains each way, with the emphasis on faster services. The 7.50am Southampton now became a semi-fast passenger train, not calling at Millbrook, Mottisfont or Clatford, and arriving Andover Junction at 9.1. The second down train, 9.45 Southampton, took just one minute longer. The following 9.55 Southampton Mixed was much slower but "must not be detained at stations for shunting after its time". From 11th February, the A&R regained a Sunday service, this time of a morning and evening train in each direction.

In April, the SM&A offered to apply for powers for an amended curve at Redbridge, this time to leave the A&R about a mile north of Redbridge Junction. It also wanted the LSWR to recognise the SM&A and A&R as a through route to the Isle of Wight, and to ensure that the route was capable of carrying such traffic in the event of either Company entering into an agreement with any Isle of Wight railway. The LSWR reaction was less than enthusiastic. It had probably decided that the projected Redbridge curve would be of more use in carrying its own trains from London via Longparish and the A&R towards Bournemouth. Writing to his Directors on 14th August 1883, Shopland said "after a long interview with Mr Scott, we left with the strong impression that he wants to obtain for his Company control of the Totton line". On 27th November, the LSWR formally declined to assist with the construction of the Stone Point line, arguing that it did not have Parliamentary powers to raise its half of the required capital.

In the July timetable, three pairs of trains were booked to cross at Horsebridge. By October a further Goods train was timed to leave Andover Junction at 9.30am for the Town, returning at 10.20. The first up passenger train now started from the Junction at 7am, and was accelerated to reach Southampton Docks at 8.10.

The South Western was keen to develop traffic at Nursling, a village between Romsey and Redbridge, even before the line would be doubled. On 11th October 1883 it asked the Board of Trade to give conditional approval for the opening of the station, which had already been built:

> "Pending the doubling of the line, it is intended only to open one side of the station for a single line without sidings but when the second line is laid there will be two platforms and also sidings.....with signal connections."

It went on to ask the BoT to sanction use of the present facilities (a single platform and buildings on the down side) "on the understanding that when the whole of the works are completed and inspected, any requirements of the Inspecting Officer will be duly complied with".

Two days later, Colonel Yolland recommended conditional approval for the station to open. On the same day, the LSWR Secretary wrote to the BoT asking for permission to begin using a siding south of Nursling, serving gravel workings on the down side and reached by a south-facing connection from the existing single line. As with the new station, a signal box had been provided on the up side and the request was also for immediate use, on the understanding that any alterations deemed necessary by the official Inspection would be made. On 15th October, Thomas Gray of the BoT gave a dispensation relaxing the usual requirement for the Company to give a month's notice of its intention to bring the siding into use.

Colonel Rich inspected both the station and the "Ballast siding" in early November. He required a clock to be provided at the station, along with platform lamps and repeaters for its distant signals. Noting that the A&R was single but worked "by means of the Telegraph", he concluded, "I cannot recommend sanction of these new works unless the mode of working is altered to Train Staff and Block Telegraph." A covering letter to the LSWR from Cecil Trevor, no doubt intended to soften the blow, said the BoT would be prepared to sanction the new work on being informed that the requirements in Col. Rich's Report had been met. The station opened on 19th November to passenger and parcels traffic, all trains booked to call there including the 9.55am Southampton Mixed and the 1.35pm Andover Junction goods.

At the start of 1884, the A&R weekday passenger service amounted to seven down and six up trains, four each way providing through carriages, or at least connections, to or from Swindon Town or Cirencester (and advertised in the local press as if through services). Running times were 39–44 minutes for the 18 miles between Andover Junction and Romsey; and 71–76 minutes for the 27¾ miles from Andover Junction to Southampton Docks. While not fast even by contemporary standards, these timings represented a major improvement on the service offered in the early years.

Work on doubling the line continued through 1884, Romsey Junction to Redbridge being worked as a double line from 17th March, when the existing Train Staff and Ticket working over the Romsey–Nursling and Nursling–Redbridge sections was abolished. For the next 12 months, the A&R timetable was regularly revised, not only to accommodate work on doubling the route between Kimbridge Junction and Andover Town but also because of the changing fortunes of the SM&A. By May, five of the seven down trains had onward connections to either Cirencester or Swindon. Less attractive to passengers was the 11.1 Mixed train from Romsey (starting as a Goods train from Southampton Docks), which had a layover of 20 minutes at Horsebridge, where it crossed an up passenger service. The Mixed train had ceased to convey passengers from Southampton Docks in December 1883.

On 23rd June 1884, the SM&A merged with the Swindon & Cheltenham Extension to form the Midland & South Western Junction Railway (MSWJ), although seven years would elapse before this struggling Company's trains would reach Cheltenham. It had yet to exercise its running powers into Southampton, but Andover merchants were already receiving coal from various sources via the GWR at Salisbury. In February, F.A. Scott, based at Andover Town, was selling coals from the Forest of Dean, Radstock, Merthyr, Hucknall and Newcastle at prices ranging from 19s to 27s per ton. H. Stride had offices at the Star Hotel as well as a depot at the Town station, offering delivery of truck loads of coal or coke at any LSWR station. By November, Mr Stride's business had been taken over by William Day, whose firm continued to trade at Andover Town until the line closed.

The newly formed MSWJ Company laid the foundations for north-south freight via Andover when it defeated objections from the GWR and LSWR to its proposed competitive rates for traffic from South Wales and Gloucestershire to Southampton. After months of fruitless correspondence with James Grierson, General Manager of the Great Western, who was invariably "out of town" when B.L. Fearnley, his SM&A counterpart called to see him, the then SM&A took its case to the Railway Commissioners under the provisions of the 1873 Regulation of Railways Act.

The SM&A had contended that its newly opened route from Swindon to Andover was the shortest and quickest for freight from Aberdare to Southampton; Aberdare, Glyn Neath and Resolven to Fullerton Bridge; Gloucester and Stroud to Romsey; Gloucester and Cheltenham to Southampton Docks and vice-versa. Grierson published a reply on 21st June arguing that, although the mileages via Andover might be shorter, this advantage would be more than counterbalanced by having to trav-

ANDOVER to REDBRIDGE

A Beyer-Peacock & Co built 0-6-0 on an MSWJ service from Southampton. The engine can be seen to be minus a buffer, which would no doubt have rendered shunting operations hazardous if this had been required en-route.
(L&GRP)

erse 36 miles of single track between Swindon Junction and Andover Junction, whereas the GWR route via Reading and Basingstoke was double throughout. Nevertheless, the Commissioners ruled on 29th July in favour of the (by now) MSWJ proposals, with the exception of Aberdare–Southampton.

Meanwhile, work was progressing on the doubling of the line between Clatford and Fullerton. The formation was realigned between south of Goodworth Clatford village and Westover Farm crossing to take it further away from the River Anton and also to enlarge the radius of the curve. Together with a realignment approaching Fullerton, which brought the railway nearer the river, the effect was to eliminate a reverse curve. The line was also re-laid with standard LSWR pattern rail weighing 82lb per linear yard. Major Marindin of the BoT reported favourably on these new works on 2nd December 1884.

In preparation for doubling southwards from Fullerton, work started on 8th December to slew the existing single line from Fullerton to Stockbridge, and from Mottisfont to Kimbridge Junction. Drivers were instructed to travel at reduced speed on sharp curves and at worksites, and to be prepared to stop dead on receiving a hand signal to do so. Widening the formation on the former stretch involved construction of three overbridges at Leckford. Drivers of both up and down trains were required to sound their whistles as a warning to the men at work. Engineering trains were now running on Sundays in between the sparse passenger service, to deliver Permanent Way materials to the contractor at Fullerton. The foreman in charge was required to notify each station and junction on the route when the last trip had been made. At this time, the LSWR Engineering Department 2-4-0 locomotive "Hawkshaw" was working engineers' trains for the doubling south of Fullerton.

The newly doubled section from Fullerton to Stockbridge was inspected in April 1885 by Major Marindin, who noted that the formation had been diverted in several places to ease out curves and that the final 600 yards into Stockbridge had been re-laid with new rail on both lines. His report of 11th April also refers to the building of four new overbridges, three with wrought iron girder tops and one with a double brick arch. He commented that "the Permanent Way is now of standard LSWR pattern with 82lb double headed steel rails, 40lb chairs secured by wrought iron nails and steel

WIDER HORIZONS

MSWJ 4-4-4T No 18 between Stockbridge and Horsebridge with a Southampton service, probably in the late 1890s. The coaching stock is of varied origin and comprises MSWJ four- and six-wheeled vehicles and a bogie carriage. Seen against the white chalk, the red livery of the locomotive would have been a stunning sight. The chalk excavations were a relatively common feature of the A&R for much of its length, the excavated material having been used to provide the infill for the former canal at the time it was converted to a railway.

(L&GRP)

fishplates weighing 23lbs per pair" so this may refer to both running lines. He also observed that each 24-foot length of track was laid on nine sleepers and each 30-foot length on 11. The sharpest curve was one of 20 chains radius at Fullerton. Unfortunately, the work was still incomplete and he could not allow the new up line to be brought into use until it was connected up at both ends. Additionally, the lever frame from the existing signal box at Stockbridge had to be transferred to the newly built one, in which a Block Telegraph instrument had not yet been installed. He also asked for a field gate north of the station to be altered so that it opened away from the railway.

These requirements had been met when the Major wrote his re-inspection report on 22nd May, and the A&R was being worked as a double line from Andover Junction to Stockbridge by the beginning of June. The new up line from Mottisfont to Kimbridge Junction, a distance of 76 chains, was inspected in early July, coming into use on the 13th. Major Marindin noted that Mottisfont station now had two platforms, both new, and that interlocking gates had been fitted to the level crossing. Although not on the section inspected, Kimbridge Junction level crossing attracted his attention because its gates were still being worked independently of the signal box. He urged the LSWR to provide that crossing "with the proper apparatus" as soon as possible.

The central section of 5¾ miles between Stockbridge and Mottisfont presented perhaps the greatest engineering problems because the widened formation had to encroach on Common Marsh, and it was not offered to the BoT for inspection until 3rd November. Major Marindin's first report, dated 18th November, noted that "many of the curves of the old line have now been improved", with the sharpest now of 33 chains radius. Three new underbridges had been built, one carried partly on existing brick piers and abutments. While commenting that "the new works are well and substantially constructed", he could not sanction use of the second track until the necessary connections had been made at Stockbridge, Horsebridge and Mottisfont, and interlocking of signals completed. He also required the signal arms (then lower quadrant) to be balanced so that they would move to danger in the event of the vertical rod breaking on a signal post. He added that the LSWR had adopted balanced signal arms for some time. Provided the Company took every possible precaution for line safety while this outstanding work, "which will only occupy a few hours", was in progress, he recommended opening of the new track, subject to a re-inspection of signalling when completed.

Major Marindin's second report is dated 31st December, and noted that Stockbridge signal box now contained 12 working levers, Horsebridge 9, and Mottisfont 11. In addition, there was a two-lever ground frame at Stockbridge and a four-lever one at Mottisfont. He found the interlocking to be correct and recommended the new line to be brought into use on the understanding that the signal arms would be properly balanced within a reasonable time. The earliest reference in Service Timetables to the A&R being worked as a double line throughout appears in January 1886.

I discovered two incidents involving navvies, one being the theft in January 1884 of a shirt belonging to James Brown, engaged on the work at Clatford. Brown himself was no angel, having just been discharged from seven days' jail in default of a fine for being drunk and disorderly, to find his clothes had allegedly been sold by his landlord in Andover. On 12th May 1885, William Mott, of Stockbridge, was injured on the line at Mottisfont by a girder "which crushed his great toe most severely. He was conveyed home and attended by Dr. Loveless".

The Longparish Branch Opens

Meanwhile, the South Western had opened its seven mile branch from Hurstbourne Junction to Fullerton, with stations at Longparish (3 miles 63 chains) and Wherwell (5 miles 77 chains) on 1st June 1885. From the same date, Fullerton Bridge station was closed and replaced by Fullerton Junction, slightly further south and on the actual junction, sporting two platform faces for each route.

The branch was initially served on weekdays only by four passenger trains in each direction between Fullerton and Whitchurch, the eastern terminus chosen in order to compete with the DNS whose line had opened to Winchester with its own Whitchurch station on 1st May 1885. By July, the Longparish branch was enjoying five trains each weekday, the first train from Whitchurch and the last back from Fullerton being Mixed. The new route was double track but its passenger service was not aimed at long distance traffic, so that the last connections from both Southampton and Andover were around 3pm. A further revision in November created a round trip from Fullerton to Basingstoke in the middle of the day.

In the spring of 1888, the operating day began with a light engine running from Andover shed to Fullerton, where it collected its coaches and took them to Stockbridge to form a 7.52 train to Whitchurch, so providing Stockbridge with commuting possibilities in three directions. The first down branch train (that is, from Whitchurch) was Mixed, as was the final up train (from Fullerton) at 4.20pm. The Fullerton–Basingstoke round trip was allowed 45 minutes each way for 20¾ miles. The branch closed for the day after the 5.55 from Whitchurch had reached Fullerton, the loco running light to Andover at 6.25.

The A&R had been upgraded and gained two connecting routes, but the pattern of its own passenger services remained much as before. The anticipated through services from north of Andover had yet to start because of the MSWJ's weak financial position. The latter railway was in any case open only as far north as Cirencester, awaiting completion of its link to the GWR at Andoversford which would then create a through route from Cheltenham to Southampton. Despite generally good connections with MSWJ trains at Andover Junction, services over the A&R were still local rather than regional in character. The eccentric Mixed train from Romsey to Andover was still running (and lingering for 22 minutes at Horsebridge) in 1888. It had become purely a Goods train by 1892 as the Regulation of Railways Act 1889 had led to a great reduction in Mixed train working, these being confined on the LSWR mainly to shorter branch lines.

Development of the A&R timetable in the first seven years after the doubling was to suit freight rather than passenger traffic. By 1885 a 4.30pm cattle train ran on Mondays, when required, from Andover Town to Southampton Docks, reached at 5.58. The LSWR Special Notice for March 1885 advised that henceforth "trucks with livestock must not be attached to passenger trains but must be forwarded by this train". At first, a pilot loco was attached to the 8.30am Southampton Docks Goods in order provide motive power at Andover to work the train, the Guard travelling to Andover Town on the 12.45 Southampton Docks passenger. By 1888 the arrangements were changed so that the loco working the cattle special ran light from Northam shed at 1.47pm, reaching Andover Junction at 2.38, where it was turned and departed at 2.45 for the Town station. The cattle special was much faster than the 1.30pm Goods from Andover Junction, which called at all stations, including a conditional stop at Nursling.

Tasker's Ironworks remained a major freight customer, and wagons were conveyed by a 4.15pm service

WIDER HORIZONS

Wherwell at its peak, which was to be somewhat short lived. The location possessed a full range of facilities, as did its neighbour at Longparish, although these were scantily used. Decades later, the main station buildings survive as a private residence while the steel bridge to the north of the station carries what is now designated the B3420.

(Contemporary postcard)

from Andover Junction to Clatford, returning at 4.30 to pick up and set down wagons at Tasker's siding and Andover Town.

Vision Becomes Reality

In 1891, the MSWJ trains had at last reached Cheltenham and, the following year, that Company's position revived under the energetic leadership of Sam Fay, a former LSWR manager, who returned to his old Company in 1899 and was knighted in 1912. From the summer of 1893 it exercised its right to run its own passenger trains through to Southampton via the A&R, providing Andover with fast trains to Southampton and back. The initial service was of one train each way, the southbound being 2.45pm from Cheltenham, due off Andover Junction at 4.35, then calling only at Romsey, Southampton West and Southampton Docks, reached at 5.30. The northbound train, 2.10pm from Southampton Docks, was even faster, reaching Andover Junction at 3pm despite a third intermediate stop at Redbridge for connections from Bournemouth.

Through freight trains from the MSWJ had begun in 1892. On 1st November the LSWR bought the Southampton Dock Company, which had run into financial difficulties. A period of rapid expansion of the docks followed, including the development of Transatlantic Liner services, generating a great deal of passenger and freight traffic via the MSWJ. In the Winter 1892/93 LSWR Timetable commencing on that date, the southbound MSWJ Goods was timed to leave Andover Junction at 10.50am each weekday, calling at Romsey and Southampton Docks. Its path then became earlier so that a year later it was leaving Andover Junction at 7.15, following the 7am stopping passenger train all the way to Southampton Docks, where respective arrivals were 8.20 and 8.13. From May 1895 that Goods train became Saturdays only, although the MSWJ introduced a Tuesday to Friday service to Southampton Docks, departing Andover Junction at 11.10am. The northbound MSWJ Goods left Southampton Docks in mid evening (becoming 9.30pm by Winter 1895) running non-stop to Andover Junction and was aimed at early morning market deliveries in the Midlands.

The 1840s vision of a north-south artery through Andover had become reality now that the MSWJ linked

STOCKBRIDGE

1914-1918

As was common with numerous locations throughout Great Britain, men serving with the colours often either volunteered, or were billeted, in areas associated with good railway communication.

Stockbridge was no exception, and these views, which are believed to originate from a local resident, poignantly depict the 'flower of youth' so many of whom would be lost for ever in battle, miles from their homeland.

It is believed that the regiments represented include The Black Watch, 4th Highlanders, and the Catering Corps.

ANDOVER to REDBRIDGE

Robert Stephenson & Co built 4-4-2T No 427 on an Andover train near Stockbridge, sometime between 1897 and 1901. The alarm cord running just under the roof of the first vehicle and attached to the engine whistle can just be seen in the photograph. At the time, this was one of around nine passenger trains using the line in this direction on a daily basis, a figure that did not include services to the MSWJ.

(L&GRP)

WIDER HORIZONS

Southampton and the A&R with the Midland Railway at Cheltenham. It made sense for the MSWJ to run express passenger and freight over the route, particularly in connection with Southampton Docks, and to leave the local traffic south of Andover to the LSWR This set the pattern of services over the A&R for 65 years. The LSWR local trains were now timed around MSWJ expresses, which ran non-stop between Andover Junction and Romsey.

By this time, the local passenger services had been slightly accelerated, covering Andover Junction to Southampton Docks in 65–68 minutes. On weekdays in winter 1892/93, the earliest arrival at Waterloo from A&R stations via Andover Junction was at 1.17pm via a seven minute connection from 9.55 Southampton Docks, but it was hardly feasible to return the same day. The last service from the capital via Andover connecting to all A&R stations departed Waterloo at 3.50pm, although on Saturdays the 5.50 connected into an 8.25 SO Andover Junction–Fullerton, the latter formed of the stock off the final train of the day from Whitchurch via Longparish. Return travel via Southampton was not much better, the last connection being from the 4.55 Waterloo, with a wait of over an hour at Southampton Docks. The Sunday service remained at two trains each way and, with infrequent main line expresses, resulted in some appalling "connections", that is, the 11am Waterloo–Exeter being the only train reaching Andover Junction in time for the 6.35pm departure, and the 12.25pm Waterloo involving a wait of almost 2¾ hours at Southampton Docks for the final service of the day to Andover.

By 1894, a cattle special ran as required from Horsebridge on Wednesdays for Basingstoke market. The cattle wagons were worked from Basingstoke at 6.35am via Longparish to reach Horsebridge at 7.23.

In July 1896, the introduction of direct Cardiff–Bristol–Portsmouth trains, calling at Southampton West, brought more traffic to the Romsey–Redbridge section of the A&R, replacing the Eastleigh route as Southampton's main gateway to the west. These trains were a joint venture between the LSWR and the Great Western, involving a change of locomotive at Salisbury. The new service had been made possible by the conversion of the GWR Westbury–Salisbury line to standard gauge in 1874, and the opening of the Severn Tunnel in 1886. Before long, however, Eastleigh was to become a regular destination and route for trains from Andover.

On a less happy note, Stockbridge suffered a severe economic setback in 1898 when the racecourse closed after part of the site was inherited by a woman who was vehemently opposed to horse racing. The railway naturally lost incoming passenger business, but the district was to remain an important centre for racehorse training with the result that Stockbridge goods yard retained a steady traffic in horseboxes.

Early in the 20th Century, Eastleigh became very much the operational hub of the railway system in the Southampton area. A large locomotive depot opened there on 1st January 1903, when Northam shed was closed. Marshalling yards were also laid on the down side north and east of Eastleigh station. Extensive sidings also opened at Bevois Park, between Northam and St. Denys on 16th September 1901. There was an advantage in routing trains, particularly freight, to and from Bevois Park or Southampton Docks via Eastleigh rather than Redbridge because this avoided the congested main line between Northam and Millbrook and, particularly, the cramped layout at Southampton West. Some A&R stopping trains and a local freight in each direction were now routed via Chandlers Ford to start or terminate at Eastleigh, but the basic service for the six intermediate stations north of Romsey remained at half a dozen trains each way on weekdays and two on Sundays.

The more intensive use of the A&R was a factor in an accident on 19th September 1903. On Saturday evenings, there was an additional MSWJ express from Southampton, timed about 15 minutes behind an MSWJ freight, also to Cheltenham, which conveyed perishables for the Midlands. The freight stalled on the steep gradient north of Andover Town close to the Cottage Hospital. As the passenger train approached Andover Town at 40mph, the level-crossing gates were closed to the railway. The signalman managed to open one set of gates but before he could open the second pair across Weyhill Road, the passenger loco had run through the gate on the Station Hotel side of the road. Fortunately, the Driver brought his train to a stand 100 yards behind the failed freight.

Although revenue from through traffic and the MSWJ running powers agreement was far greater than local business on the A&R, the South Western did try to develop local traffic at the Andover end of the route by extending some Longparish services to Stockbridge and Horsebridge. The introduction in 1906 of Railmotors (locomotives enclosed in a single carriage) enabled more local services to be provided because there was no separate locomotive needing to run round the train. On weekdays, these provided journeys considerably later than the last all stations train to Southampton. These Railmotors departed Andover Junction at 7.30pm for Horsebridge and at 8.30 for Stockbridge. By 1909 there were also late stopping trains, on Wednesdays only, departing Andover Junction at 9.55pm for Romsey; and from Southampton at 11.20 via Eastleigh, not reaching Andover Junction until 12.45.

Local freight traffic flourished, including the afternoon trip from Andover Junction to Clatford serving Tasker's siding. Agricultural fairs generated much sheep traffic on the line. The Wednesday cattle train was still running when required in summer 1909, the empty vans

ANDOVER to REDBRIDGE

A steam railmotor entering Andover Town with a local service, some time after 1906. Railmotors were also used on the Hurstbourne - Fullerton line at this time.

(Commercial postcard)

due off Basingstoke at 6.42am, out to Horsebridge via Longparish but returning loaded via Andover. The empties were timed to pass Fullerton eight minutes behind the empty Railmotor, which ran from Andover to Stockbridge to form the first up passenger service to Whitchurch. The cattle train (7.47 Horsebridge) was allowed 10 minutes for loading at Stockbridge, departing at 8.5, 10 minutes ahead of the first all-stations train from Southampton. It then had a clear run to Andover Junction, where the engine ran round before setting off for Basingstoke.

World War One

Southampton had played a major part in the embarkation of troops for the Boer War, and more so during the First World War, when the A&R carried numerous troop trains, either via the MSWJ or via Longparish, the latter route relieving the Waterloo–Southampton main line. Many hospital trains also conveyed wounded servicemen to the Midlands via the A&R and MSWJ lines.

On 26th June 1916, the Shell Marketing Company signed an agreement with the LSWR to store petroleum spirit alongside a siding at the south end of Andover Town goods yard.

In the Winter 1916/17 Timetable, the basic passenger service north of Romsey was nine trains each way on weekdays, of which three were MSWJ expresses. Of the six local trains, two ran from or via Eastleigh. In addition, there were variations on the Longparish shuttle to serve A&R stations north of Stockbridge. The latter town still had its commuter train to Whitchurch, now running ahead of the Wednesday cattle special, which was now recessed at Stockbridge for the first down passenger train (7.20am Southampton Town–Andover Junction) to overtake. There was also a 4.50pm Andover Junction–Basingstoke via Fullerton and Longparish. The late evening trains from Andover and Southampton had been withdrawn, probably because of manpower shortages, so that the last up stopping train now left the Junction at 7.32, followed by a MSWJ express at 8.44.

The majority of LSWR trains between Southampton and Andover ran via Nursling, where Portsmouth/ Southampton–Salisbury trains and some of the Portsmouth–Bristol/Cardiff trains also called. The 6.50am Bevois Park–Salisbury freight called, if required, at Nursling on Tuesdays to take on cattle traffic for Salisbury market. This train was diagrammed for a "Heavy

WIDER HORIZONS

Engine" of the 330 or 453 class.

North of Romsey, there were two MSWJ and one LSWR freights in each direction, plus trips from Andover Junction to Town in the morning and to Clatford in the afternoon. A light engine also ran from the Junction at 2.28pm to Fullerton to work a 3pm Goods to Basingstoke via Longparish. The local freights had long shunting allowances at goods yards, the 5.35pm Romsey being overtaken by four trains including a 7.17 Fullerton–Andover Junction passenger and a 7.5 Southampton Docks MSWJ Goods. The 5.35 Romsey also called at Tasker's siding if required.

The pattern of MSWJ Goods trains was early morning southbound, two being timed to depart Andover Junction at 4.45 and 6.3, ahead of the first stopping passenger train, which left the Junction at 6.45. There were paths for two MSWJ freights from Southampton Town at 11.20am and 2.35pm, which ran as required but the regular services both started from the Docks (as distinct from Southampton Town for Docks *station*) at 7.5pm and 9.18pm. The latter stopped at Redbridge, if required, to take on cattle wagons detached from the 5.15pm Dorchester up Goods.

LSWR Sunday services north of Romsey in 1916 were little changed from 1883, with an out and back working, morning and evening, between Southampton Town and Andover Junction via Nursling. By 1909 these had been joined by a morning MSWJ express from Southampton, plus an MSWJ Goods between Cheltenham and Romsey.

The LSWR Service Timetable from 5th May 1918 makes no reference to any passenger trains originating or terminating on the MSWJ via Andover or the GWR via Salisbury. It may well be that these had been suspended because of manpower shortages, and the paths released for troop, supply or ambulance trains. Staffing difficulties were probably the reason for the withdrawal of the Sunday morning round trip between Southampton and Andover. Evidence of a desire not to run any trains or book on crews unnecessarily is provided by a new instruction concerning the conditional Wednesday cattle train from Horsebridge to Basingstoke. All Station Masters, Horsebridge to Longparish inclusive, were now required to advise Basingstoke by telegram no later than 4pm Tuesday whether there would be any cattle to be forwarded the next morning. In the event of there being traffic at Fullerton but not Stockbridge or Horsebridge, the loco and brake van would depart Basingstoke at 7.20 instead of 6.30am. If none of those stations had cattle to be loaded, the engine and van would run direct to Andover Junction.

North of Romsey, the A&R now had six passenger trains each way plus a 6.52pm Fullerton–Andover Junction, the latter worked with the stock of the final trip along the Longparish branch. An additional freight was now timed to leave the Junction at 8.15am for Stockbridge, whence it returned at 10.15, calling at Clatford and Tasker's siding if required.

Stockbridge in LSWR days with an Andover train entering. Note the single headcode disc; these codes varied, depending upon the actual service. On the other side of the line, the tall starting signal has been provided with a sighting board against the trees. The footbridge can also be seen in front of the road bridge. (Commercial postcard)

ANDOVER to REDBRIDGE

Fullerton Junction at its most eminent, as the junction for the Longparish line, to and from Hurstbourne. As discussed on page 18, the original station at Fullerton had been closed, and replaced with Fullerton Junction station, seen here. The new station was slightly further south than the original, with each route now having two platform faces. The canopy of one of the platforms for the Longparish line is visible on the left. An Andover-bound train is entering the platform.
(Commercial postcard)

Chapter 4

THE SOUTHERN RAILWAY ERA

The 1921 Railways Act amalgamated 123 railway companies into four geographical groups. Whereas the London & South Western Railway became part of the Southern Railway, the Midland & South Western Junction was, after much deliberation, absorbed into the Great Western Railway with effect from July 1923, six months after the Act had become law. The MSWJ's running powers over the A&R into Southampton now transferred to the GWR, which was ironic in view of the LSWR's earlier determination to keep its rival out of the port. In the same month, Southampton Town for Docks station was renamed Southampton Terminus.

After the War, railway companies recruited large numbers of staff, particularly in the footplate grades, to replace men killed or severely wounded. The MSWJR was able to reinstate through services between Southampton and the North of England in 1922, albeit on a smaller scale than pre-war. The Great Western reduced the four weekday trains each way between Cheltenham and Southampton to two but it continued the through coach working from Liverpool and exploited the Andover corridor as a route for excursions to the South Coast. In the Summer 1924 Timetable there was a path for a GWR Saturday excursion, timed to reach Andover Junction at 8.45am and depart at 8.50, running via Redbridge and due in Southampton Terminus at 9.51. Excursions from Gloucester via Cheltenham to Southampton and Portsmouth continued to run on specific Summer Saturdays until the systematic rundown of the MSWJ route in 1958. Strengthening of bridges on the MSWJ in the late 1920s brought heavier GW locomotives on to the A&R with freight services. Ex MSWJ locos were gradually displaced on the through passenger trains by GW 4-4-0s of the Duke and Earl classes, and in the 1930s by GW 2-6-0s. At Cheltenham, these trains continued to use Lansdown, the former Midland Railway (by now LMS) station and the through freights started or terminated at High Street, the former MSWJ goods yard. In 1924 there were two booked freights each way on weekdays between Cheltenham and Southampton, the southbound due off Andover Junction at 7.45 and 10.50 and the northbound starting from Southampton Docks in the evening. As yet, no GWR services were booked over the A&R on Sundays.

The inter-company Cardiff–Portsmouth service via Redbridge and Southampton West, which had also been suspended during the War, was likewise revived.

The Southern Railway was not to be outdone when it came to creative timetabling on the A&R. The local passenger service gained some interesting destinations and starting points in order to make maximum utilisation of rolling stock and traincrews. The first down weekday passenger train in July 1924 started from Southampton Terminus at 6.25am, calling at all stations to Whitchurch (S.R.) via Nursling, Fullerton and Longparish. Just after 9am, at Andover Junction, an Eastleigh–Salisbury service was timed to meet one working the same route in reverse, probably for traincrew handover purposes. The down train (7.54 Eastleigh) detached a set at Romsey to work an 8.35 to Portsmouth. In the evening the 5.58pm Romsey started from Brockenhurst, and the 6.50 Whitchurch–Fullerton was extended to Southampton Terminus via Eastleigh. The majority of stopping trains on the A&R were now routed via Eastleigh rather than Redbridge, reflecting the importance of the former town as the local operational hub. In all there were now seven SR trains in each direction north of Romsey on weekdays plus the two GW services to and from Cheltenham. The down pick-up freight (7.17am Eastleigh) was overtaken at stations by three passenger trains (two SR stoppers plus the 10.5 Southampton Terminus–Cheltenham GW passenger) and also called at Tasker's siding if required.

Probably the most useful innovation was the introduction of a direct train to London via the A&R on Sundays. Starting from Andover Junction at 2.15pm, it called at all stations, except Nursling, to Southampton West, whence it departed at 3.30 and stopped at the majority of stations to Woking, arriving in Waterloo at 6.6. Introduced on 1st June 1924, it was still running as a through train in 1936. The Sunday morning trains were reinstated, this time starting from Andover Junction at 7.50 and working through to Winchester via Redbridge. All three down trains on Sundays now started from Eastleigh at 10.20am, 4.40 and 8.25pm, although the late afternoon service ran via Southampton West and Redbridge rather than Chandlers Ford.

With double track and six intermediate signal boxes north of Kimbridge Junction, the A&R had plenty of capacity to accommodate trial runs of engines overhauled at Eastleigh Works. In summer 1924 there were 10 down and 9 up light engine paths between Eastleigh and Stockbridge, mostly between late morning and mid afternoon. If an engine was delayed en-route it had to be shunted clear and then take up the next light engine path so as not to delay other trains.

The closing months of 1925 saw an effort to improve the appearance of Andover Town station. The *Andover Advertiser* referred to the new footbridge and better arrangement of poster boards, commenting "the result is a great improvement in the appearance of the platforms as viewed by the passer-by along Bridge Street". It added that it doubted that the "temporary tin buildings", which had served as station offices since the line's opening, would ever be replaced "by buildings in keeping with one of the principal thoroughfares of the town" (a very prophetic statement as things turned out) but considered that their new standard of decoration would make their ugliness less obtrusive. Another marketing initiative at the start of 1926 was the publication of a combined bus and rail guide for the Andover area, available from local stationers or on the buses.

New Year 1926 also brought an unwelcome event in the form of a break-in at Fullerton booking office on the night of 4th/5th January. Station Master Ernest Green was alerted by Signalman S. Keats, who had come on duty at 6.30am on the Tuesday to switch in his box, only to find the ticket window forced open and the office ransacked. Only 13/11d and 39 copper coins (petty cash for change) were missing, however, as the safe was untouched. Mr Green notified the police and "prompt action" by Superintendent Jones of Andover led to the arrest in Winchester of two men, both of no fixed abode and who admitted taking a chisel from a Permanent Way hut near Fullerton station to force an entry.

Both men pleaded guilty when tried at Winchester Assizes in February. They had, they said, stolen the money to buy food. Ernest Birchall, 28, who had previous convictions, was sentenced to 18 months imprisonment with hard labour. He immediately asked the judge, "Can you make it three years?" His younger accomplice, described by Supt. Jones as coming from a good family and whose Counsel had made a strong plea for leniency, was bound over for £5.

Britain's railways were brought to a virtual standstill when railwaymen joined the General Strike in May in support of the miners. The Lord Lieutenant of Hampshire, Maj. Gen. J.E.B. Seely commented that the railway workers were "a most orderly section of the community but consider at present it is their bounden duty to support … the National Union of Railwaymen". He noted that railwaymen were the only large group of workers still on

South of Romsey, the intermediate station at Nursling had been opened by the LSWR on 19th November 1883. Its design was similar to both Wherwell and Longparish, while the curved top to the platform canopies could also be seen at other locations, including Shawford on the main line north of Eastleigh. Despite serving a sparsely populated area, the station witnessed far more traffic in the form of through services than the A&R stations north of Romsey did. This was because a number of the Southampton—Bristol services ran through the line south of Romsey.

(Commercial postcard)

strike in the county for a second week.

Most staff at Andover Junction had joined the strike on Tuesday 5th May, the *Advertiser* noting that, with no trains running to Southampton, the level-crossing gates at Town station were left open to road users. It also claimed "the smooth working of the road traffic showed what a great benefit it would be if the level crossing could be dispensed with altogether".

The Southern managed to run 334 trains on the Wednesday, of which two were over the A&R. A turning point came on Friday, when the strike collapsed locally at Ludgershall on the former MSWJ line after NUR officials had met with hostility from a community resenting the loss of trade from Territorial Army soldiers whose special trains were not running. The first GW train to run from Cheltenham to Southampton was on 12th May, the *Advertiser* describing the volunteer fireman as "a gentleman of independent means. He may not possess the dexterity of other members of the craft but from the way he handled coal….he was certainly not afraid of manual labour."

In an age when there was still comparatively little road traffic and most businesses relied heavily on the railways, the *Advertiser* had exposed local and national weaknesses in the rail industry that road interests would be able to exploit in later decades. Moreover, the Southern had to find ways of reducing its overheads to offset the loss of business caused by the strike. By 1927, Station Masters were withdrawn from Nursling (now coming under Romsey), Mottisfont (now supervised by Dunbridge), Horsebridge (now under Stockbridge) and Clatford (now managed by Andover Town). Redbridge also lost its Station Master, who was now based at Millbrook.

The line was serving an essentially rural catchment area as both Andover (1931 population 9,962) and Romsey (4,862) were still small market towns. Southampton (176,025) was closer to its present size but of the intermediate settlements north of Romsey, only Kings Somborne (1¼ miles from Horsebridge) had around 1,000 inhabitants. Stockbridge, although a town, had just 915 inhabitants in 1934. Nevertheless, the railway provided an important link within the Test and Anton valleys as well as between Southampton, the Midlands and North because car ownership was still outside the reach of most people and most long distance freight travelled by rail.

Local industries in Romsey that were important customers of the railway included Strong's brewery, The Hampshire Preserving Company's jam factory and Wills' nursery. The latter had opened in 1926 alongside the line south of Romsey and soon acquired a private siding for receiving fuel for its boilers, although produce was despatched via the station. Elsewhere on the line, the private siding to Tasker's Ironworks, latterly receiving coke and iron, was converted to a public delivery siding in 1930, and remaining traffic for the Ironworks was handled at Andover Town. Stockbridge, which continued to be a racehorse-training centre long after the closure of its own racecourse at Danebury, sometimes received horsebox specials. One, consisting of five horseboxes and a utility van, arrived on 2nd August 1934 via Eastleigh from Singleton, on the soon to be closed Chichester–Midhurst line, behind ex LBSCR C2x class No 252. The Summer 1936 Timetable provided a Q path (a slot in the timetable for a special train to be run at short notice according to traffic requirements) for a 7.3am Stockbridge–Andover Junction horsebox train.

In 1931, Fyffes bananas began arriving at Southampton Docks and special trains to the Midlands were worked via the A&R and the MSWJ. These helped to sustain the line as a trunk freight route for 27 years.

The Longparish branch, however, succumbed to bus and car competition as its route to Andover was less direct and its train services infrequent. It closed to passengers on 6th July 1931 and freight was also withdrawn north of Longparish. Now that Fullerton was a less complex junction, it was deemed not to require a Station Master and came under Stockbridge, where Frederick Bale took command of all stations from Horsebridge to Longparish. The branch might have survived longer had the projected north to west curve been built at Redbridge, thereby creating another Waterloo–Bournemouth route.

Motive Power and Special Trains

In the 1920s, Adams 0460 4-4-0s were frequently seen on local passenger trains over the A&R, but their days were numbered, the class becoming extinct in 1929. By the early 1930s A12 0-4-2s and various Adams (C8, X2, X6) and Drummond (K10, L11, T9) 4-4-0s shared the SR passenger services over the line and were often deployed on excursions. The normal formation for the SR local trains was a three- or four-coach non-corridor set. Passenger traffic was boosted on Saturdays by Southampton football supporters travelling to home games, particularly from Andover Town. The GWR trains departing Cheltenham around 10am and returning from Southampton Terminus at 4.30pm were well timed for supporters living in Andover, and had more seating capacity than a SR non-corridor set.

Local freight services were worked by A12s or Class 700 0-6-0s shedded at Andover or Eastleigh, while longer distance freights, such as banana trains from Southampton Docks to Cheltenham, were usually powered by GWR 2-6-0s. By 1933 Churchward 43xx, 53xx and 63xx 2-6-0s, and the new Collett 73xx variety, were working the early morning freight from Cheltenham to Southampton Docks, returning with the 10.10 Southampton Terminus–Cheltenham passenger train via Redbridge.

ANDOVER to REDBRIDGE

Drummond C8 4-4-0 as Southern Railway No 293 at Andover Town on a local Eastleigh freight. The fact the starting signal is in the 'on' position implies that shunting is about to start, or has recently taken place, and the train is halted briefly before its next action. This particular engine entered traffic in 1898 and lasted in service until February 1935. On the headcode disc, the number 279 referred to the loco duty number from Andover Junction. The point rodding that can be seen on the left-hand side of the picture led to a ground frame that operated a crossover and access from the south end of the yard. This was released from the Town Signal Box. To the right, a store for Messrs J. Bibby & Sons can be seen.
(R.K. Blencowe Collection)

THE SOUTHERN RAILWAY ERA

Romsey Station viewed eastwards, with part of the commodious goods yard visible on the left. In the distance it is just possible to discern the junction signals routing trains left on the original route to Eastleigh and right via the newer line to Nursling. Interestingly, the original route has the taller arm, implying its greater importance. (Lens of Sutton)

Eastleigh duty No 293, with Adams T6 class 4-4-0 No 685, waiting at Romsey with a 'down' train for Andover. (Up trains ran south from Andover.) When this photograph was taken on 22nd April 1935, this particular engine had less than a year to remain in service, and was withdrawn in February of the following year. The fact that machines in their final years were used for A&R services indicates the lack of importance felt by the Southern towards the line at this period.
(H.F. Wheeler Collection / Roger Carpenter)

ANDOVER to REDBRIDGE

This time it is a Southampton Terminus - Andover via Redbridge service that is depicted entering Romsey (the different headcode will be noted). In charge is another Adams' design, A12 No 598, at the head of vintage LSWR stock.
(National Railway Museum/Box 380)

The versatile 700s were deployed on freight, passenger and special passenger trains alike. On 5th April 1936 No 690 passed Eastleigh, bound for Southampton Docks, with 22 empty LMS banana vans in tow. Sister engine 368 was the motive power for an 11-coach corridor troop train from Tidworth to Southampton Docks on 1st October that year. Nearly 10 years earlier, on 7th October 1926, Black Motor No E327 had headed a troop special from the MSWJ line to Eastleigh consisting of eight non-corridor coaches, six horseboxes and two vans.

The A&R saw many military specials in the 1920s and 1930s. Those originating on the Southern tended to be destined for Amesbury, Bulford or Tidworth, especially the latter when a Tattoo was held. Between 4th and 11th August 1934, two troop and four excursion trains ran to Tidworth in connection with the Tattoo, two from Weymouth being T9-hauled while ex LBSCR C2x 0-6-0s brought eight- and six-coach trains from Chichester and Brighton respectively. Troop trains reaching the A&R via the MSWJ tended to be heading for ports, not only from the Midlands to Southampton Docks but also from Salisbury Plain camps to Dover or Shorncliffe. Their motive power tended to be GW or SR Moguls and S11 or L12 4-0s. Six non-corridor specials ran from Weyhill and other MSWJ starting points to Dover or Shorncliffe on 20th September 1935, Maunsell U 2-6-0s being the motive power in four cases. Collett 22xx 0-6-0 No 2255 had worked 18 wagons of Army equipment from the MSWJ to Southampton Docks on 1st June the same year.

Great Western excursions via Andover continued to run to Southampton, Bournemouth and Portsmouth. On 14th July 1933, two 10-coach holiday specials ran from Swindon to Portsmouth for Swindon Works employees and their families, both trains passing Eastleigh behind T9 4-4-0s, although two years later 63xx Moguls worked the same two trains (and a third Works special for Bournemouth) over the A&R. By 1934, the GWR was running excursions of seven or eight corridor coaches with dining car from Cheltenham or Gloucester to Bournemouth and Portsmouth.

By contrast, the Southern catered for the local market for excursion traffic, running specials from Andover to the coast, such as two trains of 11 corridor coaches each from Andover Town to Bournemouth on 20th June 1934. George Woodward recorded these as conveying children (presumably from a group of local schools or

THE SOUTHERN RAILWAY ERA

Eastleigh based A12 No 609 at Andover Town on what is possibly Eastleigh duty No 306 (goods Eastleigh to Andover Junction, then return with the 6.46pm passenger service). In the distance, the level crossing gates can be seen closed across the railway, indicating that the train was in the course of shunting the yard. The increasing difficulties experienced with this level crossing are discussed on page 35. *(National Railway Museum/Box 229)*

Sunday schools) and hauled by L11 No 169 and K10 No 150 respectively. Ten days later, the same K10 loco powered a 10-coach special from Andover Junction bound for Hayling Island on behalf of the Ancient Order of Foresters, which was celebrating its centenary. Brighton and Weymouth were also regular destinations for excursion trains from Andover but, when A12s were used, they would be relieved by another loco at Eastleigh because of their limited water capacity. In the reverse direction, Tidworth Tattoo was the magnet for excursions from stations on the South Coast.

Pigeon specials were also evident in the 1930s, George Woodward recording three heading for Southampton Docks via the MSWJ, Stockbridge and Eastleigh behind GW 2-6-0s in the summer of 1936.

In the Summer 1935 Timetable, the weekday passenger service on the A&R north of Romsey consisted of eight SR stopping trains each way, including a morning trip from Andover to Horsebridge and back, plus two GW services each way via the MSWJ. The latter started from Southampton Terminus at 10.13am and 4.36pm; departures from Cheltenham (LMS) were at 10.29am and 1.35pm. The two southbound GW trains filled what otherwise would have been a large gap in the Andover–Southampton service. The first of these, due off Andover Junction at 1.8pm, called at all stations to Romsey, while the later one was timed behind the 4.30pm Andover Junction stopping train so it called at Andover Town and was then fast to Romsey. Two down stoppers now started from Weymouth at 2.25pm and Fawley at 5.16pm, although these offered protracted journeys for any through passengers, not reaching Andover until around 6.30 and 7.30 respectively.

A year later, the Andover–Horsebridge round trip was still running, and a late evening service was provided on Saturdays, 10.38pm Andover Junction–Romsey and 11.35 return. The Guard had to collect tickets and extinguish station lamps. On certain Saturdays, a GW excur-

ANDOVER to REDBRIDGE

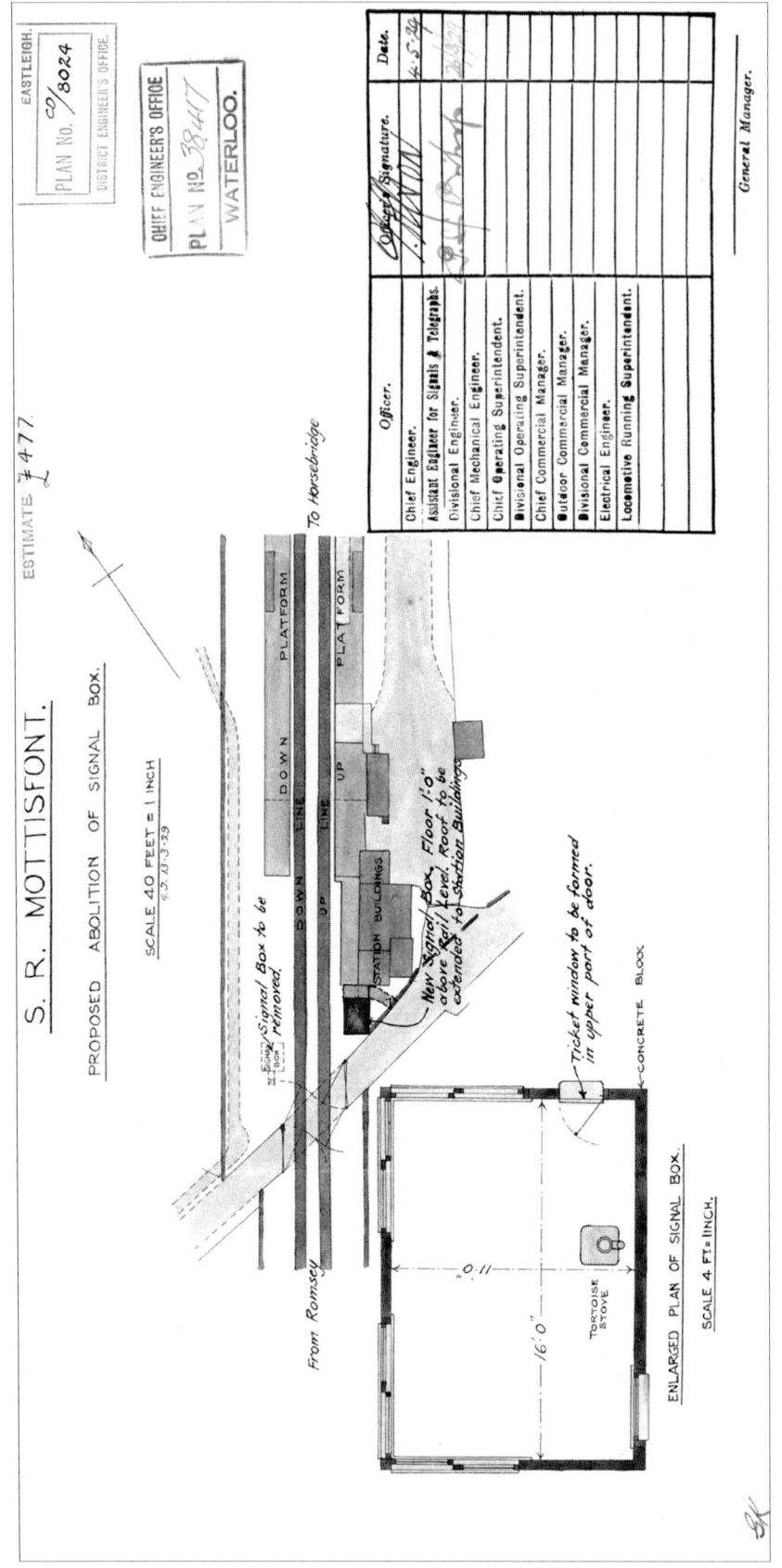

An interesting plan found in the archives was this 1929 proposal for the removal of the signal box at Mottisfont to a new site. The reason for such action has not been established and, as the line was reasonably straight both sides of the location, there would appear to have been little obvious advantage in visibility. For whatever reason, the work was not carried out.

sion (7.10am from Swindon) was timed to depart Andover Junction at 9am, running to Southampton Terminus on two dates and Portsmouth & Southsea on four. The return departure from Portsmouth was 8.30pm, pathed behind the 8.53 Eastleigh–Andover stopper. The Southern ran a dated 10.20am Bulford–Bournemouth train on three summer Sundays, routed via Andover and Eastleigh to avoid reversal. It called at all stations to Eastleigh and its return working was detached there from the 8.53pm Bournemouth–Surbiton. The normal Sunday service still featured the 2.15pm Andover Junction–Waterloo that was introduced in 1924, and a 4.20pm Winchester (SR)–Andover Junction, both via Redbridge.

Freight over the A&R in summer 1936 included two GW services starting from Cheltenham at 4.5 and 7.35am. The former was due away from Andover Junction at 7.30, between the first two up passenger trains, and called at Millbrook and Southampton Docks. The second was more of a local goods, departing the Junction at 12 noon and calling, when required, at Clatford to return the key that unlocked the ground frame for Upper Clatford (formerly Tasker's) siding. Although booked to run to Romsey, it would terminate at Stockbridge if it was loaded to no more than 12 wagons on leaving Andover Junction.

Problems with Level Crossings

Increasing rail (and road) traffic no doubt influenced the decision of Andover Borough Council, in the summer of 1935, to press, via the County Council, for additional signals at Andover Town, with a view to reducing the time that the level-crossing gates were closed to road traffic when a train was due, or in the station. The longest delays to road vehicles occurred with down trains because once the bell signals for "Train entering section" had been received from Clatford signal box, the Andover Town signalman had to open the gates for the train. Special Instruction 92.B-1929 required this to be done three minutes before the train was due to arrive after being signalled. The running time for a down passenger train between the two stations was then four minutes. Up trains created less of a problem for road users, partly because of the short distance from the previous box (Andover Junction East) and the falling gradient, but also because a local instruction permitted the gates to be opened for the road once the train was at a stand in the station.

A Signal Sighting Committee met on 6th August and recommended provision of a calling-on signal under the down home signal at Andover Town, plus a banner repeater for the down starting signal. These would have allowed down trains to draw into the platform while the gates remained open to road traffic but the recommendations were overruled by the SR's Chief Engineer. His own suggestion seems to point to cost being the main factor:

"If it were possible to modify the instruction by retaining the home signal at danger until the train approaches it, the cause of the complaint might, to some extent, be met without expenditure on the Company's part. The County Surveyor's proposal to move the down starting signal back and lengthen the platform could not, of course, be entertained."

On Monday 19th August, a survey of the time that the gates were closed to road traffic for each train was taken on behalf of the Southern Divisional Superintendent. These ranged from a little over a minute for light engine movements to three or four minutes for GW freight trains such as 4.5am Cheltenham and 7pm Southampton Terminus–Cheltenham. In the case of down passenger trains, the gates were opened and closed to the railway twice, in the first instance on the approach of the train after it had belled out of section at Clatford. The gates were then reopened to road traffic immediately after the train had come to a stand at Andover Town. The road was closed a second time, usually for 1½ minutes or less, when the train was ready to depart. On 28th August, the SR informed the County Surveyor that it did not appear that any alteration was called for, but assured the Council that "all possible steps will be taken to reduce the occupation of the crossing to a minimum".

On 21st April 1936, an accident occurred at Westover accommodation crossing, between Clatford and Fullerton, which would generate correspondence about safety for a further 23 years. The 10.29 Cheltenham–Southampton, comprising two GWR bogie coaches and a LMS bogie van behind Duke class 4-4-0 No 3285, "Katerfelto", ran into a herd of cows that were being driven from the water meadows on the up side of the crossing to the farm on the down side. Three of the beasts were killed. Subsequent statements by the traincrew and Permanent Way staff described the weather as drizzle with a boisterous wind.

When asked by the Guard why the cattle were crossing when a train was due, the drover, a Mr Day, replied "I did not hear (the train)." The accident was witnessed by Farmer I. Bevan, owner of the cattle, who was proprietor of Westover Dairies and also a member of Andover Rural District Council. He conceded "there was some fault" but claimed the train should have stopped. Two of the carcases were blocking the down line, but Lester Whitemore, booking clerk at Stockbridge who was travelling on the train, walked to Fullerton to warn the signalman to caution down trains. The train continued on its way, within 15 minutes of the collision, no passengers or staff having been injured. A joint SR/GWR inquiry held at Fullerton station three days later exonerated the

ANDOVER to REDBRIDGE

A12 No 614 at Fullerton Junction, probably around the time of closure of the line between Hurstbourne and Fullerton to passengers, which took place from 6th July 1931. After this, the route was still open to goods for a while, but this was curtailed between Hurstbourne and Longparish from 29th May 1934, leaving the stub end to be served from Fullerton. It is unlikely that the single coach (which accommodated 3rd class passengers only) had many occupants.
(Lens of Sutton)

crew and judged Mr Day responsible for the accident. He was dismissed from his job, losing his tied cottage as a result.

Driver Frederick Gale of Andover told the inquiry that he worked this service one week in five. He had sounded the whistle as the train rounded the curve preceding the crossing, adding that his first sight of the crossing would be behind some willows on the up side. Permanent Way Inspector Cannon pointed out that up trains used to have 18 chains' visibility of the crossing, but this had reduced to about 200 yards after the willow trees, located off railway property, had matured.

The Southern Railway accepted that the willows might have hindered visibility but deferred action to remove them in view of Mr Bevan's claim for £75 compensation for the loss "of three of my best cows". He also asked the SR to destroy rabbits living on railway property, which he claimed were "playing havoc" with a wheat crop near Fullerton. An internal memo noted that Westover crossing was used four times daily by cattle and twice daily by horse and cart. By contrast, Upper Westover crossing was stated to be used only twice per year and was suggested for closure.

For more than 20 years after the accident the SR and BR discussed possible improvements to the safety of the four crossings between Clatford and Fullerton. In BR days consideration was given to installing a telephone circuit to Clatford signal box, although, in 1948, the cost of £270 was regarded by the Divisional Operating Superintendent as difficult to justify when other crossings were said to have "circumstances on a par (with Westover) or even worse".

The policy in the SR's Southern Division had been to provide farmers and other regular crossing users with extracts from Working Timetables showing all scheduled trains and Light Engine movements, but later correspondence acknowledged the difficulty of giving prior notice of amended or special trains, let alone late running ones. The practice was discontinued early in the Second World War for that very reason (no doubt because of the need to run military trains at minimal notice) and also because it was felt that giving one particular farmer such informa-

THE SOUTHERN RAILWAY ERA

Former Adams 460 class express design No 0478 at Wherwell on 30th April 1928. The wonderfully evocative view has captured the character of the line so well. It had been singled as far back as 13th July 1913, while towards the end of its days boasted a daily timetable of three passenger services northbound but only two southbound. The 'route was also one where Bradshaw seemed unable to decide which was an 'up' train and which was a 'down', it hardly mattered anyway. Duties however were almost exclusively in the hands of locomotives and crews from Andover Junction.

(H.C. Casserley, courtesy of R.M. Casserley)

tion created a precedent.

Later in 1936, the Air Ministry had requisitioned 550 acres of the Leckford Estate to build Chilbolton airfield, much to the disappointment of John Spedan Lewis, the Oxford Street retailer who had bought the estate in 1928. The airfield brought extra traffic in servicemen and supplies to Fullerton station.

World War Two

The Second World War brought a massive volume of troop, supply and hospital trains to the line via Southampton Docks. Some of the ambulance trains ran to Foss Cross, a remote station on the MSWJ in Gloucestershire, which was two miles from an American military hospital. With all routes to Southampton under great pressure, up and down goods loops were provided on the Romsey side of Kimbridge Junction, where a new signal box was commissioned on 21st May 1943, together with a box at Awbridge at the Romsey end of the loops. The war also gave a new lease of life to the Longparish branch, following a decision by the Air Ministry to create a major ammunition store in Harewood Forest. This also resulted in the provision of additional sidings and signals at Fullerton to accommodate the increased traffic over the branch.

It was on 7th October 1941 that Squadron Leader Pool of the Air Ministry telephoned the Southern Railway headquarters to ask for extra sidings in the Longparish–Fullerton area. Meetings were held between R.A.F., Air Ministry and SR officials at Fullerton and Longparish on 22nd October when draft plans for the new railway facilities were examined.

Works agreed for Fullerton were costed at £7,400 and comprised:
- A new siding, to hold 31 wagons, connected to the Longparish branch
- A new siding on the formation of an old one (behind the down platform), able to hold 40 wagons and connected from the down line at the Clatford end of the station
- Alteration to existing dock siding, reconstruction of dock and removal of adjacent siding
- Reinstatement of a branch platform face as a loading dock at the Stockbridge end
- Construction of an end dock for loading from platform on to lorries
- Widening and extension of existing roadways in the goods yard.

This, and £6,915 expenditure at Longparish, where the branch was to be re-laid towards Hurstbourne for a distance of 917 feet to provide a shunting neck, were approved by the Ministry of War Transport. A special train run from the Fareham direction to Andover Junction on 7th April 1942 may well have conveyed senior railway personnel to inspect the work, as the formation included a saloon vehicle, a brake composite coach and an LNER First Class sleeping car, hauled by T9 No 119. Authority for the work to proceed was given by Sir Eustace Missenden, SR General Manager, on 26th May. A month later, a Signal Sighting Committee proposed three additional signals at Fullerton, namely a Branch Home, Branch Starter and Down Advance. The last mentioned would be 685 yards from the signal box and, to give it an approach view of 350 yards, four trees on the Clatford side of Westover crossing would be felled.

Some years later, when the history of the railway was being reported in the local press consequent upon its pending closure, one of the newspaper articles referred to Fullerton station having been taken over in wartime as the temporary HQ of the Administration and Planning Departments of the Docks and Marine Authority evacuated from Southampton, with offices alongside the Longparish bay and also in a disused carriage nearby. There is no other confirmation of this though.

Additional trains and disrupted locomotive diagrams resulting from the war brought a number of locos to the A&R from depots well outside the area, although many of these were GW engines running in after an overhaul at Swindon Works, such as 3443 on 22nd October 1941 and 3389 of Hereford on an afternoon train to Cheltenham on 19th June 1942. The 10.10 Southampton–Cheltenham was normally worked by the GW engine off the early morning freight from Cheltenham but when the latter was heavily delayed, an SR loco might be found to work the GW passenger train, for example, on 11th August 1942 when K10 "Small Hopper" 4-4-0 took it to Andover Junction.

SR locos were also to be seen on through services between Southampton and the MSWJ. During May 1943, the 3.50pm Marlborough–Southampton (which had been cut back from Cheltenham in 1941) was worked by U class 2-6-0 No 1636 on several occasions. Moguls of the U and N classes were observed shunting at Andover Junction after working in from Eastleigh and then being used as required to shunt at Andover Town or assist trains struggling up the bank from Town to Junction. June 1943 saw D15 4-4-0 No 471, a member of the last class to be designed by Drummond, work from Romsey to Andover Junction.

The GW Manor class, introduced in 1938, was working regularly over the A&R with Cheltenham trains by 1944, and continued to do so until the MSWJ route closed in 1961. They were lighter and slimmer than the other GW 4-6-0s and therefore permitted over the MSWJ, which the Great Western classified as a Blue route.

SOUTHERN DAILY ECHO, Monday 21st May 1928

DEAF MAN'S FATAL SHORT CUT

Killed by Express at Stockbridge

CORONER ON BREAKING A RULE

In attempting to take a short cut over the railway lines instead of using the footbridge at Stockbridge railway station on Friday afternoon a deaf man named Joseph Henry Smith (48), Mount Cottage, Wherwell, was knocked down and killed by the 1.4 p.m. express train from Andover. At the inquest held by Mr. P. E. J. Talbot at the Poor Law Institution, Stockbridge, on Saturday, the jury returned a verdict of Accidental Death.

Mr. R. Proudfoot (Southampton) represented the Southern Railway Company. Frederick James Sullivan, 3, Whitworth Road, Gosport, carpenter, a half-brother, stated deceased was a pensioner of the Royal Marines, having been invalided out of the service as he was stone deaf. Witness was working at Stockbridge station and deceased came to see him there. Witness left him a few minutes before one o'clock and it was his intention to catch the 1.23 train back to Fullerton on his way home. Deceased was not a man likely to commit suicide.

WARNING SHOUT NOT HEARD

Alan Row, The Nest, High Street, Stockbridge, said about 1.20 he was on the road bridge over the railway and looking down towards the station he saw Smith come through the goods yard and through the gate on to the platform. He went round under the footbridge as if to cross the rails. Witness saw him until he got close to the rails and his view was then obscured. A train was coming from Andover and witness shouted twice, but Smith took no notice whatever. On crossing over the bridge to see if he could see the man, witness noticed pieces of a coat on the line, but not the man.

William J. Parsons, porter at Stockbridge station, said he knew Smith and took him to his brother. He afterwards saw him at the White Hart about 12.30, and witness left at 1.20. Deceased was then putting on his coat preparatory to leaving and he asked him to get him a ticket. He knew Smith intended to go by the 1.23 train to Fullerton, and before leaving, witness told him if he were going by that train to "buck up". He did not get the ticket. When witness left the hotel, Smith was perfectly sober. Witness went on to perform his duties on the down platform and while there he heard someone shout from the bridge at the same time the express was coming in from Andover. The train passed through the station at about 35 to 40 miles an hour.

NO BUSINESS ON LINE

Proceeding, witness stated that after the express had gone he looked down the line and saw something in a heap about 60 yards on the Southampton side of the bridge. On going there he saw it was Smith, who was terribly injured. There was a notice near to the point where Smith went on to the line stating "Passengers must cross the line by the bridge". No servant of the company was on duty at the time on the side where deceased entered.

The Coroner: He had no business on the line? - No, people should go over the bridge. The Coroner: But they don't all go - We get most of them over that way. Answering Mr. Proudfoot, Parsons said to get to the place where deceased was about to cross the line he would have to pass the bridge. Had he looked to his right as he entered the platform he could have seen the express train coming, and to get to the place where he was going to cross he would have his back to the oncoming train.

NOT SEEN BY DRIVER

The driver of the express, James William New, 68, Millway Road, Andover, said the train passed through Stockbridge at about 35 miles per hour. He was keeping the usual look-out, but saw nothing. When he arrived at Romsey he was informed by the stationmaster that he had knocked down and killed a man. He could see nothing on the engine, but at Southampton when he got underneath he could see blood and pieces of flesh. The engine had a right-hand drive, but had he had a left-hand drive engine, as he had the previous day, he should have seen the man. If he had seen deceased when his train was at the other end of the platform he could not, however, have stopped, as before he could shut off and apply the brakes he would have been through the station.

In reply to Mr. Proudfoot, witness said he had the whistle open and blew twice going through. In summing up, the Coroner observed that deceased only did what a good many people had done before. They would take a short cut, especially if in a hurry. Deceased had no right to be where he was - he was really trespassing. Though they did not look upon deceased as being a foolish man, people would break the rules - he had done it himself.

The Jury returned a verdict as stated. Mr. Proudfoot, on behalf of the Southern Railway Company, expressed regret at the accident and sympathy with the relatives - a sentiment with which the Coroner and the Jury associated themselves.

ANDOVER to REDBRIDGE

Freight from the Midlands bound for Southampton Docks, in the charge of Great Western 63xx No 6341, coming off the A&R at Kimbridge Junction to join the Salisbury—Eastleigh route on 17th August 1938. Trains and loads such as these would become commonplace over the following years.
(National Railway Museum/Box 290)

Chapter 5

LATE SOUTHERN TO EARLY BR

In the final Southern Railway timetable before Nationalisation, the weekday passenger service between Andover and Romsey consisted of nine up trains (eight on Saturdays) and eight down. Two each way were GWR services to and from Southampton via the MSWJ; these ran via Nursling, as did two Andover–Portsmouth services in each direction. The other weekday trains ran north of Romsey only, starting or terminating at Eastleigh in some cases. There were two Sunday services each way, all in the early evening except for 11.42am Romsey. The second down train started from Winchester (SR) at 4.10pm, ran via Southampton Central, and connected at Andover Junction into a Yeovil Town–Waterloo semi-fast, enabling people who spent the weekend in the Test Valley to return to the Home Counties, or vice-versa.

Local commuters were catered for by two trains timed to meet at Romsey at 8.10am. The first down passenger train, 7.54am Eastleigh, carried workers into Andover and the opposite flow was carried by 7.30am Andover–Romsey, where reasonable connections were available to Eastleigh, Southampton, Portsmouth and Bristol. From Fullerton and Clatford the local travel trend was towards Andover rather than to Romsey or Southampton. A12 Jubilees were still to be seen working local trains as late as 1946. The class became extinct in 1948.

The A&R south of Romsey was not vastly busier in terms of scheduled passenger trains (considering that it was part of the main line from the South Coast to Salisbury and Bristol). In winter 1947 there were a dozen passenger trains via Nursling in each direction during the week and five each way Sundays. About half of the weekday trains called at Nursling, but none on Sundays. As well as Bristol expresses, there was the SR Brighton–Plymouth train, conveying a Portsmouth portion and running non-stop between Southampton Central and Salisbury.

Post 1950, following a revision of regional boundaries, SR engines started working certain services over the former MSWJ line. SR T9 No 282 (with British Railways displayed on the tender), pauses at Andover Town on a Southampton train, at the head of WR stock on 14th May 1951. (T.C. Cole)

30125 departing south from Horsebridge. This was the engine that was involved in the run through incident at Rooksbury level crossing, which is described on page 85. The first carriage in the train is Bulleid stock.
(P.J. Cupper)

LATE SOUTHERN TO EARLY BR

63xx No 6341 approaching Stockbridge non-stop with the 10.15am Cheltenham Lansdown to Southampton Terminus service on 26th October 1957. After June 1958, there was only one fast service left to and from the former MSWJ, although in the opposite direction, a quirk of the timetable showed the corresponding down train pausing for a minute at Fullerton Junction of all places, its only stop between Romsey and Andover Town. (Denis Cullum)

North of Romsey, the SR train service pattern on the A&R was not unlike that on secondary GWR routes – infrequent; a mixture of origins and destinations; and patchy connections. Large gaps in Andover–Romsey services during the late morning and early afternoon meant that a traveller missing a connection at Andover Junction or Romsey could be stranded there for hours. Clatford had gaps of four to five hours in its service during the middle of the day, although it was possibly the least busy A&R station north of Romsey. One connection that must have caused some nail-biting was from a Plymouth–Waterloo express due in Andover Junction at around 1pm, into the 10.10am Cheltenham–Southampton, which was due to leave the Junction a few minutes later, for example, 1.3pm SX in Winter 1947. At least this would have been a cross-platform connection between trains on either side of the up island platform. Retiming in 1949 made the connection a little safer but if it was missed, southbound passengers had to kick their heels until after 4pm for the next service to Romsey.

Long distance travel via the A&R was frustrated not only by the shortcomings of its own timetable, but also because few West of England expresses called at Andover Junction, unlike today when all Waterloo–Exeter trains do so. Thus a journey between say Stockbridge and Devon usually involved changes at both Andover Junction and Salisbury. There were several ways of reaching Waterloo from the A&R, via Andover Junction, Eastleigh or Southampton, according to the time of day, although the first route often involved an additional change at Basingstoke. Despite its infrequent connections to the West, some people preferred the Test Valley route, and not just for its scenic beauty. Jack Morris, a railwayman living at Chandlers Ford in the early 1950s, used to take his family that way to Devon because there was less of a scramble for seats on an express at Andover Junction than at Salisbury. He recalls that T9s invariably hauled his train on the A&R, usually the second down service (8.33am Southampton Terminus via Eastleigh) which made a convenient connection into the 9am Waterloo–Plymouth.

Nationalisation from 1st January 1948 brought few changes to the route and its workings. The whole of the A&R became part of British Railways Southern Region while the entire MSWJ route transferred from GWR to BR Western Region ownership. Unfortunately the legislation had been rushed and one of its weaknesses had been the guarantee of a 4% interest payment on British Transport Commission stock, which the Transport Act had given to the former shareholders of the four private

GOODS

Top: U class 2-6-0 No 31802 nearing Fullerton on freight in October 1957.
(Denis Cullum)

Bottom: Another U class engine, this time No 31619 on an Eastleigh bound service on 17th August 1955. Judging from the headcode, it might well have originated at Bulford.
(J.H. Aston)

The private owner wagon depicted in the background was owned by A. Rhools Trist of Guildford (although lettered C. Emmence of Horsebridge) and carried the number 9.

SERVICES

Top: Occasional visitors to the A&R line were the Q class 0-6-0s, a number of which were based on Eastleigh. This picture shows No 30542 on a service of banana vans from Southampton Docks.
(Ron Grace)

Bottom: Apart from Stockbridge, goods traffic originating from, and destined for, the intermediate stations was sparse, and followed the national trend in reducing still further in the 1950s. It is unusual then to find a photograph (albeit slightly distant) of a wayside yard being shunted. This is taking place at Horsebridge on an unknown date in BR times. In charge is what appears to be a standard class 76xxx.

A wonderfully evocative view of Andover Town on a Saturday lunchtime in 1962, with shoppers about to board the train destined for Southampton.

(Rod Hoyle)

Companies in exchange for their shares. The interest had to be paid whatever the financial position of BR, which was worsening because of falling passenger traffic (due partly to the reintroduction of long distance motor coach services in 1946), staff shortages and substantial pay awards. The result was that any plans BR might have to improve services were overshadowed by the demands of its parent body, the BTC, to produce economies. Hence the creation in 1949 of the Branch Lines Committee, whose remit was to identify thinly trafficked lines for closure.

Local passenger trains south of Andover continued to be worked by M7 0-4-4Ts and T9 4-4-0s, with L11 4-4-0s putting in appearances. In mid 1948, L11 No 30442 was allocated to Andover sub-shed for working local freights on the A&R and the Longparish branch until its withdrawal in 1951. This class, although younger than the T9s, became extinct in 1952, by which time Eastleigh had acquired four Maunsell L1 4-4-0s to replace a diminishing stock of Adams and Drummond locomotives. Wainwright L 4-4-0s were observed during 1952, particularly on the last down train of the day, 7.45pm Portsmouth & Southsea–Andover Junction. On 2nd August L class No 31776 headed six corridor coaches from Bournemouth, presumably a return excursion. Ivatt 2-6-2Ts were also evident from 1952. In winter 1952/53 an Ivatt 2-6-2T at Andover shed was diagrammed for Turn 267, which included a late afternoon or early evening trip from Andover Junction to Romsey or Eastleigh after a morning on the Tidworth branch. On Saturdays, the 2-6-2T worked the 6.40pm Andover Junction–Eastleigh before retiring to Eastleigh shed, but the SX diagram was much more intensive, changing from Tidworth duties to the 4.12pm Andover Junction–Romsey, then a train to Southampton Terminus, thence to Alton and back to Eastleigh.

In the Winter 1948 Timetable, the weekday service north of Romsey was still nine up and eight down passenger trains, plus two freights each way. The early morning express freight from Cheltenham, due off Andover Town at 8.4am, was scheduled to pass Kimbridge Junction at 8.55. Up and down local freights were booked to meet at Fullerton at 10.15am, being allowed eight minutes running time between Clatford and Fullerton in either direction compared with five for a stopping passenger train.

GWR 43xx 2-6-0s and Manor 4-6-0s generally worked the trains originating or terminating on the

LATE SOUTHERN TO EARLY BR

MSWJ. By 1949 the 3.50pm Marlborough–Southampton Terminus (4.41pm Andover Junction) had reverted to its pre-1941 starting point of Cheltenham Lansdown. Wartime economies were gradually reversed as demobilisation raised manpower levels.

The Impact of Changes to MSWJ Workings

Regional boundary changes effective from 2nd April 1950 transferred all lines south of the Reading–Westbury–Taunton main line to the Southern Region, which now extended along the MSWJ route as far north as Grafton. Eastleigh-based U class 2-6-0s were tried out on some Southampton/Andover–Cheltenham passenger trains in April 1952, but the work soon reverted to their WR counterparts. The following year, the ex MSWJ shed at Andover was closed and permanent diagrams were introduced for U and N class locos from Eastleigh on Southampton–Cheltenham services. The MSWJ timetable was now constructed around loco and rolling stock diagrams starting and ending at Eastleigh rather than just Swindon or Cheltenham, although some MSWJ work remained with both Western depots. Cheltenham crews continued to work some Southampton trains as far as Andover Junction but did not have route knowledge over the A&R.

One example of this change was Andover Locomotive Turn 269. In winter 1952, a 43xx 2-6-0 was diagrammed to work the 7.30am from the Junction to Romsey, then the 8.32 Romsey–Eastleigh and the 9.2 Eastleigh–Southampton Terminus, due there at 9.22. Its next duty was the popular 10.10 Southampton Terminus–Cheltenham, returning with the 3.20pm freight from Cheltenham to Andover Junction. From the Winter 1953 Timetable, this sequence of trains was diagrammed for a U class 2-6-0.

The A&R had gained and lost journey opportunities from the Winter 1952 Timetable. The 9.30am Andover Junction–Romsey gained a connection from Swindon, but connections from Cheltenham (and places north) into the 6.35pm Andover Junction–Romsey were wiped out now that the incoming train started from Swindon Town. The two direct Cheltenham–Southampton trains continued to run, but the 4.30pm Southampton Terminus–Cheltenham became the final A&R service to places north of Andover because the 7.45pm from the Junction to Swindon was withdrawn. Overall, the effect was to reduce the usefulness of both routes for long distance

Push-pull working on the A&R line survived for certain services until the advent of dieselisation. 30481 propelling its train away from Clatford in the direction of Romsey, with what might well be the 5.42pm Andover Junction to Eastleigh service. The photograph was taken sometime after October 1957, a period that saw a purge at a number of locations where former LSWR lower quadrant signals were still in use. These were often replaced by standard upper quadrant arms as seen here, on the original post.
(D.W. Winkworth)

travel.

New BR Standard Class 4 4-6-0s (75xxx) and 2-6-0s (76xxx), also Eastleigh-based, found their way on to the line, as did 2-6-4 (80xxx) and 2-6-2 (82xxx) tank locos from the same stable. The tender engines worked passenger and freight trains via the MSWJ, while the Standard tanks were tried out on some of the local passenger trains south of Andover Junction. T9s nevertheless remained very much in evidence on these trains. Dai Evans, then a Driver at Andover, recalls that enginemen preferred the SR Moguls to the 76xxx series for the Southampton–Cheltenham trains because the latter type made heavy weather of the seven mile climb from Cheltenham to Andoversford. WR locos fresh out of Swindon Works after an overhaul often worked local trains over the A&R after a running-in turn to Andover Junction.

Resourcing Freight Services

On the eve of Nationalisation, the railway was still important to the local economy, as evidenced by the movement of a complete farm from Warwickshire to Clatford on 27th November 1947. Mr A.E. Harman of Norman Court Farm, Upper Clatford, received nine pedigree Guernsey cattle, a herd of pedigree Large White pigs (including four sows with litters), poultry, horses and eight farm cats, the latter conveyed in a specially constructed crate. The cows were milked during the 115 mile journey and the churns sent to the dairy soon after arriving at Clatford station around 10am. In all, 26 wagons were consigned to Andover Town, where heavy farm machinery was unloaded and the remainder of the train sent in batches to Clatford under the supervision of Mr F. Wasley, the Town Station Master.

Local freight trains were often worked by 700 class 0-6-0s and T9s, including trips to Longparish, worked by a loco and crew from Andover Junction. In the Winter 1952/53 Timetable, loco Turn 266 covered local freight workings and was rostered for a T9, which came off shed and worked as follows:

9.37am Andover Junction–Fullerton–Longparish, arriving Longparish at 11.5.
11.45 Longparish–Fullerton, arriving at 12 noon.
12.14 Fullerton–Romsey, arriving at 2.16pm, shunting at stations as required.
Mondays to Fridays
2.35pm Romsey–Nursling freight, arriving at 2.55, returning as 3.14 from Nursling, due in Romsey at 3.24pm, shunting as required.
6.5pm Romsey–Eastleigh freight, arriving at 6.39. Loco to shed.
Saturdays
3.30pm Light Engine Romsey–Eastleigh shed, arriving at 3.48.
4.40pm Light Engine Eastleigh shed–Southampton Terminus.
5.28pm Southampton Terminus–Portsmouth & Southsea passenger, arriving at 6.37.
7.45pm Portsmouth & Southsea–Andover Junction (via Redbridge) passenger, arriving at 10.4pm.

In the opposite direction, local freight was serviced by Eastleigh loco Turn 295, as follows:

Mondays to Fridays - L1 class 4-4-0.
6.40am Eastleigh–Andover Junction freight, arriving at 10.45. Loco to shed.
3.16pm Light Engine Andover shed to Andover Town, then shunting until 4.55pm.
5pm Andover Town–Andover Junction freight, arriving at 5.5.
6.40pm Andover Junction–Eastleigh passenger, arriving at 7.50.
Saturdays - Q class 0-6-0.
6.40am Eastleigh–Andover Junction freight, arriving at 10.45. Loco to shed.
5.30–8pm shunting at Andover Junction.
8.50pm Andover Junction–Eastleigh freight, arriving at 10.25. Loco to shed.

Sunset Over Longparish

The freight-only stub from Fullerton had survived on the strength of traffic to and from the ammunition dumps in Harewood Forest. For this reason, the Branch Lines Committee had decided in 1952 that the line should be retained, subject to further review if the Air Ministry depot at Longparish should close. After the depot closed on 31st January 1955, the Committee put forward a case for closure. It noted that remaining freight, now that the ammunition had been cleared, was mostly iron and steel for Messrs Kennedy & Kemp, tractor engineers of Longparish. The firm received sheets, strips and springs by train, forwarding ironwork such as chains. The Committee claimed that the tractors themselves were no longer forwarded or received by rail, although this is contradicted by Ron Grace, who began his railway career as a junior porter at Fullerton in 1955. Considering the highly rural area served by the branch and the absence of any traffic at Wherwell station, which was officially still open for freight, annual revenue for the branch of £5,014 (based on 1954 traffic levels and excluding Air Ministry traffic) was quite respectable against expenses of £10,437. No savings were expected in rolling stock, nor in heavy items of repair and renewal over the next 10 years if the line were to remain open. In this case at least, the Branch Lines Committee did not make the kind of

SUNSET OVER LONGPARISH

The final days of the freight only service on the stub end of the Hurstbourne line from Fullerton.

Top: This view was taken on 17th August 1955 and shows 700 class 0-6-0 No 30306 waiting at the one remaining branch platform, with just a brake van as its train.
(J.H. Aston)

Centre: 30288, an Eastleigh based T9 on a train of just three wagons at Wherwell, probably around the same period. The neatness of the track and ballast, even after so many years of minimal usage, is apparent. It was noted that expenses were twice that of any revenue

Right: Following the withdrawal of freight services from Hurstbourne and Wherwell, the truncated remains of the line were used for various purposes including the storage of condemned stock, and for testing new DeMUs. This picture from 19th April 1963 shows former 4-Sub EMU No 4352 sitting at the end of the line awaiting scrapping. At the other end was another 4-Sub, No 4348. One Eastleigh driver recalled that, when he was tasked with eventually collecting the stock for scrap, they had been standing for so long, and were so difficult to move, that the resultant jolts shook the glass out of a number of windows of the train. (R. Joanes)

ANDOVER to REDBRIDGE

For a time in the 1950s, a number of former SECR L1 class 4-4-0s were transferred to Eastleigh to augment the depleting ranks of T9 class engines, to work similar duties. It was not a popular choice and for really little reason other than tradition. One member of the class, No 31787 is seen here at Fullerton on an Andover to Portsmouth service.
(Brian Hart)

disingenuous claims so typical of the Beeching era that line closures would avoid spending vast amounts on track and signalling renewals within a few years.

Longparish was still forwarding 46 and receiving 460 parcels to and from stations beyond Fullerton in 1954 (compared with 66 and 481 respectively in 1953) but this traffic was expected to remain on rail. BR considered that alternative railheads at Andover Town, Fullerton and Sutton Scotney (the latter on the DNS) could handle any freight on offer at Longparish, and traffic losses from closure were predicted at only £400 per year. Five posts (a goods porter at Longparish, junior porter at Fullerton and three Permanent Way) would become redundant when the branch closed, although a Track Lengthman would be retained to maintain fencing, control pests and deal with other legal liabilities until the formation of the line could be sold. As things turned out, lifting of the track and disposal of the land was some way off because BR needed somewhere to store redundant wagons before they could be scrapped. (Aside from the storage of condemned and redundant wagons, the stub end of the branch was also used as a temporary home for withdrawn electric units for some time. The Longparish line was chosen for this as an alternative to the recently closed Bluebell route in East Sussex, which was deemed a political embarrassment after having to be re-opened following an initial objection to its closure. Possibly BR felt it prudent not to appear to reopen the entire Lewes–East Grinstead route a second time, which would have been a possibility if the track were used for temporary wagon storage.)

Nevertheless, the last revenue-earning train over the branch ran on 28th May 1956, powered by T9 No 30288, hauling one wagon of steel and a brake van to Longparish, and seen away on its return journey by Mr Whitemore, the Stockbridge Station Master. Ron Grace transferred to Eastleigh because his post at Fullerton was surplus to requirements.

Local Freight on the A&R

At this time, all A&R stations were handling freight, although Romsey was the only station between Andover Junction and Redbridge equipped with a crane. All except Fullerton and Nursling were still able to handle livestock. Andover Town, which had a substantial goods shed and sidings for timber merchants Messrs P. M. Combes, was particularly busy. Coal merchants Messrs Corrall and Day both had offices between the main station building and footbridge at Andover Town.

Fullerton despatched bulk loads of eggs from a packing station at Chilbolton, the wagons being berthed in the long siding at the north end of the station. These wagons were marshalled into a pick-up freight by the Horsebridge travelling shunter, for many years Bert Rogers, who also shunted Stockbridge yard. The local freight train might spend an hour at each yard.

Tractors and farm machinery repaired by Messrs Kennedy & Kemp had their rear wheels replaced with half-tracks for the rail journey to and from Fullerton. County Tractors, of Fleet, was a regular customer. Sugar beet was railed from Fullerton to various factories where it would be converted to animal feed. Inward freight at Fullerton included coal, animal feed and fertiliser, while many parcels arriving there had continued their journey in the brake van of the Longparish freight until the latter branch closed.

Fullerton goods yard was adjacent to the Longpar-

LATE SOUTHERN TO EARLY BR

Arguably a more suitable modern steam engine for branch and cross country work was the Ivatt 2-6-2T design, a number of which were allocated to Eastleigh. No 41304 of the class paused at Horsebridge with a 3-coach Bulleid 'cross-country' set on 17th August 1955. The striped lamp-posts and canopy supports, a reminder of the wartime years, will be noted.
(J. H. Aston)

ish branch, but there was also a refuge siding behind the down platform where the 6.40am Eastleigh–Andover pick-up freight would be stowed so that the 8.33 Southampton Terminus–Andover passenger train could enter the station. This siding, and the long one north of the station on the up side, had been installed at the expense of the Air Ministry but were now in use for regular freight. When asked to consider taking the two sidings out of use, the District Operating Superintendent pointed out that the egg traffic, increased fertiliser traffic from Messrs Smith Bros and coal traffic formerly dealt with at Longparish, were putting great pressure on the facilities at Fullerton. He added that when special and troop trains were run, the 6.48am Cheltenham High Street–Romsey freight was shunted on to the Longparish branch. He recommended that the up siding and 1,200 yards of the branch be retained. It would not be possible to retime the 6.40 Eastleigh freight, but it too could be recessed in the up siding if necessary.

In the Summer Timetables of 1956 and 1957, the 6.48 Cheltenham was non-stop from Andover Junction on Saturdays, although allowed 55 minutes for the 18 miles to Romsey, as it was not fully fitted. During the week it called at all goods yards south of Andover, with a long sojourn at Horsebridge for the 10.5 Cheltenham–Southampton passenger to overtake it. The freight was not due in Romsey until 2.16pm. A freight trip from Romsey left at 2.35 for Nursling, calling at Wills' siding from 2.38 to 2.47.

Despite the healthy freight traffic at Fullerton, its signal box was by this time open only as required, generally in the mornings, for recessing freight trains, shunting the yard, or when the Longparish branch was occupied.

The porter signalman would get a call from Stockbridge, Horsebridge, Mottisfont or Clatford, usually in the morning, advising him to 'switch in' at Fullerton.

Stockbridge and Horsebridge boxes were also switched out except when access to sidings was required. Andover Town, Clatford and Mottisfont boxes were open for all trains because they controlled level crossings. The A&R north of Kimbridge Junction was closed at night. Thus a special (presumably of troops) from Tidworth to Southampton Docks on 12th January 1952, worked by a WR 2-6-0, travelled out via the A&R but returned in the late evening via Basingstoke. Staffing was also frugal at the intermediate stations, Stockbridge being the only one between Andover Town and Romsey with a Station Master.

Clatford goods yard was serviced by the Andover Town travelling shunter and whatever locomotive was available to shunt both yards. Often this was a WR loco which had brought a freight train (such as 6.48 Cheltenham) into Andover Junction. These included 43xx 2-6-0s, 45xx 2-6-2Ts and 57xx pannier tanks. On 25th October 1956, 0-6-0PT No 3666 assisted T9 No 30707 from Andover Town to Junction after the latter had failed with bent coupling rods while working the 5.16pm Fawley–Andover passenger. 30707 was a regular performer on the A&R and had bent its coupling rods only the previous month.

Express Freight Trains

Long distance freight included banana trains from Southampton Docks to the Midlands and North. Ron Grace recalls an engine sometimes being sent from An-

ANDOVER to REDBRIDGE

dover Junction shed to Fullerton, where it would attach to the rear of a banana train to bank it up the 1 in 66 incline between Andover Town and Junction, for instance an N class 2-6-0 assisting a train hauled by an Eastleigh Q class 0-6-0. The Q and Q1 classes could work banana (and passenger) trains because these locos were equipped with steam heat connections to provide heat to all the wagons and assist ripening of the cargo. In 1955, 1956 and 1957 there were 'Q' paths for banana trains from Southampton Old Docks at 11.30am, 2.30 and 3.40pm, all via Nursling and including two-minute stops at Fullerton for the attachment of a banking engine. Three banana specials run over the A&R in May 1955 comprised 42, 37 and 40 wagons, out of 606 wagons loaded with bananas at Southampton Docks over a three-day period. Jack Herbert, then a Passed Fireman at Gloucester Horton Road, used to cover spare turns at Cheltenham and recalls Cheltenham crews occasionally working a 63xx 2-6-0 through to Southampton, piloted over the A&R by SR men, in order to return north with a banana special. Any suitable motive power would be deployed to get the perishable cargo away as soon as possible after the docking of a Fyffes boat.

During the early to mid 1950s, the first express freight train over the A&R was the 4.10am Cheltenham High Street–Southampton Terminus, generally worked by a Cheltenham 2-6-0 or Manor class which returned on the 11.30am empties from Bevois Park, although an Eastleigh N or U class was often used instead. Peter Cupper has recalled watching the 4.10 Cheltenham arrive at Southampton Terminus about 9.30, when wagons would be detached and shunted by the resident B4 0-4-0T before the WR loco took the remainder of the train to the Old Docks. In winter 1952, a Cheltenham 43xx was diagrammed to work this train and ran light from the Docks about 11am to Bevois Park sidings to collect its return train, which was due in Andover Junction at 1.12pm.

In summer 1956, there were two fitted or semi-fitted freights each way on weekdays between Cheltenham and Southampton or Eastleigh. The 4.10 Cheltenham was due at Andover Junction at 7.42 and followed the second passenger train of the day to Romsey before continuing to Southampton via Redbridge. Its formation was loco, wagons for Romsey, Portsmouth, Eastleigh and transfer, Southampton Terminus, Southampton Docks, brake van. In summer 1957 it was starting from Washwood Heath at 2.15 as a fully fitted express (XF) service. The other fast southbound freight at this time was 3.20pm Cheltenham–Eastleigh, running to Swindon in the path of a passenger service withdrawn in 1952. Departing from the Junction at 8.50, it was due in Eastleigh yard at 10.27. Cargoes on these southbound freights included Bass beer and Fry's chocolate for export via Southampton, and steel used in the construction of Marchwood power station.

In the opposite direction, the 11.30am Bevois Park–Washwood Heath had no traffic stops between Andover Junction (where its load could be increased) and Cheltenham, although it had three booked crossings with passenger trains on single-track sections of the MSWJ. The 7.4pm Southampton Docks–Cheltenham, which often carried imported timber, did not reach Cheltenham High Street until 1am. This wide spread of freight paths made little difference to signal box hours on the A&R, but required 20-hour opening of boxes on the MSWJ north of Cirencester. This would strain the economics of the MSWJ route as its passenger traffic decreased, and hence undermine the viability of the A&R as a major freight route between Southampton and the North. Another weak link in this north-south chain was that the length of freight trains over the A&R was limited by the length of passing loops on the MSWJ.

Chapter 6

THE DAWN OF THE DIESELS

In 1952, a Railway Executive committee chaired by Mr H.G. Bowles of the Western Region had recommended the construction of lightweight diesel multiple units to replace a number of steam-hauled secondary passenger services. This was the objective face of BR's search for economies – one of investment as opposed to the more negative approach of the Branch Lines Committees. Hampshire was among the areas that the Bowles Report proposed for DMU operation because many of its passenger services were by then worked by elderly locomotives and coaches, not least on the A&R.

Three years later, the Government approved in principle a Modernisation Plan, which included expenditure of £285m for new coaches and 4,600 DMU vehicles. While most Regions favoured diesel mechanical multiple units, the Southern preferred diesel electric units as its eventual standard passenger trains on non-electrified routes. A decision was made to fit the engines above the floor and while this would reduce seating capacity compared to that of a diesel mechanical set, it would allow the DeMUs to maintain higher levels of speed, so as not to cause delay to electric multiple units and steam-hauled expresses. The SR did not envisage its basic diesel set as just a branch line vehicle, and its first batch of DeMUs replaced steam-worked expresses as well as stopping trains on the Charing Cross–Hastings line. Construction of the Hastings sets had started in 1955 and a scheme to convert stopping passenger services in Hampshire to diesel operation was added on.

The initial batch of 18 two-car sets (numbered 1101–1118) for the Hampshire scheme was built at Eastleigh Works, where No 1101 made its first public appearance at an Open Day in August 1957. Each set comprised a motor brake second class car housing the 500hp engine, parcels compartment and five passenger semi-compartments; the other vehicle was a driving trailer composite, including five second class semi-compartments, two toilets, two first class compartments and a final second class (smoking) compartment, which had no access to the toilets and which was immediately behind the driving cab. Total seating capacity was 127 per set, considerably less than on a three- or four-coach loco-hauled train.

Training for the first phase of the Hampshire diesel programme had begun in March, using the brand new Hastings set 1005, running between Eastleigh, Romsey, Stockbridge and Fullerton. Further trials on the A&R were undertaken in August using newly built Hampshire sets 1101 and 1102. The workings to Fullerton ran into the Longparish platform, but not on to the branch proper (which was by then used for storing condemned wagons as well as electric sets that were awaiting scrapping).

The first stage of diesel passenger services in Hampshire began on 16th September, when 10 sets took over stopping trains between Portsmouth, Southampton and Salisbury. At the same time, an interim hourly service was introduced between Portsmouth, Eastleigh, Romsey and Andover Junction, using steam traction, generally of three-coach Bulleid sets and calling at all stations. The frequency of service via Stockbridge was greatly improved, but connections for Southampton were poor at Romsey, although better at Eastleigh. The Western Region continued to run two trains each way between Cheltenham and Southampton via Redbridge, and these provided the fastest journeys from Andover to Southampton or vice versa.

The A&R gained six trains between Andover and Portsmouth, filling significant gaps between mid morning and late afternoon. The 11.25 Andover Junction–Eastleigh was extended to Portsmouth and retimed to start at 11.42, xx.42 becoming the standard departure from Junction for most of the day. Eastleigh provided connections with Winchester and Southampton, partly compensating for missed opportunities at Romsey.

The interim steam service was a more complicated operation than using push-pull sets because the Romsey bay at Andover Junction had no runround loop. Trains from the Romsey direction therefore ran into the down main platform. Another locomotive had to be ready to take the set on its next working to Portsmouth while the locomotive that had just arrived was serviced. Up trains either started from the island platform or were shunted into the Romsey bay. Dennis Cullum, who worked in the SR Waterloo Headquarters, saw five different three-coach sets hauled by a total of seven locomotives (three T9s, two M7s, a U class and a Standard Class 4 2-6-0) provide six trains to and from Portsmouth when he walked the route with a lineside pass on 26th October, the penultimate Saturday of the interim steam timetable. Set 812, for instance, was powered by 76013 on its 9.53am Portsmouth

Previous page: T9 No 30726 entering Horsebridge with Bulleid 'cross-country' set No 818 during the final week of the interim steam interval service, November 1957. Although some modernisation did occur to the signalling on the line in the 1950s, a number of locations north of Romsey retained their lower quadrant LSWR arms right to the very end.

(P.J. Cupper)

ANDOVER to REDBRIDGE

Leaving Fullerton for Clatford and Andover, taken looking north from the A3057 road bridge.

(Rod Hoyle)

leg, returning as 11.42 Andover behind 30726, which in turn was relieved by another T9, 30732, to bring the train back as 1.53pm Portsmouth. One diesel set could have accomplished all three workings, and soon the basic service via Stockbridge, excluding the WR Cheltenham trains, would be operated by just three diesel sets. The justification for conversion to diesel operation had been the prospect of reduced rolling stock mileages, faster turnarounds, concentration of all maintenance at Eastleigh (where a new four-road DMU shed was built) and fuelling at Eastleigh and Fratton.

For rail users there would be more frequent, regular interval services, but not at Nursling, where the station closed on 16th September, a victim of bus and car competition. Nursling signal box was switched out from this date, opening thereafter on summer Saturdays only until final closure on 25th March 1965. The last trains to call at Nursling on Saturday 14th September were the 2pm from Cheltenham headed by U class 2-6-0 No 31618, and the 7.25pm Portsmouth & Southsea–Andover Junction, worked by sister engine 31803. A dozen or so villagers turned out to see off the latter, but less than three months passed before the 7.25am Romsey–Southampton Terminus stopped in error on 9th December.

The Test Valley is Converted to Diesel Operation

When the second phase of the scheme began on 4th November, a further eight two-car diesel sets entered

THE DAWN OF THE DIESELS

service, enabling the Portsmouth–Eastleigh–Andover and Eastleigh–Winchester–Alton routes to be dieselised. The entire Hampshire diesel operation was now based on 17 of the 18 two-car sets being available for traffic, giving little scope for handling peaks. Today's train operators, subject to fines for delays and cancellations, would no doubt regard 94% availability as uncomfortably tight. By the autumn of 1958, availability had been eased to 14 out of 16 sets in traffic at any one time with two others undergoing tyre returning in Eastleigh Works because of the very high mileages run (at a rate of 120,000 miles per set, per year, in the Winter 1957/58 Timetable).

The faster schedules enabled xx.53 departures from Portsmouth & Southsea to reach Andover Junction at yy.29 compared with yy.34 on the interim steam services. Most of the acceleration was east of Eastleigh, particularly in the Portsmouth direction. Running times over the A&R itself were little changed from the interim schedules, although a few significant changes were made to suit the DeMU diagrams. One set was cycled via Salisbury each night, resulting in the last down train, 8.53pm Portsmouth, continuing from Andover Junction at 10.31 to Salisbury, whence it started next morning at 6.16 to run as 6.42 Andover Junction. In steam days, for instance Winter 1955, a Salisbury T9 had worked a train via Andover to Eastleigh in the same path, but had returned much earlier in the evening.

Other alterations were influenced by the need to maintain an effective timetable. The 2pm from Cheltenham, due off Andover Junction at 4.40, would have clashed with the 4.42 DeMU so the WR train now ran non-stop from Andover Town to Romsey. The diesel train now started at 4.48, calling all stations to Eastleigh, where it terminated Mondays to Fridays.

Reaction to the DeMUs in the first few months was mixed. Commuters used to four-coach loco-hauled

An example of the steam interval service. 76013 has charge of the 9.53am Portsmouth and Southsea to Andover Junction service and has just left Fullerton on 26th October 1957, with Bulleid set No 812. The train is just passing the original Fullerton Bridge Station. This had been opened with that name on 6th March 1865. The suffix was dropped from October 1871, and the original station was closed when the replacement Fullerton opened as a result of the new line to Hurstbourne on 1st June 1885. This new station later carried the suffix Junction from May 1889 until 7th July 1929.

(Denis Cullum)

Andover Town showing evidence of the inconvenient relationship between rail and road users at the level crossing. The headcode 47 referred to services between Andover and Portsmouth, regardless of up or down workings.

(Rod Hoyle)

trains in the Southampton evening peak were not amused at having to travel in two-car sets. Other complaints included the noise from the diesel engines and rough riding. The Hastings sets had been fitted with silencers – or more accurately 'mufflers', basically boxes filled with steel wool and placed over the exhaust pipe, so reducing the noise level from 94 to 90 decibels, and the Hampshire sets were likewise modified. 22 centre trailers and four new three-car sets were ordered in the autumn of 1958, although not delivered until November 1959. When the trailers were fitted to the original 18 two-car sets, they were fitted with 600hp engines to improve the power to weight ratio. At 56 tons, the DeMU power cars were about 60% heavier than those of diesel mechanical multiple units going into service on the London Midland Region.

From 5th May 1958, with diesel modifications in progress, the A&R had reverted partly to steam haulage in order to release sets for the Alton route. Alternate diesel services from Portsmouth terminated at Eastleigh, connecting with trains to Andover worked by M7 0-4-4Ts with push-pull sets in an effort to keep as close as possible to diesel timings. A shortage of push-pull sets at Bournemouth in March 1959 resulted in a brief reappear-

THE DAWN OF THE DIESELS

Horsebridge, with modern (for the period) traction, but the infrastructure and operating practices of an older period. An unidentified unit awaits departure north for Stockbridge and Andover.

(Rod Hoyle)

ance of Standard Class 3 2-6-2Ts (82xxx) hauling three-coach sets on the Romsey–Andover route.

The increased frequency of trains reopened old anxieties about the safety of farm crossings. Mr Cooper, tenant of Westover Farm, who had asked in 1949 for improved warning facilities at Westover crossing, now made representations for warning bells to be installed. In discussions with the District Traffic Superintendent's Office (DTSO), he advised that the movement of cattle across the line was confined to Westover and Wherwell crossings, mainly between April and October. His principal concern was about Westover crossing, where up trains had limited visibility.

On 21st October 1957 the DTSO wrote to the Chief Operating Superintendent, Waterloo, detailing the safety devices then available at each of the four crossings in a 15 chain stretch between Fullerton and Clatford. The letter noted that Lower Trent crossing (at 4m 11ch) had not been used for some time but that a bell, intended to warn crossing users, was activated by a treadle in the down line 64 chains away and had been observed to ring for 95 seconds before the arrival of a steam hauled passenger train; the writer suggested that this warning period might be shorter with a diesel unit, which could run faster up hill. He added that the bell had evidently been installed in LSWR days because of the restricted sighting due to the line curvature and a cutting.

Concerning Wherwell crossing, the letter referred to its regular use for moving 100 or so cattle grazing in the water meadows on the up side of the line between Wherwell and Lower Trent crossings, adding that one herd was observed to take almost three minutes to cross.

The letter concluded that, despite the more frequent train service, the situation did not justify installation of telephones at Westover or Wherwell crossings because of the expense, likely to involve a connection with Andover Town signal box because of a proposal to close Clatford level crossing and reduce the opening hours of the box there. Provision of telephones might generate a flood of applications from other local farmers expecting the same. Instead it suggested provision of a whistle board on the Clatford side of Upper Westover

ANDOVER to REDBRIDGE

The use of a few BR 82xxx class locos was mainly confined to a brief period in 1959, although this particular engine was recorded on a southbound service between Andover Town and Clatford on 22nd May 1956.

(E. Gamblin)

crossing, to give up trains earlier warning of the four crossings.

A later internal memo referred to the risk of wrong side failures by track circuits or treadles that failed to activate warning bells.

A Signal Sighting Committee was convened at Clatford on 27th November 1957 and recommended installation of a whistle board 310 yards from Upper Westover crossing on the up side. With effect from 10th March 1958 an instruction was added to the Engine Whistle Codes of the Western Section Appendix to the Working Timetables, requiring Drivers of up trains to sound one long whistle when approaching Westover crossing. The same amendment repeated the older instruction reminding Drivers of down trains to sound the whistle continuously from the down whistle board to Lower Trent crossing.

Erection of the up line whistle board was deferred by restrictions on capital expenditure that had gripped BR in the spring of 1958. Nevertheless, the Chief Solicitor's Department, while stating that the law required crossing users to ascertain that it was safe to use the crossing on each occasion, accepted that these particular crossings presented a special case:

"The difficulties…..arise because in actual fact the user <u>cannot know</u> whether it is safe to cross or not because of the way in which the railway was constructed. There is, therefore, a duty upon the (British Transport) Commission to take special precautions. Until recent years, it has been thought that whistle boards and the corresponding whistling of approaching trains for an appropriate distance is sufficient to satisfy the requirements of the law. I am in no doubt that the very least that is required of the Commission is to have these boards and to do their utmost to see that drivers are in fact causing the whistle to be sounded as they approach these four crossings."

Adding that a Court of law might well find liability against the Commission in the event of an accident at one of these crossings if there had been a failure to take special precautionary measures, the letter went on to suggest installation of telephones at Westover and Wherwell crossings.

Faced with these arguments, the Operating Superintendent recommended expenditure of £37 on the up line whistle board, which was installed on 15th October.

Financial Crisis and the Rundown of the MSWJ

Throughout the 1950s, BR experienced difficulty recruiting and retaining staff because pay rates had fallen behind those offered by other industries. In 1958, a Joint Advisory Board of senior BR and Trade Union officials appointed an Independent Pay Inquiry Committee, chaired by Mr C.W. Guillebaud, Reader in Economics at Cambridge University, to examine the case for improving the relative position of railway wages to those of other skilled manual work. The Committee offered an interim increase in pay of 3% soon afterwards and this was accepted by BR and the trade unions early in June. Unfortunately this triggered a major financial crisis of which the root causes were falling revenue and the continuing burden of interest payments on BTC stock.

Although both passenger and freight traffic on the railways had been boosted by petrol rationing in the aftermath of the Suez crisis, reflected in improved results in 1957, these gains were largely wiped out by the Government's decision that September to restrict credit and freeze investment in nationalised industries. With industrial output falling, particularly in the coal and steel industries that provided the lion's share of rail freight, BR found itself having to finance a pay rise of slightly above inflation when its bread and butter was disappearing. Rising car ownership, falling passenger revenue and the lib-

THE DAWN OF THE DIESELS

Typical of the final period in the life of the MSWJ was a Southern Mogul type at the head of perhaps three WR coaches. U class 2-6-0 No 31619 leaving Mottisfont for Romsey and eventually Southampton Terminus with the 1.56pm ex Cheltenham on 25th May 1957.

(C. Saunders / R. Blencowe)

eralisation of road haulage as a result of the 1953 Transport Act, weakened BR's ability to offset the effect of a larger pay bill. While there was evidence of increasing passenger numbers and income on routes that had recently enjoyed regular interval diesel services, these were as yet too localised to produce a dramatic increase in revenue nationally.

While the Southern Region could reduce the frequency of its lavish suburban services without causing much hardship, the directive that costs had to be reduced by 14% as a matter of urgency created a dilemma elsewhere on the rail network. If the SR were to trim its Hampshire diesel services, which were of generous frequency for a largely rural area, it would convey a message that future phases of the Hampshire scheme were not essential. There was a risk that the additional trailer cars and three-car sets envisaged for later phases would be shelved or reassigned to other routes. If big savings were required in train movement and staff costs, the easiest targets would be the longer rural and secondary main line routes on which business had suffered from unimaginative timetables and where costs were relatively high because of long signal box opening hours. There were many such routes on the Western Region, where services generally were not lavish outside the commuting areas of the big cities, so that any hastily arranged cuts were likely to create huge gaps in timetables, with a disastrous effect on revenue. It was easier to market shorter routes such as Andover–Portsmouth, because the local travel patterns were well known and custom would be encouraged by the hourly service. Cross-country travel was less predictable, requiring good connections, faster timings and co-operation between different BR regions if an attractive service was to be provided. In the case of the MSWJ route, three regions, including the London Midland which ran the connecting expresses from Cheltenham, were involved. The MSWJ was also vulnerable because it was still entirely steam-operated and there was a national shortage of Firemen and Cleaners, partly due to a peak of retirements among Drivers who had joined the railway just after the First World War. All these factors encouraged the Southern to concentrate on its own service south of Andover and the Western to plan the rundown of the MSWJ route, now entirely under its management following a further change of Regional boundaries on 1st February. It had already removed early and late freights (the 2.15am Washwood Heath–Southampton in September 1957 and the 7.4pm Southampton Docks–

ANDOVER to REDBRIDGE

Stockbridge. A consequence of the introduction of the diesel services were 'stop' boards informing the driver of the service where to come to rest. The rear of one of these can be seen at the base of the footbridge. (Rod Hoyle)

Cheltenham) to eliminate night operations over the MSWJ.

Accordingly, the axe was now being sharpened for the thinly trafficked MSWJ and DNS lines, this despite their potential for long-distance travel. What both those routes needed was to develop their through traffic, a point made by correspondents in *Railway Magazine*, but neither Region's management had the necessary vision, although the DNS was still regarded as having a future for inter-regional freight. On the very day that the interim pay award took effect, 30th June 1958, many WR routes had their services slashed in order to achieve drastic savings in overheads. Among the casualties were one of the two Cheltenham–Southampton trains, and both return workings, including the popular 10.10am from Southampton Terminus.

The Cheltenham trains were the fastest through the Test Valley, complementing the regular interval stopping services and maintaining the A&R as a gateway to the Midlands and North. This gateway was effectively closed from 3rd November, when the track layout at Lansdown Junction, Cheltenham was altered so that trains coming via the MSWJ could no longer run into Lansdown station, where connections had been made with trains to the North of England and Scotland. Of course, the remaining through train (now 2pm Cheltenham St. James) could still connect from the North at Malvern Road station but any thoughts of developing that connection for passenger or freight via Andover was far from the minds of WR Management desperate to cut costs.

At the start of the Summer 1958 Timetable there was just one daily through freight each way between Southampton and Cheltenham, the down train normally starting from Bevois Park at 11.45am (although it could run instead as 11.30 from the Old Docks). Either version ran via Eastleigh and was due to pass Kimbridge Junction at 12.20, reaching Andover Junction at 1.10. This was allowed to convey up to 39 wagons plus brake van, but Andover Junction could increase this load to 50 for the MSWJ portion of the journey. The up train started from Cheltenham at 3.20pm, Mondays to Saturdays, and

THE DAWN OF THE DIESELS

Horsebridge in in early 1960s, replete with standard green enamel notices. The canopy-support columns have been repainted since the view on page 51 was taken.

(Rod Hoyle)

was due off Andover Junction at 8.50, following the 8.42 DeMU. Additionally, there was a Q path for a 2.48pm Southampton Docks–Cheltenham, catering for banana traffic, which ran via Redbridge to reach Andover Junction at 4.15. Local freight was served by a round trip departing Eastleigh at 6.45am, returning from Andover Junction at 1.10pm. These had to be pathed around the hourly diesel passenger service, especially in the case of the down train which was booked to dwell two hours at Romsey until 9.10, with 20–30 minute waits at Stockbridge, Fullerton and Clatford for passenger trains to overtake it. At Fullerton the overtaking train was the 10.10 Southampton Terminus–Cheltenham until the latter was abruptly withdrawn. The 6.45 Eastleigh was limited to 25 wagons north of Romsey because of siding lengths at some goods yards. The 1.10pm Andover Junction had replaced the 6.48am Cheltenham in servicing all goods yards from Clatford to Romsey.

The express freight trains were withdrawn around the same time as the track remodelling took place at Cheltenham. Thereafter, the A&R north of Romsey carried only local or diverted freight. With incredible timing, this abandonment of through freight came just as BR achieved what may have been a post-war record despatch of freight in one day from Southampton Docks: 12 trains totalling 523 wagons, mainly laden with bananas, citrus fruits and meat, on 2nd November. More freight was precisely what it needed to revive its fortunes, but as one part of BR was doing its utmost to win and move traffic, others were reducing the number of routes available to carry it.

The winter 1958/59 Timetable brought an unusual working to the A&R in the form of a Saturday passenger service diagrammed for a WR 45xx 2-6-2T. This was the 1.3pm from Andover Junction, returning at 4.50pm from Southampton Terminus. Both trains were a remnant of the Cheltenham services that had been curtailed in the summer. This round trip remained steam-hauled even after delivery of three-car DeMUs brought an end to push-pull working between Eastleigh, Romsey and Southampton from 4th January 1960. On 14th May 1960 the restored ex GWR 4-4-0, 3440 "City of Truro" traversed the A&R on a railtour to Southampton Docks via the MSWJ. This loco had been a regular performer over the DNS in 1957/58 following its liberation from York Railway Museum in 1957.

Closure of the MSWJ to passengers (and entirely between Ludgershall and Savernake) on 11th September 1961 came as little surprise. Any lingering hopes of the A&R remaining a feasible link between Hampshire, the Midlands and North had now vanished. In its final years, the remaining northbound train (7.50am Andover Junction–Cheltenham St. James) had a connection from the Romsey direction, due in Andover Junction at 7.10, while the return working, 1.56pm Cheltenham St. James, valiantly ran through to Southampton Terminus to return the loco, usually an N, U or Standard Class 4 2-6-0, to Eastleigh. Sunday services had run over the MSWJ south of Swindon in the final timetable, worked by WR 2-6-0s and, thanks to the DeMU services on the A&R, had enabled Wiltshire people to have a day away at Portsmouth.

Kimbridge Junction. The 20mph restriction applied to trains leaving the Salisbury route and turning north towards Andover. *(Rod Hoyle)*

Chapter 7

A HOSTILE CLIMATE

By the end of 1962, the line had developed a significant passenger business from five years of hourly services. Despite the loss of modest through traffic when the MSWJ route closed, the A&R itself had gained from the rerouting on 18th June of most of the trains via its original metals to provide regular direct services to and from Southampton Central. This was achieved by extending the stopping Portsmouth–Southampton trains to Andover. The first weekday train from Andover continued to run via Chandlers Ford to Eastleigh, and was well patronised by young people attending the Eastleigh Technical College. Another benefit was an increase in Sunday services to 10 each way. The Saturday afternoon steam workings ceased from that date with the closure of the sub-shed at Andover Junction, although steam locos were still seen on freight and excursion trains as well as covering diesel failures.

The Summer 1962 Timetable was marketed by a green-covered timetable booklet, covering all the Hampshire DeMU routes and quoting a selection of local fares and season ticket rates. Phase 2 of the dieselisation scheme, including Reading–Portsmouth services via Eastleigh, was at last up and running, about two and a half years later than originally envisaged. The booklet referred to the routing of Andover trains via Southampton as a benefit, although the decision may have been influenced by the need to free up paths on the Eastleigh–Fareham line for the new Reading service.

The freight picture was less favourable. North of Romsey, the A&R had ceased to be a freight artery when the MSWJ had been run down in the late 1950s, although its own double track route was available for diversions and as a link between Eastleigh yard and the military branches to Bulford and Ludgershall, the latter now the freight-only stub of the MSWJ from Andover. Even at Andover Town, the busiest goods yard on the line, there had been a heavy decline in traffic, from 5,000 wagons in 1938 to 1,400 in 1962; coal traffic received fell from 17,000 to 7,500 tons over the same period. Clatford goods yard had closed in 1961. Fullerton was still receiving coal and fertiliser by rail but Ron Grace recalls that the egg traffic had now ceased.

It was unfortunate that freight services were withdrawn from Horsebridge and Stockbridge on 7th and 21st January 1963 respectively, two months before publication of the Beeching Report, which proposed four of Hampshire's dieselised passenger services for closure. Those lines were Alton–Winchester, Eastleigh–Romsey, Southampton–Fawley and Andover Junction–Romsey. With little regular freight between Andover Junction and Kimbridge Junction, the cost of maintaining 15 miles of double track and five intermediate signal boxes was borne mainly by the passenger trains which, although very well supported in the peak hours and moderately at other times, were probably not profitable because of the low intermediate population. The Beeching mentality did not see the line's capacity for additional or diverted traffic as an asset. Rather, the lack of through freight services was simply an added argument for closing the line.

It was not only BR Management who now saw the line as just a liability. The *Andover Advertiser* went further, implying that the Beeching proposals offered a wonderful opportunity for road users because closure of Andover Town station would remove "the thoroughly unpopular Bridge Street level crossing."

> "Few tears will be shed over this and many Andoverians will feel that the loss of the Romsey line will be a cheap price to pay to be rid of the inconvenience of the level crossing."

Routes that had been seen as promising candidates for development only a few years earlier were now threatened by what looked like an abrupt change in Government policy. One reason was the appointment of Ernest Marples as Minister of Transport after the 1959 General Election. He had direct personal involvement with the road construction industry and pursued policies that would increase public spending on roads at the expense of the railway system. The recommendations of the Guillebaud Committee for a substantial increase in railwaymen's pay no doubt hardened Government thinking in favour of reducing the network. In 1961, the Ministry of Transport had created its Railways B Division specifically to process proposals to close uneconomic lines.

The Southern Region lost little time in preparing a statutory closure proposal for Andover–Romsey, and it was published on 2nd August 1963. Local railwaymen had already been informed officially at a staff consultation meeting held at Andover Junction on 19th July that the line would close to passengers from 7th October if no objections were lodged with the South East Area Transport Users' Consultative Committee by 21st September. It was reported that closure would eliminate 23 posts.

In trying to mobilise opposition to the proposals, the local branch of the National Union of Railwaymen attacked the basis of BR's financial case, which quoted the passenger service as earning £20,500 and costing £47,900 per annum. BR admitted that revenue was calcu-

Passengers joining a Romsey bound service at Andover Town in September 1964.

(Rod Hoyle)

lated in terms of journeys made between Andover and Romsey multiplied by the average fare paid. So although a high proportion of journeys were to Southampton, Portsmouth and other destinations south of Romsey, only the value of fares to Romsey southbound or Andover northbound would be counted. This gave a very distorted picture of the financial health of lines that contributed a great deal of revenue to the remainder of the network. It also seemed to rest on the assumption that people travelling south of Romsey would either use the proposed substitute buses and connect into trains there, or travel from Andover Junction to Southampton via Salisbury, a distance of 42 miles compared to 25 over the threatened route. Yet this was the normal basis on which the revenue effect of proposed closures was estimated.

BR also expected to save £100,000 over the next five years on track, signalling and bridge renewals that would be avoided if the line were closed. The local NUR branch countered this by saying that very little had been spent on the route and its stations over the previous 10 years. A number of 25mph speed restrictions were in force, and concrete sleepers that had been unloaded earlier in the year were removed by Engineering trains after lying unused. The state of Andover Town, Stockbridge and especially Fullerton station exteriors seemed to confirm this impression of neglect, the latter being one of the most dilapidated on the Region. This did not seem to indicate positive marketing of the hourly diesel services but was no doubt indicative of BR's desperate financial position from the late 1950s. Dieselisation had got off the ground just before BR went into a financial straitjacket, and might not have happened had it been delayed a year or two. The real reason for dieselisation had been to save on operating costs at a time when it was becoming more difficult to recruit staff, and the impression of service expansion masked an underlying search for economies. The Branch Lines Committee had considered singling the route north of Kimbridge Junction as early as 1952, and BR was progressing the abolition of Clatford level crossing at the time of dieselisation. Closure of Nursling station had probably been identified as a saving to help justify the financial case for the diesel service. BR's reluctance to spend £37 for a whistle board at Upper Westover crossing, and its Winter Sunday closure of Fullerton and Horsebridge stations from 15th September 1958, all suggest that the financial position was very different from the impression given by new trains running more frequently. Peter Noyce believes that Andover–Romsey might well have closed along with the MSWJ had the Hampshire DeMU scheme not already been in place. Andover was still a relatively small town (population 17,000 in 1961) and the expansion plans might not have been known to BR officials preparing the MSWJ closure.

The haste with which BR was seeking to close

The run down appearance of the up-side platform canopy at Fullerton in July 1964 did little to enhance the image of the railway.

(Rod Hoyle)

Andover–Romsey was in contrast to the situation regarding the other three dieselised lines in Hampshire that Beeching had condemned. The Romsey–Eastleigh line and the Fawley branch both carried heavy freight traffic, while Alton–Winchester would be needed for diversions during the proposed electrification of the Bournemouth main line. It is tempting to suggest that lines such as the A&R, which had experienced substantial growth in recent years through improved timetables, were an embarrassment to official thinking. The new orthodoxy decreed that rural branch lines could never succeed, yet the diesels serving the Test Valley could hardly be described as an abject failure, when BR's traffic censuses showed 5,000 passenger journeys over the line in an April week and 7,000 in a July week.

The threat to the line generated suggestions from local authorities, the NUR branch, and individual objectors for further economies in its operation. Some of these ideas were misguided in proposing singling of the track and shorter, less frequent trains. While 15 miles of double track may have seemed extravagant for an hourly passenger service, most of the intermediate signal boxes had in latter years been switched in for a couple of hours to allow shunting. Had the route been singled, each crossing place would have needed a signal box manned for all trains, resulting in higher staff costs unless early and late trains were withdrawn. The first two weekday trains from Andover were the busiest on the line. Shorter trains, such as the diesel railbuses or single railcars fa-

ANDOVER to REDBRIDGE

Evidence of economy: the signal box at Horsebridge switched out and un-manned. The starting signals in both directions showing 'off'. (J.H. Aston)

voured by some of the line's defenders, could not have coped with the morning peak into Andover, let alone the much heavier one towards Eastleigh and Southampton.

The most realistic suggestions for reducing costs involved destaffing stations, with tickets being issued on trains by Conductors. Given the short distances between stations on the A&R, it would have made sense for Andover Town to retain a ticket office for most of the day, and Stockbridge for the morning peak, but the four other branch stations north of Romsey did not justify ticket offices for the number of people travelling in later years. The idea of Conductor guards and unmanned stations now seemed to be taken seriously by the *Andover Advertiser*, which only a few months earlier had welcomed the Beeching proposals.

Some questionable economies had already been made, such as Winter Sunday closure of Fullerton and Horsebridge, then at Clatford on Sundays all year from January 1962. BR claimed that ticket sales at Clatford had never exceeded 16s 10d (84p) on a Sunday during the previous six months, against a wages outlay of £2 16s 4d (£2.81) for a porter signalman, but the value of tickets issued to Clatford from other stations does not appear to have been considered. Clatford level crossing had already been reduced to a foot crossing in 1960, and the signal box was closed from 25th February 1962. The block sections now became Andover Junction East to Andover Town; Andover Town to Mottisfont (except when Fullerton, Stockbridge or Horsebridge boxes were switched in); and Mottisfont to Kimbridge Junction.

It made little sense to close stations on Sundays as a means of justifying staffing reductions, because the paybill savings would have been eroded by loss of revenue. Many Southern Region stations had lost their Sunday services from 15th September 1958 simply because the porter signalman did not have a level crossing to operate. This exercise was implemented with little regard for potential revenue. Arguably, Fullerton, which served much of the Leckford Estate and several villages in the upper Test Valley, had more potential as a railhead than did Mottisfont, where the village was only half a mile from Dunbridge station on the Salisbury–Southampton main line, but which continued to enjoy Sunday trains all year because the signal box controlled a level crossing. Further evidence of a lack of imagination on BR's part was the Sunday closure of Chandlers Ford station, de-

Evidence of expenditure: recent relaying of both lines with concrete sleepers, but with nearly all trains running over the line diesel units, was the cost justified? (P.H. Swift)

spite a rapidly growing population (which has resulted in its reopening in 2003). As with many late 1950s train service enhancements, the benefits of the Hampshire dieselisation were diluted by missed business opportunities, decrepit stations, some poor connections and an underlying obsession with paper cost savings.

If there was a lack of enterprising management, there were certainly local staff with pride in their work and in the upkeep of their stations. The *Southern Evening Echo* referred to the prizes won by Horsebridge in Best Kept Station competitions and attributed this to the dedication of porter signalman Tom Hook.

(Rod Hoyle)

From around 1964, the Hampshire diesel units began to receive yellow panels at both ends as an interim stage from the provision of a single orange 'V'. A southbound service at Mottisfont in 1964.

(Rod Hoyle)

Chapter 8

KILLED BY WHITEHALL

When the official notice of the proposal to close the Andover–Romsey line was published on 2nd August 1963, the first objection was received by the South Eastern Area Transport Users' Consultative Committee the next day. 95 objections were lodged including those from Hampshire County Council, Andover Borough and Rural District Councils, Romsey Borough, Romsey & Stockbridge RDC, Southampton Borough Council, six Parish Councils and several Women's Institutes. Other bodies to object included Leckford Estate Ltd, the Ramblers Association and Southampton Football & Athletic Club, the latter claiming that closure would cause "serious embarrassment to supporters in the Andover district". There were 40 individual objections from Andover users, including two petitions totalling nearly 2,000 signatures. Of 35 individual objections from elsewhere along the route, 12 were from users of Stockbridge station, six each who used Fullerton and Horsebridge, three users of Clatford, just one from Mottisfont and six from Southampton.

At the time, Andover had no further education facilities and a good proportion of the commuters were young people travelling to Technical Colleges in Southampton and Eastleigh. The National Union of Vehicle Builders argued that closure would make it impossible for apprentices from the Andover area to attend evening classes in Southampton. Andover had been promised a Technical College by 1970 and BR suggested at the public hearing into the closure proposals, held at Andover Guildhall on 30th October, that the new college would reduce the demand for public transport between Andover and existing centres of further education. Andover's Town Clerk replied that this argument was nonsense because the town was planned to grow from 18,000 to 48,000 people by that time as part of a Development Plan for South East England.

Many of the individual objections were based on special needs, for instance an Andover man who travelled periodically to Portsmouth for repairs to his artificial limbs. A Bournemouth woman travelled each weekend to Fullerton to visit her sick mother. A young lady from Andover relied on the railway to attend ballet school in Southampton. The essential problem was that the proposed bus services (connecting with trains at Romsey) could not match the speed of existing through trains between Andover and Southampton.

Journeys between Andover and Eastleigh or Southampton would be increased by 30–60 minutes through having to travel by bus north of Romsey, even if bus and train connections were always achieved. In reply to an objection from a regular user of the 2.38pm Portsmouth & Southsea, BR suggested that he either: caught that train and reached Andover bus station at 5.40 compared with the existing train arrival of 4.29 at Andover Town, or left Portsmouth an hour later to connect into a bus reaching Andover at 5.57. One commuter from Andover pointed out that he would be away from home for 12 hours a day in order to do 7½ hours' work in Southampton.

Two objections related to Passengers' Luggage in Advance services, BR replying that these would continue to be provided from Andover Junction using other routes. The other commercial objection came from C.M. Jones, Managing Director of the Leckford Estate, who sent and received over £200 worth of livestock annually via Stockbridge. (Fullerton station, which was nearer to Leckford village, had not handled livestock for some time, probably since the loading docks had been adapted for Air Ministry traffic in 1942.) Unfortunately, freight facilities had been withdrawn from Stockbridge in January so the objection may have referred to seasonal traffic in animals during previous years or to consignments of poultry by passenger train. Mr Jones, incidentally, was elected to Hampshire County Council in the 1980s, becoming its Chairman in 1985.

The same public hearing also considered objections to the proposed closure of Hurstbourne station on the main West of England line between Whitchurch and Andover, one of these being inter-related to the Andover–Romsey proposals, namely Hurstbourne Tarrant WI which was concerned at the hardship to students attending Southampton University and Technical College.

BR had conducted a census of passengers using the A & R line in the weeks commencing 1st April and 27th July 1963. During the former week a total of 5,330 passenger journeys were recorded over the six weekdays (an average of 888 per day or 28 per train). On Sunday 31st March, 201 (or an average of 11 per train) used the line. The summer week was better, with 7,530 journeys over six days (an average of 1,255 per day or 39 per train). The Sunday produced 446 passengers, an average of 22 per train as the summer service provided 10 trains each way compared with nine in the Winter Timetable. With this level of custom, closure would certainly be controversial.

Understandably, some trains were much busier than others, the largest flow being of 130–200 passengers spread over the first three departures from Andover Junction (6.40, 7.22 and 8.55am), most of these returning on the 3.38, 4.37 and 5.38pm from Portsmouth & Southsea. The great majority of these people were commuting to Southampton but this could not be confirmed by the cen-

Seemingly only four passengers have alighted from this particular service seen leaving Horsebridge for Stockbridge in July 1964.

(Rod Hoyle)

sus, which did not report the numbers joining, alighting, or on board either south or east of Romsey. Thus travel to and from the most popular destinations off the branch, Southampton, Eastleigh and Portsmouth, were not recorded. Nor was any count taken of London passengers from A&R stations, and whether they connected via Andover Junction, Eastleigh or Southampton.

The morning peak into Andover was smaller but still significant. The first down train, 6.22am Eastleigh, was regularly taking 45–55 passengers into Andover, of whom about two thirds alighted at the Town station. The following 6.53 Portsmouth & Southsea, due at the Junction at 8.29, conveyed about 70–80 passengers for the Andover stations, with about 80% alighting at Town.

Some local flows (or the lack of them) were identified by the census. During the April week, not one passenger was recorded joining or alighting from the 9.55am Andover Junction at Clatford or Fullerton, which points to the local travel trend from those stations being very much towards Andover. On Wednesday 3rd April, the last down train, 9.40pm Eastleigh–Andover–Salisbury attracted just one passenger from Eastleigh but 64 from Romsey, suggesting most had come from or via Southampton. In both weeks this train often had no passengers boarding or alighting at Fullerton and Clatford.

The daily average of the two censuses for passengers **joining** at each station was:

	Southbound	Northbound
Andover Junction	85	–
Andover Town	222	6
Clatford	6	34
Fullerton	12	27
Stockbridge	29	72
Horsebridge	35	14
Mottisfont	15	13
Branch totals	**404**	**166**

Following closure of the MSWJ route in September 1961, services on the A&R were restricted to local traffic only. These became exclusively diesel operated from the Summer 1962 timetable, and from this date steam would appear only to cover for the failure of a diesel set. This was one of the last scheduled steam services, and is seen at Andover Town in the summer of 1962 behind U class 2-6-0 No 31816.

(Rod Hoyle)

ANDOVER to REDBRIDGE

The Ministry of Transport admitted that 200–250 people joining the branch trains at Romsey or beyond (for example, at Southampton) needed to be added to these totals to give a true picture of usage. The actual number of journeys was therefore about 800 per day.

Passengers joining the Sunday trains were overwhelmingly at the two Andover stations. At this time, all A&R stations except Clatford had a Summer Sunday service, but of 38 joining the first up train, 8.17am Salisbury–Andover–Portsmouth, only two had alighted by Romsey, suggesting that Andover people found the service very convenient for day trips to Southampton and beyond. Very few passengers used Mottisfont on Sundays, despite its all year service, but Stockbridge, Horsebridge and Fullerton produced a fairly even sprinkling of Sunday passengers so the impression is that leisure usage of the stations was in proportion to the populations they served.

One theme amongst the objections was the very poor proposed alternative bus service on Sundays, with no journeys before 4pm, a point noted by the TUCC in its Report to the Minister of Transport, which it completed on 18th December.

Supporters of the line kept up the pressure in the meantime. During a debate on the Harbours Bill, Horace King, Labour MP for Southampton Itchen, said that "if there are great developments in the hinterland behind Southampton Docks, the maintenance of some railways which the Minister proposes to close, becomes of great importance".

Mr Marples interrupted to say that Dr Beeching and Lord Rochdale, of the National Ports Authority, "had discussed the question at great length". Mr King continued by saying that the line was "part of the vital communication system which must remain if Andover is to expand…or Southampton Docks is to expand". Three local Conservative MPs also took up the cause in correspondence with the Minister. These were John Howard (Southampton Test); Denzil Freeth (Basingstoke), whose constituency included Andover; and Peter Smithers (Winchester), whose constituency covered Stockbridge and Romsey. Mr Freeth stressed the need to retain the track for Andover's population growth and Southampton freight. He criticised the prospect of longer journeys by bus and suggested retaining a peak hour service, with the line maintained to light railway standards.

The Ministry of Housing & Local Government, which would oversee the expansion of Andover, advised the Ministry of Transport that removing passenger and freight services from the line would deter industry from relocating to Andover, a view echoed by the Andover Joint Committee which represented the Borough Council as well as London and Hampshire County Councils.

The Ministry Deliberates

The TUCC Report reached the Ministry of Transport on 1st January 1964 and was then considered by a Working Party of civil servants from the MoT who consulted other Departments with an interest in the case, such as the Ministry of Housing & Local Government. Its deliberations were summed up by its Chairman, Mr J.H.H. Baxter, in an internal memo dated 22nd April:

> "This difficult case turns mainly on the hardship issue. The Working Party divided over it, the majority including myself believing that it could not be alleviated by the proposed bus services. Parliamentary Secretary will no doubt wish to consider this aspect with special care. On the basis of the majority view, I must recommend refusal. There is also a strong S. E. Study aspect. MHLG (Ministry of Housing & Local Government) are against closure in case it would prejudice the large-scale developments planned for Southampton. Allied these two elements present a strong case for retention, though the latter by itself might not."

Another handwritten memo of the same date was addressed to the Parliamentary Under-Secretary to the Minister and probably represented the pro-closure faction. While agreeing that "this is certainly a difficult case", it made the single point that "as the freight service had already been withdrawn, the amount of money at stake is £75,000 per annum plus £100,000 on renewals". The figure for renewals was said to comprise £91,075 for track, £600 for signalling and £12,350 for bridges, stations and other assets.

In the event, the Under-Secretary, Tom Galbraith, came down in favour of the line. In a memo to Ernest Marples he wrote:

> "After a good deal of thought I have come to the decision we <u>should</u> refuse closure. The growth of Southampton and possible use of freight instead of via Newbury may soften the blow. Dr. B. may take badly so it might be appropriate to discuss at next policy meeting."

Unfortunately his convictions were not supported by his master when the Nationalised Transport Policy meeting discussed the Andover–Romsey case:

> "E.M. said he was shocked at the high

The same engine as seen in the view on page 71. Having turned at Andover, it is setting off across the main lines to the junction with the A&R route heading south, which lay immediately beyond the signal box.

(Rod Hoyle)

loss on this line for the sake of 80–100 regular daily passengers. This would mean a very large subsidy from the Exchequer for each regular passenger. Parl. Sec. (C) had recommended refusal of consent but the Minister said we must support Dr. Beeching where we can. After discussion it was agreed that the case could be referred to RRT by Parl. Sec. (C)......E.M. said hardship must be related to the amount the taxpayer had to pay and the Committee should be asked to give their guidance on the relevant figures."

This was a serious, and possibly fatal, blow to the line. Mr. Marples had clearly aligned himself with Dr. Beeching's policies, and the Ministry itself seemed to have accepted the dubious costings (which ignored the value of ticket sales to destinations beyond Andover or Romsey) as the basis for any further argument. Even the line's supporters in the Ministry seemed concerned not to upset Beeching. The fate of the line now rested with the Road-Rail Transport Committee, chaired by Lord Blakenham, which scrutinised contentious rail closure proposals.

A further memo, in the same hand as the equivocal one of 22nd April, instructed Mr Baxter to draft a paper to the RRT: "This should contain no firm recommendation but should bring out clearly the financial consequences of refusing consent". A subsequent memo from Mr Baxter referred to the draft as "giving the fullest possible statement of user journeys". Adding that the TUCC had tried to establish "the important journeys made", he concluded that "Essentially the 80–100 regular commuters and the other 100 long journeys are the core of the problem and these figures…are not disputed".

Mr Baxter expressed concern at the proposed journey times between Andover and Eastleigh which would average 100 minutes outward and 87 minutes return, compared to 50 minutes by the existing train services. Andover–Southampton journeys would average 90 minutes compared with 50 by direct train. Paragraph 7 of his draft neatly summarised the disadvantage of replacing trains with buses:

> "Unfortunately the problem cannot be solved merely by devising a better alternative service. The existing train service is a modern diesel service and any bus service is bound to take substantially longer. *The alternative journey times set out in….RRT (64) 13 can scarcely be improved on.* A journey of 18–20 miles along ordinary roads cannot be achieved, even by a fast bus, in much less than one hour."

Despite the arguments in that paper, the battle was all but lost by 2nd June when Tom Galbraith noted tersely: "At last meeting of RRT members wished to close Andover railway line but were concerned at extent of hardship. They asked for figures which this paper supplies and which I recommend be circulated." He was referring to a revised paper to RRT, which removed the italicised sentence above now that an additional evening bus from Romsey to Andover, connecting out of a train from Eastleigh, was proposed for the benefit of students attending the Technical College there.

Other alterations made to Mr Baxter's draft included the addition of a sentence playing down the higher cost of having to buy separate bus and rail tickets. Reference to a 70% increase in the cost of day return travel from Andover to Eastleigh was now followed by an unreasoned statement, "it must be expected that, if the service were retained, rail fares would be likely to be increased."

Paragraph 16, which suggested possible economies in the train service, was toned down and the idea of increasing longer distance season ticket rates "which compare so very favourably with the buses" struck out. Worst of all, paragraphs 18 (advocating use of the line for freight in connection with developments at Southampton to offset losses on the passenger service) and 19 (which presented the dilemma of hardship versus costs as an open question) were replaced by a new paragraph 17:

> "Withdrawal of the service would leave a substantial number of users with much increased journey times and higher fares. But retention would cost the taxpayer some £70,000 per annum in addition to the capital expenditure on renewals. When the Minister discussed the case with me before going abroad, he gave great weight to the subsidy of perhaps £200–300 per annum which each regular user would in effect receive from the Exchequer if the line were retained."

The game was almost over, but the Ministry needed to satisfy itself that it had done something to provide for all the students and school children whose travelling would be disrupted by closure of the railway. When RRT met again on 9th June, it resolved to invite the Department of Education & Science to consult on the effect of the closure, but very soon afterwards RRT members were sent a letter in Ernest Marples' name advising them that the Secretary of State for Education & Science took the view that additional bus services would not result in unreasonable extra travelling time, and hence the effect on school children and students "would not be such as to justify reconsideration of the conclusions reached by RRT on 9th June". A letter of 16th June from Mr P.T. Sloman of DES expressed surprise that his Department had not had the opportunity to express a view until this late stage, although he wrote again on 2nd July to advise that Hampshire County Council would be providing a direct bus service from Andover to Eastleigh Technical College for 26 full time and 50 day release students then using the railway. This would cost about £600 per annum more than train fares. He also understood that the County Council was considering boarding arrangements in Southampton for four full-time students (three from Andover, one from Horsebridge) at the city's Technical College. 31 pupils were using the line to travel to Andover, two-thirds of whom were from Stockbridge, and it was considered that their journeys would be only about 15 minutes longer by bus. While repeating the argument that additional bus costs and longer journeys did not override the conclusions reached at RRT, he added, "on the other hand, nothing in this letter means that some

A final view of life at Rooksbury Crossing near Andover. The signs depict the various stages of ownership through LSWR to SR days. (Rod Hoyle)

light railway arrangement might not be very welcome".

Operation of the line as a light railway had already been suggested by Denzil Freeth and some of the objectors. He and the other MP whose constituency was directly affected, Rear Admiral Morgan-Giles (then MP for Winchester), appear to have been among the first to be informed of Mr Marples' decision to authorise closure. Writing to Rear Admiral Morgan-Giles on 14th July, the Minister noted "your predecessor (Peter Smithers) was particularly concerned about the development needs of the area and the retention of the railway track to meet possible future needs". So the decision as published on BR posters on 7th August mentioned that the Minister had asked BR to notify him if it decided to remove the track, and also that closure could not take place before specified additional bus services were provided.

The Axe Falls

Reaction to the decision was of anger and frustration, particularly in Andover. Within days, Romsey Borough Council had lodged an objection with the South Eastern Traffic Commissioners to the granting of licences for the additional buses. It argued that the connections from bus to train at Romsey depended on buses arriving on time as the Station Master was authorised to

ANDOVER to REDBRIDGE

Fullerton, forlorn and forgotten in 1965.
(Rod Hoyle)

hold only the first three up trains. Secondly, children going to school in Romsey would have to return on the 4.20pm bus, which would exclude them from extra-curricular activities. Thirdly, the A3057 was unsuitable for additional traffic, and improving it would spoil the beauty of the Test Valley. A fourth ground of objection would be the loss of all Sunday public transport between Romsey and Stockbridge, as no buses were required by the Minister to cater for such journeys. Finally, the overall reduction in public transport arising from the closure would deter people living north of Romsey from attending sporting activities in Southampton.

These arguments cut no more ice with the Traffic Commissioners than they had done with Mr Marples, and closure was confirmed for 7th September. The final Timetable (effective from 15th June) provided 16 southbound and 15 northbound trains each weekday, with nine southbound and ten northbound on Sundays. The imbalance on Sundays was because the last northbound train worked through to Salisbury, whence it formed a 6.14am Salisbury–Portsmouth & Southsea during the week. Connections at Andover Junction from the A&R into the majority of up Waterloo expresses were good or reasonable. Connections into down West of England expresses tended to be tight (for example, 10.27/10.29am) or narrowly missed (for example, 2.28/2.18 and 4.29/4.18pm), the natural hazard of regular interval arrivals trying to connect into infrequent departures. The opposite flow (from the West of England to the Test Valley) fared better because of the hourly xx.42 or xx.55 departures from the Junction. The date fixed for the Andover–Romsey closure was also the date when Andover Junction would gain a regular interval service of Waterloo–Exeter semi-fasts.

The last passenger trains ran on Sunday 6th September, with services starting or terminating at Swanwick via Portsmouth & Southsea because of engineering work. A Locomotive Club of Great Britain railtour headed by Standard Class 3 2-6-2T No 82029 also traversed the line. The final southbound train departed Andover Junction at 9.1pm, formed by DeMU 1105. It was timed to pass the last northbound train, 19xx Swanwick–Salisbury, between Clatford and Fullerton. The northbound train, worked by set 1127, was witnessed by crowds of about 40 at Stockbridge, small groups at Fullerton and Clatford, then seen off by a large gathering at Andover Town, where 110 tickets were issued for the short trip to the Junction. With its horn sounding, this train drew into Town station, where the Mayor of Andover, Councillor G. Lynn, placed a wreath in the Driver's cab. The Mayor and Mayoress rode in the cab to Junction station, where many more people were waiting, and the Last Post was played as passengers alighted. Simpler tributes had been paid along the route by people flashing torches or waving from their gardens.

The level-crossing gates at Andover Town would now open only when freight trains needed to run between Junction and Town stations. South of Andover Town, the line was now closed completely through to Kimbridge Junction. There would be very few trains to delay motorists at the crossing, but the *Andover Advertiser* recorded that, on Monday 8th September, the road traffic still tailed back to the floral clock! Town signal box was reduced to ground frame status from 29th September, the down line remaining in use from Junction and worked as a siding. In order to access the goods yard, which was on the up side, both platform lines were converted to a runround between the two trailing crossovers, and a stop block positioned at 1m 2ch on the up line, about half a mile north of Rooksbury Crossing.

The Minister had required the track to be retained so that he could consult with MHLG at a later date on the implications of the South East Study for expansion of Andover. Naturally people who wanted the line reopened felt they had nothing to lose by asking him to reconsider his decision. T. Hanbury-Ward of Andover described himself as a loyal Conservative who did not sign petitions without good reason. Arguing that Southampton was the gateway to England and to the world, he said "the ruthless pruning of its railway connections…is a very grave mistake." Aware of Mr Marples' interest in cycling, he added, "if you took a trip down the Andover–Romsey road on your famous cycle, you would discover what a hazardous journey it would be, especially in win-

Horsebridge in March 1965. Intact and ready for the revival that was destined not to occur. (Rod Hoyle)

ANDOVER to REDBRIDGE

Stockbridge abandoned and awaiting the attention of the demolition contractors. At this time, BR's activities in removing redundant lines were explained by them with some irony: "...a working railway blends harmoniously into the landscape, while a closed line presents a melancholy sight that must be removed...". Few would argue that the scene here was anything other than melancholy. *(Rod Blencowe)*

ter when the mist often lies heavy in the Test Valley".

The reply from A.C. Morrison of MoT on 24th September referred to "300 daily users being subsidised by the taxpayer at £250 each per year" if the line had remained open. Hopes of reversing the decision rose when a Labour government was elected on 15th October, because the incoming Prime Minister, Harold Wilson, had pledged shortly before that his party would halt all major rail closures pending a national transport review. Andover Trades Council wrote to the new Minister of Transport, Tom Fraser, on 16th November, asking for the line to be reopened because "closure has virtually cut off the people of Andover and district from Southampton and the South Coast unless long and often tedious bus journeys are undertaken".

Unfortunately, the Wilson administration had already disowned its election promise to halt, let alone reverse, the closure programme. Replying on 27th November, MoT referred to a statement Mr Fraser had made a few weeks previously: "You will see that (the Minister) has no power to require the restoration of a service which has already been withdrawn." This did not deter County Councillor A.H. Clark, Chairman of Andover NUR branch, from writing on 27th February 1965, enclosing letters from local people who had experienced particular hardship since the line closed. These were a young Andover man who worked at the Ordnance Survey and had been forced to find lodgings in Southampton; and two women (one at Longstock, one at Goodworth Clatford) whose visits to their elderly mothers in London were restricted by poor bus and train connections. Mr Clark pointed out that, with no Sunday buses to Romsey, passengers from Andover could only travel via Winchester, so that a journey to Southampton, which used to take 45 minutes by direct train, now took two hours.

He and other correspondents received standard replies from the Ministry, attaching Mr Fraser's statement of 4th November. The reply to J.H. Burke of Andover, 7th July 1965, was a little more revealing:

> "The Minister has been advised that he has no power to require the restoration of services which have already been withdrawn. The track on this line will be retained for the time being…so that the position can be reviewed when development prospects for the area have been clarified."

The first sentence suggests that it was civil servants who had laid down the position to the Minister rather than the other way round. Very likely it suited them to continue closing railways so that they could pursue an agenda of road building more easily. Soon after the 1966 General Election, the MoT was preparing a new policy for the disposal of disused railways with a view to using the land for new roads. On 3rd May, its Highways

Division wrote to D. McCreadie of Railways B Division, referring to a letter of 11th January 1965, which had refused BR permission to dispose of the Andover–Romsey trackbed because of "regional planning prospects":

> "Highways had no comments to offer at the time but they are now interested in the future of the line because if it remains in use, they will need to build a new bridge for the Andover bypass."

Mr McCreadie replied that a decision would be needed on whether the roads or the regional planning aspect was more important. Cases for disposal of railway formations would in future be referred to the Economic Planning Council. In a subsequent letter to Ministry of Housing & Local Government, which had objected to the disposal of certain closed railways including Andover–Romsey, he explained that under the new policy, BR was free to remove track, signalling, station sites and accesses on all closed lines, even on those where MoT had previously asked it to retain the track and formation. Exceptionally, he had asked BRB to retain the track and formation of Andover–Kimbridge Junction and Enborne Junction (Newbury)–Winchester because the MoT expected to reach a definite view on the need for those lines by the autumn.

Almost certainly this decision was influenced by information from the Highways Division that use of the trackbed in Andover would reduce the number of river bridges needed on the proposed Eastern Distributor Road by two, saving £80,000, and also reduce the cost of the Andover bypass by £20,000. The section of line still in use to Andover Town station now also interested the Borough Council, which by November had written to MoT withdrawing its previous objections to closure of the line and removal of the track. It now wanted to use part of the route to build a distributor road. This dismayed Andover RDC, whose Finance & General Purposes Committee met on 11th November and agreed to oppose any attempt to dispose of the track. Expressing the hope that the line would be reopened at some future date, the Committee decided to convey this view to BR. Councillor J.L. Morgan said that, once the link between Town and Junction stations was broken, the line would never be used again.

Closure had been a particularly bad blow to long distance travellers in the intermediate area, whereas Andover and Romsey still had other rail routes. The local stations had provided a sorely missed gateway to the amenities of cities and seaside resorts, as expressed by a Goodworth Clatford housewife at the time of the Minister's decision:

> "The railway means as much to us as the Tube did to me when I lived in London... we shall truly be complete cabbages (and) may just as well be in complete isolation, especially on Sundays, when we could enjoy ourselves."

During 1966, at least three trains worked on to the southern end of the disused line. An Engineering train from Eastleigh worked to Horsebridge on 7th and 12th January, possibly to collect track materials. On the night of 14th July the Royal Train, carrying the Queen and Duke of Edinburgh from Truro to Bournemouth, was stabled at Mottisfont. The LNWR/LMS Royal Train was used, consisting of 10 carriages hauled (on the WR portion of the journey at least) by D1045 "Western Viscount" and an unspecified D8xx Warship diesel.

At this time, the thrice-weekly freight to Andover Town was worked by a Basingstoke crew and an Eastleigh locomotive (normally a BR Standard Class 4 2-6-4T) outbased at Basingstoke. Starting each weekday from Basingstoke yard at 5.30, the train conveyed freight for the two Andover stations and Ludgershall. After shunting for several hours at Andover Junction, a trip to Ludgershall was made, due back at Junction at 12.52. A trip to the Town would then be made if required and any traffic collected there would return from Junction at 14.15, reaching Basingstoke up yard at 15.5.

The last freight to Andover Town ran on 18th September 1967, when Type 3 (now Class 33) diesel loco No D6541 hauled a train of two wagons and a brake van back to the Junction. The *Andover Advertiser* named the Driver as P. Parker and the Secondman A. Rowe, both of Basingstoke. In the guard's van was Inspector T.E. Fleming. Two shunters, A.H.D. Blackwell and D. Teppett, also returned to the Junction, presumably in the brake van. The train was ready to depart at 12.55, when Signalman Ron Bundy worked the level-crossing gates before locking the signal box for the last time, commenting, "I'm sure the line could have been made to pay – especially with all the new population coming to Andover". The newspaper added, "We will never know, now that the line is truly redundant."

Track lifting began in the autumn of 1967, the demolition trains working towards Kimbridge Junction. All track was removed by the end of 1969. In Andover itself, most of the formation has been obliterated for road building, and the Stockbridge station site has completely vanished beneath a roundabout and approach roads, the trackbed ending abruptly north of the town near the Leckford Estate boundary. Apart from this and within the Andover town boundary, much of the disused formation is intact and might one day be reopened if the political will should arise.

ANDOVER to REDBRIDGE

Stockbridge, July 1969. *(Rod Hoyle)*

Chapter 9

THE LINE DESCRIBED

The A&R descended about 180 feet in 15 miles from Andover Junction to Kimbridge Junction but by far the steepest gradient was the stretch of 1 in 66 falling for about ¾ mile from Andover Junction to the Town station. This was the most taxing section for trains travelling in the down (northbound) direction, particularly for freights, which sometimes required banking. The next steepest section was 1 in 100 falling from Romsey Junction for about ½ mile towards Redbridge.

Using the canal bed for the majority of the railway formation kept road underbridges to a minimum. Two of these were in built-up areas of Andover and Romsey, where embankments were required to clear existing roads and align the A&R with the levels of the LSWR lines which it joined. There were, of course, numerous bridges over the rivers Anton and Test.

A feature of the A&R was the diversity of station architecture, possibly reflecting the work of different contractors. The main station buildings at Clatford and Stockbridge were fairly similar, but each of the other five A&R stations was very distinct in its style.

Andover Junction to Fullerton

At **Andover Junction**, up (southbound) passenger trains generally departed from the bay at the east end of the down main platform or, if originating on the MSWJ route, tended to use the outer face (Platform 4) of the up island platform. There was no runround in the bay so it was less convenient for down trains worked by tender engines.

The junction for Romsey was on the girder overbridge immediately east of the station. The A&R curved sharply away from the Waterloo line on an embankment and shortly afterwards crossed Charlton Road on another girder overbridge. The embankment ran behind Junction Road, giving passengers a view of the infamous Workhouse and then descended about 75 feet to Bridge Street,

Andover Junction on 26th October 1957, with T9 No 30726 approaching the junction station from the branch, hauling the 8.53am service from Portsmouth.
(Denis Cullum)

ANDOVER to REDBRIDGE

The descent from Andover Junction towards Andover Town, 1962.
(Rod Hoyle)

Opposite page, top: Busy times at the Town station on 20th July 1956 as a T9 and BR Standard interrupt the flow of road traffic.
(E. Gamblin)

Opposite page, bottom: Looking through the station from the south toward the level crossing.
(T.C. Cole)

where the level crossing was immediately before **Andover Town** station (68 chains from Andover Junction). A footbridge, originally a lattice wooden structure, rebuilt in concrete during Southern Railway days, spanned the north end of the platforms, with separate staircases to allow pedestrians to cross when the gates were closed to road traffic. The signal box was alongside the staircases on the up platform.

The station retained its original 1865 buildings on the up platform until their demolition after closure. Their spartan appearance, with corrugated ends, was perhaps not the best promotion for rail travel from such a central location, although billboards alongside the footbridge enabled special fares to be prominently displayed. The up platform had a small waiting shelter of timber with a large flat roof sloping backwards and forming a small canopy. Both platforms were sharply curved but crossovers were provided between the platforms so that shunting or run-round movements would not extend over the level crossing. The station was used to film scenes of a silent version of *"The Ghost Train"* in the mid 1920s, with booking clerk Lester Whitemore standing on the roof to shoot water from a hose to represent rain.

The goods yard was reached by a trailing connection from the up line, and access was controlled by a ground frame on the down side as the view from the signal box was partly obscured by the station building. A loading dock with cattle pens was alongside the Romsey end of the up platform. The yard included a substantial brick built goods shed and a corn store, the latter being used by Cullen Allen & Co. Adjacent to these premises, a petroleum spirit store was opened by Shell in 1916 for a rental of £30 per annum and 5% of the cost of a siding. Storage tanks were erected between the road and the headshunt at the Romsey end of the station.

ANDOVER TOWN

Level Crossings over sidings — Level crossings for vehicular traffic in the goods yard at Andover Town pass over the unloading road at a spot situated between the goods shed and cart weighbridge, also over the two outer sidings at points situated between the goods shed on one side and Messrs Compton's warehouse and adjacent coal pens on the other side.

Wagons must not be loose shunted over these level crossings, but must remain attached to the engine, and a man, provided by the Station Master, must be stationed in a suitable position for the purpose of warning drivers of road vehicles, and other persons as necessary, and safeguarding the level crossings whilst shunting operations are in progress in the respective sidings.

Dock — Bogie coaches are prohibited alongside the dock.

THE LINE DESCRIBED

ANDOVER to REDBRIDGE

Left: Bulleid Pacifics were infrequent visitors to the line between Andover and Romsey. This view shows No 34051 'Winston Churchill' displaying the West of England route headcode, possibly having been diverted via Andover Town.

Bottom: The south end of Andover Town and a glimpse at the yard facilities. Ivatt Class 2 No 46519 was another unusual visitor, and was allocated to Croes Newydd in Wales at the time. The stock is clearly of SR origin so this might have been a special working, possibly originating on the MSWJ line.

(Both: Ron Grace)

THE LINE DESCRIBED

> **Tasker's Siding** - The points leading to and from this siding, which is situated on the Down Line side about 1 mile west of Clatford Station, are worked from a ground frame controlled by an Annett's Key which is interlocked with the Down Advanced Starting Signal at Clatford.
>
> A competent man must be sent with each Goods Train or Light Engine required to stop at the Siding, who must first obtain the Annett's Key from the lock provided at the Down Advanced Starting Signal. On completion of the work at the Siding he must return to Clatford with the Annett's key, which must be replaced in the lock, and the single lever operating the slot on the Down Advanced Starting Signal must then be secured in its normal position.
>
> A gate, which must be kept across the Siding except when wagons are being worked to or from the Siding, is provided at the Company's boundary.
>
> The key of the gate is held by the Station Master at Clatford.
>
> All Goods Trains and Light Engines requiring to stop at the Siding must be block-signalled in the usual way, and after doing work at the Siding, must go forward to Andover Town, in no case being allowed to return on the wrong line to Clatford.
>
> The Main Line is on a gradient of 1 in 137 falling towards Clatford.

South of Andover Town, the railway occupied the canal bed for most of the 13½ miles to Mottisfont. The direction of the route had been southwards from Andover Junction, but it now turned westwards, keeping just north of the River Anton on a gently falling gradient. Soon after the line began to take a southerly course again, it reached Rooksbury level crossing (1m 40ch). This was a manned crossing of a private road serving a few residences at Rooksbury Mill alongside the river on the up side. It was equipped with two 14-foot gates fitted with red targets and lamps. Wicket gates were also provided for pedestrians. The large gates were secured by padlock and opened as required for road users by the resident gatekeeper. The gatehouse, on the down side, contained a block relay bell, but there were no signals or whistle boards specifically protecting the crossing.

On the morning of 5th March 1951, there was a fog in the Andover area and a fog-signalman was in position at the down distant signal, 1030 yards from the signal box but still some 175 yards on the Andover side of Rooksbury crossing. Double block working was in force on the up line as no fog-signalman was available to stand by the up distant signal.

On that day, the 7.56am Eastleigh–Andover Junction stopping train, formed by M7 No 30125 and a three-coach set, was running two minutes late after adverse signals at Kimbridge Junction but had not lost further time despite the fog. The Clatford porter signalman offered the train to Andover Town at 8.36, and it was immediately accepted. The Town signalman then opened his level-crossing gates for the train and cleared his (lower quadrant) down home signal. The "Train Entering Section" code was belled from Clatford at 8.48, two minutes after the train departed there.

At some point between the two bell codes being transmitted from Clatford to Andover Town, the gatekeeper, Mrs. Smith, returned to the crossing after seeing her daughter to a nearby bus stop. She found two cars waiting to cross and telephoned the Andover Town signalman to ask whether it was safe to allow the cars to cross. He replied in the affirmative, then immediately realised there was a train in section but it was too late because she had rung off and gone out to the gates.

The cars cleared the crossing and Mrs. Smith was standing in the six foot, swinging the down gate back towards its normal position when she became aware that

For many years, pannier tanks were allocated to the GWR shed at Andover Junction, primarily for working local services on the Tidworth line from Ludgershall. Under BR too, it was not unusual for one to be borrowed to shunt the yards at Andover Town or Clatford when necessary. This view was taken at Clatford Yard.
(Ron Grace)

a train was approaching. In an instant the train appeared out of the fog and smashed through the down gate, missing her by about a foot. She was unhurt, although severely shaken.

Driver Soper had noticed his engine quiver on the approach to the down distant signal and on seeing a white object on the ground, braked hard and brought his train to a stand just short of the signal. When he saw the remains of the gate lying in front of his engine, he walked back towards the crossing after the fog-signalman had appeared and advised him that the distant signal was still on. Having established that nobody was injured, he returned to his train and took it forward to Andover Town.

At the internal inquiry a week later, the Andover Town signalman admitted his error and was held responsible for the incident. The inquiry also considered that signalman and gatekeeper needed to reach a clear understanding of the whereabouts of a train, as originally instructed to the signalman by Area Inspector Vine. The Station Master had modified this instruction so that it became sufficient for the gatekeeper to seek permission from the signalman to open the gates. Where down trains were concerned, permission would be refused only when the train had actually left Clatford. The inquiry panel noted that the Clatford signalman also undertook platform duties and had to despatch trains before returning to the box to send "Train entering section" messages to neighbouring boxes. If Andover Town were to authorise the Rooksbury gatekeeper to unlock the crossing just before a "Train entering section" code came in from Clatford, the train might therefore reach the crossing within two minutes of such permission being given, as a stopping train was allowed four minutes from leaving Clatford to arriving at Andover Town. Incidentally, the inquiry panel included Stephen Townroe for the Locomotive Department, who later became Motive Power Superintendent at Eastleigh; and Rupert Shervington for the Operating Department, later to become Chief Operating Manager for the Southern Region.

British Railways soon gave serious consideration to destaffing the crossing, partly as an economy measure, but, in January 1953, the District Traffic Superintendent acknowledged that there had recently been a significant increase in use of the crossing as four Rooksbury Mill residents now owned cars, and there was extensive cultivation of nearby watercress beds. He repeated concerns aired at the inquiry that the station duties of the Clatford signalmen would delay the sending of signal box codes concerning trains that had already left the station. He suggested instead that when Clatford box offered "Is line clear?" to Andover Town for a down train, the signalman should advise Andover Town when he expected the train to arrive at the latter station. The Andover Town signalman would then enter this time in the Remarks column of his Train Register and use this as the basis for giving or declining permission for the operation of the gates at Rooksbury. BR had even considered a suggestion in 1952 from residents that they be given the freehold of the gatehouse and employ their own crossing keeper, but was concerned that the building was only six feet away from the down line. In later years, the tightening of procedures for using the crossing was not popular with road users, particularly after the closure of Clatford box in 1962 created long block sections such as Andover Town–Mottisfont for much of the day.

About ¼ mile south of the crossing was Tasker's

An Andover train departing from Clatford on 24th May 1957, comprising Bulleid stock. On the left can be seen the diminutive River Anton. The point rodding beside the track afforded a mechanical release (through Lever 10 in the signal box) to a two-lever ground frame, which controlled entry to the north end of the yard. The signal visible for the opposite line was No 12, the up home, which was located 131 yards from the box.

(H.C. Casserley)

THE LINE DESCRIBED

Clatford signal box, which contained a frame of just 13 levers. Although at first glance it is similar to the boxes at Horsebridge and Mottisfont, the design of the structure here was different, there being no belvedere for example. This might be because of various changes that had been made during its lifetime. Following closure of the signal box, the associated level crossing was closed permanently across the roadway although still available for pedestrian use.
(Lens of Sutton)

siding, reached from a trailing point on the down line, and provided with a catch point on the actual siding. Access was controlled by a ground frame at 1m 58ch. The siding opened in 1867 to serve the Waterloo Iron Works, which William Tasker had established in 1815. The works produced agricultural machinery and was the largest exhibitor at the Southampton show in June 1869, which many villagers visited via Clatford station. Latterly the private siding received only coal and coke for the foundry and, in August 1933, was converted to Upper Clatford public siding. The Annett's key to the ground frame and the siding gates were held by Clatford signal box. As there was no connection to the up line, train movements were made outward via Clatford and return via Andover Town, where the signalman collected the key, which was sent back to Clatford on the first stopping train.

Passing through Upper Clatford, the line continued southwards, keeping slightly west of the Anton. **Clatford** station (2m 70ch) was at the north end of Goodworth Clatford village. The main station building, situated at the south end of the down platform, was L-shaped with gable roofs and of brick construction with typically Hampshire wall cladding. Entrance to the platform was through a distinctive arch in the single storey extension. The up platform had only a wooden shelter with a sloping roof. The level crossing at the south end of the station was operated by a capstan wheel in the signal box, situated between the up platform ramp and the crossing. From 20th June 1960 the level crossing was closed except to pedestrians, horse riders and motorcyclists, in order to reduce the opening hours of the box. The gate control mechanism was removed and Whistle boards provided on the approaches to the crossing at 320

Clatford in its final days after the signal box had been closed and removed. The section was now Fullerton to Andover Town. A guide to the site of the station was given to drivers by means of white marker lights positioned 1070 yards north and 1050 yards south of the platforms. In 1961, at the same time as the signal box was closed, the goods yard and its associated connections were also secured out of use.
(E. Wilmshurst)

ANDOVER to REDBRIDGE

BRITISH RAILWAYS
Southern Region

London West Divisional Superintendent's Office, WOKING.	**Southern Divisional Superintendent's, office SOUTHAMPTON CENTRAL**

(JOINT SPECIAL CIRCULAR NO. 1)

BANK ENGINES ASSISTING AT REAR OF DOWN FREIGHT TRAINS BETWEEN FULLERTON AND ANDOVER JUNCTION.

The working of a bank engine between Fullerton and Andover Junction at the rear of a down freight train is permitted in clear weather or during fog or falling snow, in accordance with the following instructions:-

The bank engine must be coupled to the rear of the train, and the Driver must be alert and so regulate the running that the bank engine keeps buffer to buffer with the rear brake van throughout the journey, and when running on the portions of falling gradient and of level line between Fullerton and Clatford must reduce the power of assisting so as to avoid undue pressure at the rear.

The limit of load beyond which banking is necessary from Fullerton is the maximum load authorised for the respective classes of engines from Andover Town to Andover Junction as shown in the Southern Division Working Time Tables of Freight Trains.

When a bank engine is used at the rear of a freight train the double load will be the maximum for the train engine plus the maximum that the assisting engine can haul; but the maximum number of vehicles on a train so formed must not in any case exceed 60.

In the case of a freight train from Fullerton proceeding beyond Andover Junction the combined load should not exceed the maximum for the train engine beyond Andover Junction.

When assistance is required for a freight train from the direction of Romsey to the Western Region via Andover Junction, worked by a Southern Region engine as far as Andover Junction only the Station Master at Andover Junction must request the Western Region to provide, if possible, an engine which must be sent to Fullerton beforehand and there placed in a siding. In that case, the engine which works the train to Fullerton must be detached at that station, run round, and be coupled at the rear, and the train must be headed by the Western Region engine previously sent to Fullerton. In the case of a freight train from the Southern to the Western Region worked by Southern Region engine throughout, and also in the event of the Western Region being unable to provide an assisting engine from Fullerton to Andover Junction for any other of their freight trains required to be banked, the assistance of a Southern Region engine must be obtained, and this engine will be attached to the rear of the train.

The Signalman at Fullerton must previously advise the Signalmen at Andover Town and Andover Junction East by telephone when a down freight train is to be assisted at the rear and the Signalman at Andover Junction East must not give "Line Clear" for such train until "Line Clear" has been obtained from Andover Junction West. The "Bank engine in rear of train" signal (1 pause 4 pause 1) must also be sent by the Signalmen at Fullerton, Clatford, Andover Town and Andover Junction East Boxes in accordance with Regulation 6 of the Standard regulations for train signalling on double lines.

The Signalman at Andover Junction West must accept the train over the Down Main Line to his Down Starting signal (No. 8) at which signal (situated 526 yards west of Andover Junction West Signal Box) the train must be brought to a stand and the bank engine uncoupled and disposed of as required.

NOTE The foregoing instructions supersede those contained in Special Circular No. 15 S.D. dated 24th January 1944 and Special Circular No. 60 S.D. dated 20th April 1944 issued by the Southern Divisional Superintendent.

16th February 1949.

THE LINE DESCRIBED

76010 recorded near Fullerton on an MSWJ line service on 2nd April 1957. At this time, the regular interval service had been introduced onto the A&R and, consequently, the MSWJ services had to fit around these improved services. The result was a resurgence of almost non-stop running of MSWJ trains south of Andover, most now calling at Stockbridge and Romsey only. To the left are a brand new pair of standard SR concrete permanent way huts. The curved roof of the larger building allowed these to be transported to the site already assembled, while remaining within the loading gauge.
(G. Daniels)

yards away in the down direction and 424 yards in the up. Drivers approaching the crossing were instructed to sound the whistle (or horn in the case of a diesel unit) at the boards. Additionally, Drivers of up trains stopping at Clatford, or of any trains detained or checked at the up starting signal, were required to sound the whistle before starting away.

The signal box was a typical LSWR Type 1 structure, not unlike that in use today at Crediton, Devon, except that Clatford box was built on a brick base. The small goods yard on the down side, north of the station, was taken out of use in April 1961.

Keeping just east of Goodworth Clatford, the railway was almost level for about 1½ miles. After an overbridge in the village centre, it turned slightly further west of the river to keep away from the flood plain. At almost a mile from the station, the line ran between water meadows on the up side and downland on the down. It traversed a series of four accommodation crossings serving dairy farms, the keys being held by the tenant farmer. These were Upper Westover (3m 67½ch.); Westover (3m 74ch), the scene of the 1936 accident; Wherwell (4m 11ch) and Lower Trent (4m 34ch). For up trains, like the one in that accident, visibility at Westover and Wherwell was hampered by their location on the inside of a curve but, since LSWR days, down trains had activated a warning bell at Lower Trent crossing operated by a treadle adjacent to Fullerton down section signal, 685 yards from the signal box. A notice on each side of Lower Trent crossing read as follows:

L.S.W. Railway.
Persons must not cross the railway while the alarm bell is sounding. The alarm indicates that a train is approaching from the direction of Fullerton and does not sound when a train is approaching from the direction of Clatford. The alarm is intended as an additional precaution but does not exonerate the public from keeping a good look out for trains coming from either direction.

Pressure from farmers concerned at the greater perceived risk from quieter, more frequent diesel trains introduced in 1957 persuaded BR to erect a Whistle Board 310 yards north of Upper Westover crossing on 21st October 1958, and Drivers of up trains were instructed to whistle continuously from this board to the crossing. Down trains were already covered by an instruction requiring Drivers to whistle from an existing Whistle Board south of Lower Trent crossing.

Soon after Lower Trent crossing, the route descended into a shallow cutting flanked by a stretch of woodland on the down side. After another half a mile, the line went under the A3057 at Cottonworth to enter a small peninsula between the converging Anton and Test rivers. The 1865 **Fullerton Bridge** station (5m 30ch) was of brick and is still standing; it is now a private residence. The 1885 station (**Fullerton Junction**), which replaced it at 5m 38ch, was built in the 'V' of the junction with the converging line from Hurstbourne. Its single storey wooden buildings originally sported platform canopies, but half of that on the up A&R platform was removed in later years to give a very dilapidated appearance to the station. The main building was on the up A&R platform and had a small canopy over the entrance from the fore-

FULLERTON

Top: Fullerton viewed from the north, with the original station building on the immediate left. *(Denis Cullum)*

Centre: A closer inspection of the north end, showing the station offices, which were between the canopies on either side of the island platform. Removal of part of the canopy fronting the up platform took place between 1955 and 1957. *(H.C. Casserley)*

Bottom: With the Longparish line platform no longer in use for passengers, the opportunity was taken to erect a wooden shed-type building - possibly in the 1940s. It is believed that the air-raid shelter in the distance was provided at the same time. A local resident recalled that, during the war, railway office staff from Southampton, were temporarily based in a coach at Fullerton Junction. This coach travelled to and from Southampton each day attached to a regular passenger train. *(J.H. Aston)*

JUNCTION

Top: A wonderful staff view, which was probably taken sometime between 1900 and 1914. Sadly the names are not recorded. The number of men was typical of those employed at wayside stations where, despite limited revenue, wage costs were equally low.
(Commercial postcard)

Centre: Recorded from the south end during the period that the Hurstbourne line was open, three of the four platform faces are clearly visible. Note that the signal box does not appear to have a nameboard.
(Lens of Sutton)

Bottom: A closer view of the end of the signal box, taken in BR days. By now it sports a covered entrance and landing onto which the steps have been repositioned. The dates for these changes are not recorded. At one time Fullerton Signal Box had a frame of 28 working levers, but this was reduced to 19 operating levers after closure of the Longparish line to passengers.

court. The station drive was reached from the A3057 at Cottonworth and ran alongside the goods yard.

The signal box, a LSWR Type 3 structure with a gantry type walkway in front of the windows, was just south of the down platform. The down sidings, used mainly to recess slower freight trains, were reached by a trailing connection north of the station, access being controlled by a ground frame which was released by lever 14 in the signal box. Most freight loaded or unloaded at Fullerton was dealt with in two long sidings on the up side, one of which was a trailing connection from the up line and the other leading off from the Longparish branch. In its later (freight-only) days, the branch was accessed off the up line only, so that shunting of the yard and of the branch freight involved use of the running lines because there was no headshunt. For several years after its closure to freight, the Longparish branch was used to store condemned wagons, diesel and electric multiple units. It was finally taken out of use in 1960.

Fullerton to Stockbridge

The hamlet of Fullerton was on a minor road just west of the A3057, but three larger villages, Chilbolton, Wherwell (which had its own stopping place on the Hurstbourne–Fullerton line for some years), and Leckford were within 1½ miles of the station. A pedestrian walkway was provided between the cess of the up line and a long garden wall to enable Chilbolton and Leckford residents to reach the station without a lengthy detour to the station driveway via Cottonworth. Just south of the station throat the line crossed the Test on a plate girder bridge and soon afterwards passed under the middle of three brick arches of Testcombe Bridge, which carries the A3057 over river, railway and a remnant of the canal just before the road takes a sharp bend to head south-westerly towards Stockbridge. On the west bank of the Test below the bridge is the Mayfly public house, formerly the Seven Stars, and just downstream of its garden the Anton joins the Test, which changes in character to a more meandering river in a broader valley.

Fullerton's down home signal, 184 yards from the signal box, had a second co-acting arm at the top of a very tall post because the main arm was obscured by Testcombe bridge. Ron Grace recalls having to climb the post to replace the lamps on a weekly basis and also whenever a Driver had reported a lamp as having gone out.

Between Testcombe bridge and just north of Stockbridge, the railway ran through the Leckford Estate, taking it through some of the most attractive water meadows and downlands in Hampshire. For a short distance, river, railway and road were very close together, but the Test then veers westward through a series of copses. It divides into two channels that converge south of Leckford village and then divide again near Longstock. This stretch of the river is excellent for trout and has numerous private fishing beats flanked by thatched fishermen's huts. Some of the beats were reached by accommodation crossings over the railway. The line was also crossed by three plate-girder overbridges constructed during the 1885 doubling. All three (Bridges 12, 13 and 14) are standing today, one known as Whiteshape bridge carrying a road from the A3057 to Longstock, a village where wild fowl walk in the roads and famous for its water gar-

Fullerton down home signals recorded by Rod Hoyle in 1965. The co-acting arm was provided to afford visibility both from afar and also if a train was held close by. Originally, a second stop signal would have been fitted to the right of the top platform to control trains destined for the Hurstbourne platform. Rod recalls that, when he set out to take the photograph, he climbed half way up the ladder with the intention of recording the scene from the top. The amount of sway up there persuaded him to changed his mind! (Rod Hoyle)

THE LINE DESCRIBED

South of Fullerton, what is the now the A3057 crosses over the railway and River Test before passing "The Seven Stars" (renamed "The Mayfly" some years later). The bridge over the railway was one of several with twin arches, each of which were built to standard gauge formation and did not reflect the original intention for a broad gauge line.
(Commercial postcard)

den. Old chalk pits are in evidence on the east side of the A3057 either side of Leckford.

The Estate, now covering 4,000 acres, is a highly successful cattle, sheep and arable farm thanks to its development by John Spedan Lewis (1885–1963), the Oxford Street retailer who purchased it in 1928 and came to live at Leckford Abbas, the mansion above the road on the up side of the line. His social agenda included plans (unrealised) to develop Leckford into an educational centre but he did bring about improvements to housing in the village, having been shocked by the poverty of many of his tenants. He is best known as the founder of the John Lewis Partnership, which exists to return the profits from JLP stores back to its employees (who are known as Partners). In 1937 he set up a holiday camp, now called Leckford Camp, about two miles east of Stockbridge so that Partners of modest means could enjoy self-catering holidays. Since 1948 JLP Partners, spouses and guests have been able to stay at the Abbas and participate in a variety of pursuits including golf and fishing. In that year the Partnership's *Gazette* advised that Partners could be met at Fullerton station and recommended those based in London to travel on the 5 or 6pm departures from Waterloo on a Friday to reach Fullerton (via Andover Junction) at 7.8 or 7.51; or on the 9.30am Waterloo on the Saturday, arriving Fullerton at 11.40. Sunday trains on the A&R were very sparse prior to conversion to diesel operation, so the suggested return services were the 5.39pm from Fullerton, connecting via Andover to Waterloo (arrive 8.22) or the 5.50 direct service from Andover Junction. Partners were charged 5/- per night bed and breakfast, lunch being 2/- extra.

The weekend breaks appear to have been popular, as the charges had increased significantly by 1952. In a subtle change of wording, perhaps aimed at Partners who had come to expect a lift from the station, the *Gazette* now advised, "taxis can be ordered to meet visitors at Fullerton (fare 5/-) or at Andover Junction (13/-)". Recommended travel was out via the 6pm Waterloo on Fridays and back on the 5.35pm at Fullerton on the Sunday. It now cost Partners 8/- to stay for the first night and 6/- thereafter, with a charge of 4d for morning tea and 3/- for lunch.

I did not discover any requests for a station or halt

Alf Offer with "Prince" and "Topsy" at Leckford in the 1920s. It is believed that Alf ran his own business receiving supplies at the local station, probably Stockbridge, and making regular visits to the various outlying villages and hamlets.

(Jim Turton)

to be provided at Leckford although by 1886 newspapers were being dropped from passing trains for the village shop. The village houses are painted in the dark green colours of the Partnership and, apart from the Abbas, the most distinctive building is St. Nicholas church with its low flat tower.

South of Whiteshape bridge, the terrain becomes flatter and the water meadows more marshy. At 8m 52ch **Stockbridge** station was reached, north of a brick overbridge at the east end of the town which is largely one long street on the A30 Salisbury road. Stockbridge developed as a bridging point of the Test where the main roads from Andover, Romsey, Salisbury and Winchester converged. It has little industry besides a fish hatchery and is surely a contender for Britain's smallest town. The population (of the Civil Parish) was variously recorded between 800 and 1,000 during the 20th Century, but the town is now officially quoted as having fewer than 550 people. It would have grown larger but for the surrounding marshy ground and the loss of its racecourse which brought a considerable rail traffic during its June season. Despite its small size, the town boasts specialist shops and is well worth a visit.

When this section of line was doubled in 1885, a new signal box, basically of the LSWR Type 3, but with a "beehive" roof vent, was built on the down side north

700 class 0-6-0 No 30309 approaching Stockbridge on 2nd September 1962 with the Andover to Eastleigh leg of the "South Western Ltd" organised by the Southern Counties Touring Society. Enthusiasts' special workings appear not to have used the line much over the years, although 3440 "City of Truro" was recorded on 14th May 1960. Two other specials involving steam also took place on 18th April 1964 (30548) and 5th September 1964 (82029), the latter date was also the final day of scheduled services on the line.

(P.H. Swift)

THE LINE DESCRIBED

Stockbridge in the 1930s. The old A30 runs in from the bottom left, with the road to Romsey running parallel with the railway south of town. Much of the town remains the same today, although the course of railway has been obliterated by changes to the roads. The station yard appears well stocked with wagons including straw, and there appear to be three cattle wagons at the loading dock. The White Hart public house, which is still open today, can be seen in the picture. This inn was referred to in the story on page 39. (Aerofilms)

STOCKBRIDGE

Station staff posed on the platform. Although undated, the view is probably in the period 1900 to 1914. At this stage the canopy possessed a distinct hipped style that was later replaced, it is believed in around 1925.

This view was taken after the erection of the footbridge, before which passengers would have used the road bridge. Circa 1910.

The Station Master and staff, circa 1900. It is believed that those present include Harry Bragg, Mr Marsh, and Booking Clerk Harry Lobb.

Background view: An unknown group posed on the platform, with a pair of horseboxes in the background.

STATION

Third from left, Archie Moore, and, it is believed, Station Master Lovelace (seated). The view also depicts the station clock, a wonderful array of contemporary posters, and the station seat proudly proclaiming the name of the station. Circa 1900.

Station Master Prince and staff on the forecourt, circa 1890. On the far left is William Kimber, while on the far right is Albert Noyce.

STOCKBRIDGE

The collection of views on these two pages and on pages 96 and 97, are from the collection of Ron Kimber. His relative, William Kimber spent a total of 44 years working on the railway at the station. Born in 1863, he commenced work in 1881 and retired as the leading Porter-Signalman in 1925 at the age of 62.

Staff interviewed in connection with this book recall a number of fascinating aspects of the railway and of life in the town in earlier years. These include when Chipperfield's Circus had winter quarters at nearby Wallop, and would arrive in a special train at Stockbridge. It is recalled that it was not unusual to see the elephants being walked away from the station and along the High Street. At least three coal merchants also used the station on a regular basis, these were Mr. Turton, who originated from Andover, George Jeans, also from Andover, and Wood & Co from Southampton. The first two named were later taken over by SCATS.

Another type of regular traffic was race horses. Notwithstanding the fact that the local course closed in 1898, a number of trainers had stables in the area and would send their animals by train to various distant meetings. These included Vernon Cross and A. Pearce.

Opposite page: Stockbridge signal box and interior. In the centre of the block shelf is the block switch to enable the box to be switched out of circuit if required, and on either side are the two Preece block instruments. A frame of 16 levers was provided, one lever of which, No 12, operated on the standard LSWR push-pull principal.

THE FAMILY ALBUM

Station Master Lester Whitemoor and family outside the main buildings. Lester was in charge here from the mid 1940s.

THE LINE DESCRIBED

STOCKBRIDGE

ANDOVER to REDBRIDGE

The main station buildings were on the down (or Andover) side of the line and approached via a wide roadway. It appears that the exteriors of the buildings were slate hung from the outset, a feature that they had in common with Clatford. Outside were extensive toilet facilities, a throwback to when race goers had generated much income. In later years the nearby renowned trout fishing had also attracted a "good class of passenger".

(Denis Cullum)

The platform canopy was replaced by one of a much simplified design, probably in the 1920s. The upper floor of the building was given over to accommodation for the Station Master and his family.

(Lens of Sutton)

Viewed from the north end in BR days, you can just see the 2-lever open air ground frame that controlled the trailing crossover just under the bridge. A collection of platform barrows can also be seen under the canopy.

(Lens of Sutton)

THE LINE DESCRIBED

A general view of the yard area seen from the signal box. On the far left is a water tank that was provided for washing out the loading dock, the metal tank of which was probably provided from the LSWR Wimbledon works. The large store shed was used for agricultural products, while in the background is a concrete store erected around 1957 for Messrs Bibby. No railway goods shed was provided.

30033 on the 11.44am Portsmouth to Andover train with set No 829 on 26th October 1957. The starting signal can be seen, and is of SR rail type construction, while still retaining an LSWR lower quadrant arm.

(Denis Cullum)

A final view of Stockbridge, with 31802 running light toward Andover on 26th October 1957. There appears to be no record of a regular U class light engine movement on the line at this period, so it might be that the engine was being sent to cover a failure, or to bank a train from Fullerton.

(Denis Cullum)

76006 working the 11.00am Andover Junction to Poole service via Eastleigh on 4th July 1958. This was a somewhat circuitous route for a train that had originated from Swindon; possibly it was a 'Trip Special'. The location is south of Stockbridge, where the railway runs parallel with the A3057, which was, not untypically for the period, devoid of motor traffic. *(Denis Cullum)*

of the station. A ground frame south of the overbridge controlled a crossover obscured by that bridge and by the station footbridge. The bridge also obscured the up starter signal, which at one time was provided with a sighting board, though latterly replaced by an upper quadrant signal on a taller post. The main station building, a hipped roof structure with cladded walls as at Clatford, was on the down platform. At one time it had a canopy which was raised in the middle, but that was replaced by a standard SR flat-sided type. The main goods yard was on the up side, parallel with the present primary school, and included a double slip. There was a horse dock alongside the down platform, reached by a trailing connection near the signal box.

Stockbridge to Romsey

After leaving Stockbridge, the line skirted Common Marsh to its west and lightly wooded, steeply rising downland to its east. Common Marsh is now a National Trust site rich in insect and bird life between the railway trackbed and the Marsh Court River, a tributary of the Test, the main river now keeping well to the west of the line. Along this section towards Hoopers Bottom, about a mile north of Horsebridge, the railway was on a low embankment, presumably to prevent flooding of the track and rotting of sleepers. This was one of the most level sections of the route, descending only a dozen or so feet in 3¼ miles from Stockbridge to Horsebridge.

The line skirted a long shallow cutting on the up side, with the Park Stream, another tributary, converging on the down side about half a mile below Hoopers Bottom. The railway bridged this stream, which then meandered away to the east via Horsebridge Mill. Still heading south-west, the line passed under a girder bridge carrying a local road to Houghton, and then made another crossing of Park Stream immediately before entering **Horsebridge** station (11m 63ch).

The main station building was on the up platform and had a high pitched single gable roof for the station house, attached to a single-storey platform building, which had a flat roof with a skylight. The saw-tooth canopy was supported by decorative iron columns. The signal box, standing near the Romsey end of the up platform, was a LSWR Type 2 structure of timber on a small brick base and sported a "beehive" roof vent. A small goods yard with loading dock was reached by a trailing connection from the up line. The down platform had a

THE LINE DESCRIBED

Probably recorded not long after the turn of the century, this is the approach to Horsebridge from the north, taken from the road bridge carrying a minor road from Horsebridge village towards Bossington. Horsebridge Water Mill was nearby and might have afforded traffic for the railway in years past. Passing under the line is the easternmost of the three channels of the River Test that will eventually combine further south. Beyond the station was a modest goods yard, which had three sidings and an end loading dock. Horsebridge is the only location on the A&R that was known to have a coal merchant possessing his own goods wagons (see the background view on pages 44/45) although there might have been others elsewhere. The tiny hamlet of Horsebridge itself would have been unlikely to have generated much traffic alone, but this was also the nearest stopping place to the village of Kings Somborne, approximately one mile distant. It was then a relatively busy location at a time when any means of outside communication was welcome.

(Commercial postcard)

Viewed from the opposite end of the site on 22nd May 1957, the bridge that afforded the vantage point for the previous photograph is now visible. The signal box possessed a frame of 14 levers, including two push/pull levers (numbers 6 and 10). Number 4 in the frame was a spare.

(H.C. Casserley)

The signal box seen on the previous page on 22nd May 1957. It had originally possessed exposed framework, which is just discernable in the previous view. In keeping with SR practice however, this was covered with lapped timbers, probably in the 1920s. It is believed that the enclosed veranda was added at the same time.
(H.C. Casserley)

Left: Apart from the usual offices, a small brick-built goods shed was provided alongside the main station buildings. The clock will also be noted; a statutory requirement from the Board of Trade required these to be fitted at all passenger stations.

Bottom: The exterior of the station. As at Clatford, Stockbridge and Mottisfont, it also afforded accommodation for the Station Master. In later years, a BR lorry, based at Andover, would collect and deliver parcels from the station on the 'zonal' system.

wooden waiting room next to a barrel-vaulted corrugated-iron store.

For many years, the adjacent hostelry was named the Railway Inn and early in the 20th Century its proprietor, J. West, was delivery agent for the LSWR. Horsebridge itself was a hamlet, the station serving larger villages on the downs at Kings Somborne, over a mile away on the A3057; Houghton, a similar distance to the northwest; and Broughton, about three miles west.

At the south end of the station the line crossed the course of the old Roman road from Winchester to Old Sarum. There was a short stretch of 1 in 200 falling gradient and then the route was level for about ¾ mile until Brook Down, where there was another descent of 1 in 200. The last mile into Mottisfont was level. The landscape was again largely downland to the east and water meadows to the west. About 1½ miles south of Horsebridge, an easterly channel of the Test converged on the down side at Lower Brook. Here also the A3057 converged on the up side, having kept well to the east of the line since Stockbridge. A chalk quarry was passed close to the Mottisfont up distant signal, which was 1249 yards north of the signal box.

Mottisfont station (14m 26ch) was at Stonymarsh, where a minor road from the A3057 to the B3084 crossed the line at the south end of the station. The village, famous for its medieval Abbey and duck ground, is about half a mile to the west, and only slightly further from Dunbridge station, which remains open today on the Salisbury line. The latter station is in Mottisfont parish, whereas Mottisfont station was in the parish of Michelmersh. BR was persuaded to rename the surviving station "Mottisfont Dunbridge" in 1988 but it reverted to plain Dunbridge in 1994.

The main station building at Mottisfont was set back from the up platform because new platforms were built on both lines during the 1885 doubling. Wooden shelters, with canopies supported on decorative angle brackets, were provided on each platform. The small goods yard north of the station was entered via a trailing point from the up line or a single slip from the down, the latter being operated by a ground frame. The signal box, an LSWR Type 2 with "beehive" vent, was not unlike that at Horsebridge and stood at the south end of the

Mottisfont station viewed from the signal box on 2nd November 1957. The board crossing that was used by passengers can be clearly seen. As at Clatford, this was in the direct view of the signalman. (The crossing at neighbouring Horsebridge was at the other end of the platform.) The station buildings can be seen on the right. T9 No 30732 is paused at the station with the 12.42pm Andover Junction—Portsmouth service.

(G. Daniels)

ANDOVER to REDBRIDGE

Left: 7810 "Draycott Manor" at the head of the 4.26pm Southampton Central—Cheltenham, leaving Mottisfont on 25th May 1957. Opposite the engine is the small goods yard, which consisted of a single siding only, and was accessible from either end. A ground frame was also provided near to where the engine was recorded. Goods facilities were withdrawn from Mottisfont from 3rd October 1960.

(R.K. Blencowe)

Right: A closer view of the tile hung station building, and some platform subsidence. It is believed that the settlement problems were historic, being caused by slow compacting of the infill on the canal bed after the line was built.

(H.C. Casserley)

THE LINE DESCRIBED

Above: Mottisfont seen from the approach roadway that led from the A3057 to the village of the same name. The lamp post - minus its "tilley" type lamp during daylight will be noted, as will the statutory closure notice. (Rod Hoyle)

Opposite page: Mottisfont signal box, which survived to the end of the line despite the proposal referred to on page 34. The signals at the location are of LSWR style with lattice posts, although north of the location, the up distant retained a wooden post and slot from the days when slotted signals had been the norm. There were a total of 13 levers, including two spaces (numbers 8 and 9), while number 10 (the down advanced starter, necessary here due to the northern exit from the goods yard) was also slotted from the ground-frame. (D. Clayton)

ANDOVER to REDBRIDGE

down platform, next to the level crossing.

Just after the level crossing, the line crossed the Test and descended gently to Kimbridge Junction (15m 7ch), where the main line from Salisbury converged. The flat-roofed, brick signal box of ARP design was opened on 21st March 1943 and abolished after the Andover line was lifted. For the next three miles the A&R used the Salisbury–Eastleigh route, which had opened in 1847, saving the expense of a second station at Romsey. The imposing station at **Romsey** (18m 6ch) is of yellow brick and was designed by William Tite. The main building on the down platform has an arch in the chimneystack nearest to the Southampton end. The old canal, which the A&R had left behind just north of Mottisfont, runs under the embankment between the station and Romsey Junction.

Above: One of several bridges carrying the railway over the water meadows and tributaries of the River Test between Mottisfont and Kimbridge.

Taking the northern section of the A&R route from Kimbridge Junction on 24th May 1957. The curvature at this point necessitated the provision of a check rail and its associated speed restriction. The bracket signal had once also carried an arm for a series of sidings and loops installed for wartime traffic in 1943.   *(H.C. Casserley)*

THE LINE DESCRIBED

Kimbridge Junction in its last days. The signal box seen here came into use on 21st March 1943, replacing an earlier structure on the opposite side of the line. It was closed from 14th June 1967, after which the lifting barriers seen were brought into use (although on this particular occasion, a flagman was necessary). *(Rod Hoyle)*

Early days at Romsey, when a location such as this might employ 20 or more men. *(Commercial postcard)*

ANDOVER to REDBRIDGE

Romsey signal box recorded circa 1960. This box controlled the junction of the original Bishopstoke (Eastleigh) to Salisbury line and its connection with the southern section of the A&R through Nursling to Redbridge for almost a century. Today the junction still exists but is administered by remote control from Eastleigh. Romsey signal box also survives on a nearby site as a working museum, with regular open days held for those interested in the operation and history of the location.
(R.S. Carpenter)

Romsey to Redbridge

At Romsey Junction (18m 13ch), the Eastleigh line veers east. It was closed to passengers, together with Chandlers Ford station, on 5th May 1969 but remained technically open as a passenger route because it was used by a few Summer Saturday Cardiff–Bournemouth trains. During 1981, a weekday morning Bristol–Southampton train ran out via Eastleigh and back via Redbridge to avoid running the locomotive round at Southampton Central. From 18th May 2003 Chandlers Ford station was reopened, together with an hourly passenger service between Romsey and Totton provided by South West Trains. The LSWR signal box at Romsey Junction was in use until 17th October 1982. It has now been preserved in the grounds of a local school, and is open to the public on the first Sunday of each month, except January.

Striking south from the junction, the A&R crossed the Winchester Road on an underbridge before reaching Wills' private siding on the up side. This served A.R. Wills' Nursery, which opened in 1926, and received coal and coke for its boilers. The siding was worked by a ground frame released electrically from Romsey Junction box and was served by up trains. Catch points were provided in the siding 40 yards from the main line. The Nursery closed in the early 1980s and the land once occupied by greenhouses has been redeveloped.

The canal remnant, which passed under Romsey station, ends abruptly in the town centre, whence it lies beneath the A27 Romsey–Southampton road, courtesy of Lord Palmerston who arranged a deviation of the A&R from the course authorised in the 1858 Act to keep the railway outside Broadlands Park. At Lee, about 2¾ miles from Romsey, the canal looped eastwards and was crossed by the railway, converging with it just north of Milepost 21. Between Romsey Junction and Redbridge Junction, mileposts still record distances from Andover Junction via the A&R. A siding, opened on the down side in the vicinity of Nursling in October 1883, served gravel pits which originally provided ballast for the LSWR and were later known as Test River Ballast Pits. In the mid 1950s, the owner was Thomas Patterson & Sons, who operated 1ft 11½in gauge tramways that closed in the mid 1960s.

Nursling station (21m 51ch) was west of most of the present village, on the north side of an overbridge carrying Nursling Lane. Its main building was on the down side and built of brick in a rather elaborate style for a small country station. Both it and the wooden shelter on the up platform had Dutch barn canopies. There was a small goods yard on the down side with cattle pens, north of the station. There was also a refuge siding on the up side between the station and signal box, which was an LSWR Type 3 structure of timber. As at Stockbridge, the road bridge obscured the up starter signal, which was fitted with a sighting plate. Nursling, which had opened on 19th November 1883, closed on 16th September 1957. The box, latterly open only on Summer Saturdays to create an additional section between Romsey and Redbridge, was closed in 1965 after a period of vandalism.

Almost immediately before Nursling station site, the line is crossed by the M27 motorway. For the final 1¾ miles into Redbridge, the railway skirts the meandering Test in its flood plain. The main road into Southampton from the Bournemouth direction used to cross the A&R at Test Gates level crossing (23m 12ch) but both box and crossing were closed on 18th November 1930

THE LINE DESCRIBED

Nursling viewed from the south, with the typical features associated with a wayside station. South of the site, a long siding to a railway owned gravel pit existed in the early years of the 20th century, while in later years, there were a number of other similar workings nearby, some with their own internal narrow gauge railway systems. (Lens of Sutton)

By the 1930s, the location was displaying a far more drab appearance, although it remained open to passengers until 1957. A group of railway cottages can be seen in the background. The main station building survives as a private residence. (Lens of Sutton)

ANDOVER to REDBRIDGE

when a new road was built. At Redbridge Junction (23m 27ch), the Bournemouth main line (originally opened as the Southampton & Dorchester Railway) converges, having crossed the Test on a viaduct.

Redbridge station (23m 42ch) is an unpretentious affair with a main building of red brick on the up platform and a concrete footbridge at the west end. On the down side was Redbridge Works, which manufactured track for the LSWR, SR and BR. It opened in 1880 and closed in 1989. Trains from the A&R continued to Southampton West (renamed **Southampton Central** on 7th July 1935 after being extensively rebuilt), 26m 13ch from Andover Junction; and **Southampton Terminus** (known from 1858 to 1896 as Southampton Docks, then as Southampton Town until 9th July 1923) at 27m 63ch.

References
Mileages quoted are generally those shown in BR Working Timetables, 1958/59 and Summer 1964.

An unidentified 700 class 0-6-0 shunting the yard at Nursling. As was typical of the period, coal was one of the main commodities dealt with although, despite the fact that the location was only a few miles from Southampton, it was at the time a sparsely populated area. Between Nursling and Romsey there was also a private siding located on the up side of the line. Access to this was controlled by a ground frame electrically released from Romsey Signal Box.

76008 hurrying past the signal box at Nursling, bound for Southampton with the Portsmouth service from Bristol. Although built and opened at the same time, the southernmost section of the A&R was always the busiest, and in later years took priority over the original route from Romsey to Eastleigh. The section north of Romsey towards Andover, while undoubtedly the more picturesque, slowly succumbed to the status of a rural branch. Although rarely referred to as such today, the section from Romsey to Redbridge was once an integral part of the A&R and still remains open to traffic.

APPENDIX A

SIGNALLING DIAGRAMS

Andover Town signal box taken from the footbridge. This concrete structure is known to date from 1923. (Rod Hoyle)

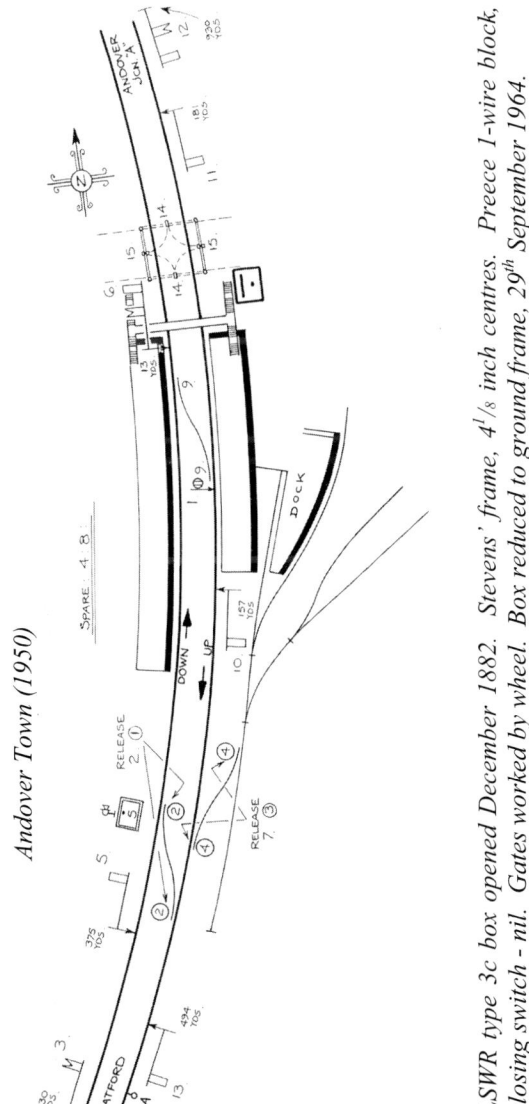

Andover Town (1950)

LSWR type 3c box opened December 1882. Stevens' frame, $4^{1}/_{8}$ inch centres. Preece 1-wire block, closing switch - nil. Gates worked by wheel. Box reduced to ground frame, 29th September 1964.

Clatford (1884)

LSWR type 1 box. Stevens' frame, $4^{1}/_{8}$ inch centres. Line doubled to Andover Town, September 1884. Preece 1-wire block to Andover Town. Tyer's tablet to Fullerton. Line doubled to Fullerton by June 1885. Levers 14 & 15 removed from frame. Gates worked by wheel. Preece 1-wire block.

APPENDIX A

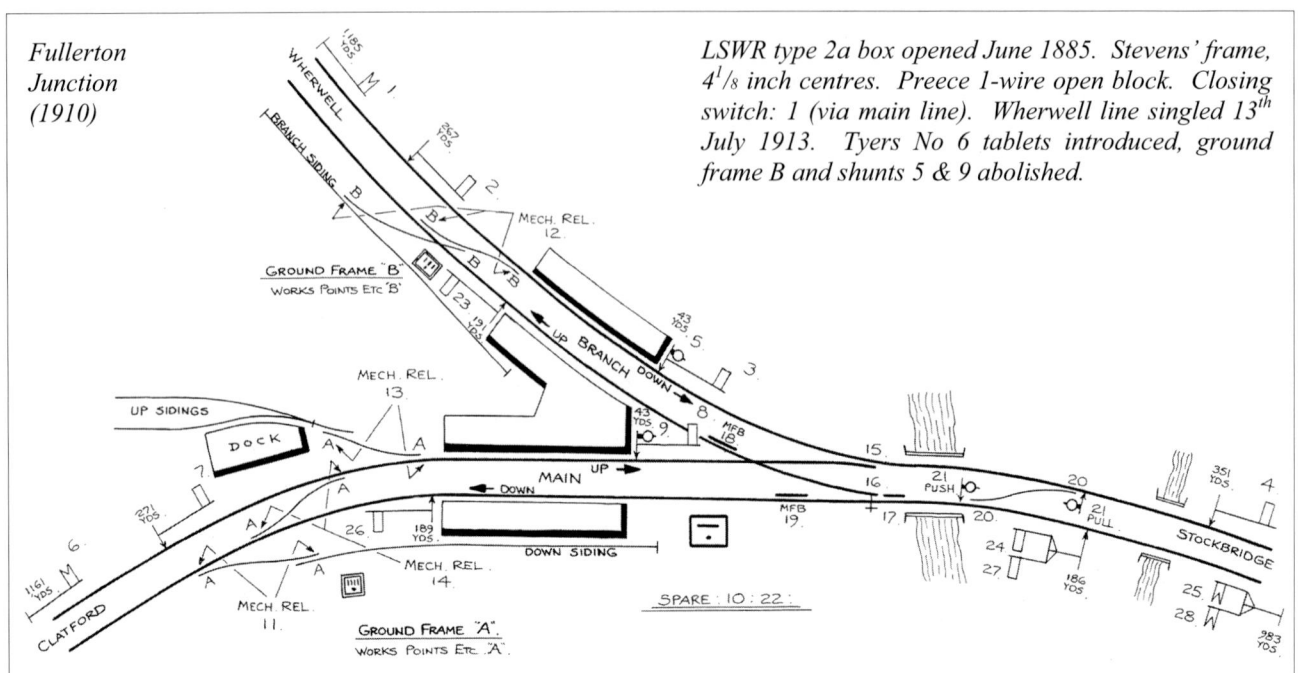

Fullerton Junction (1910)

LSWR type 2a box opened June 1885. Stevens' frame, $4^{1}/_{8}$ inch centres. Preece 1-wire open block. Closing switch: 1 (via main line). Wherwell line singled 13th July 1913. Tyers No 6 tablets introduced, ground frame B and shunts 5 & 9 abolished.

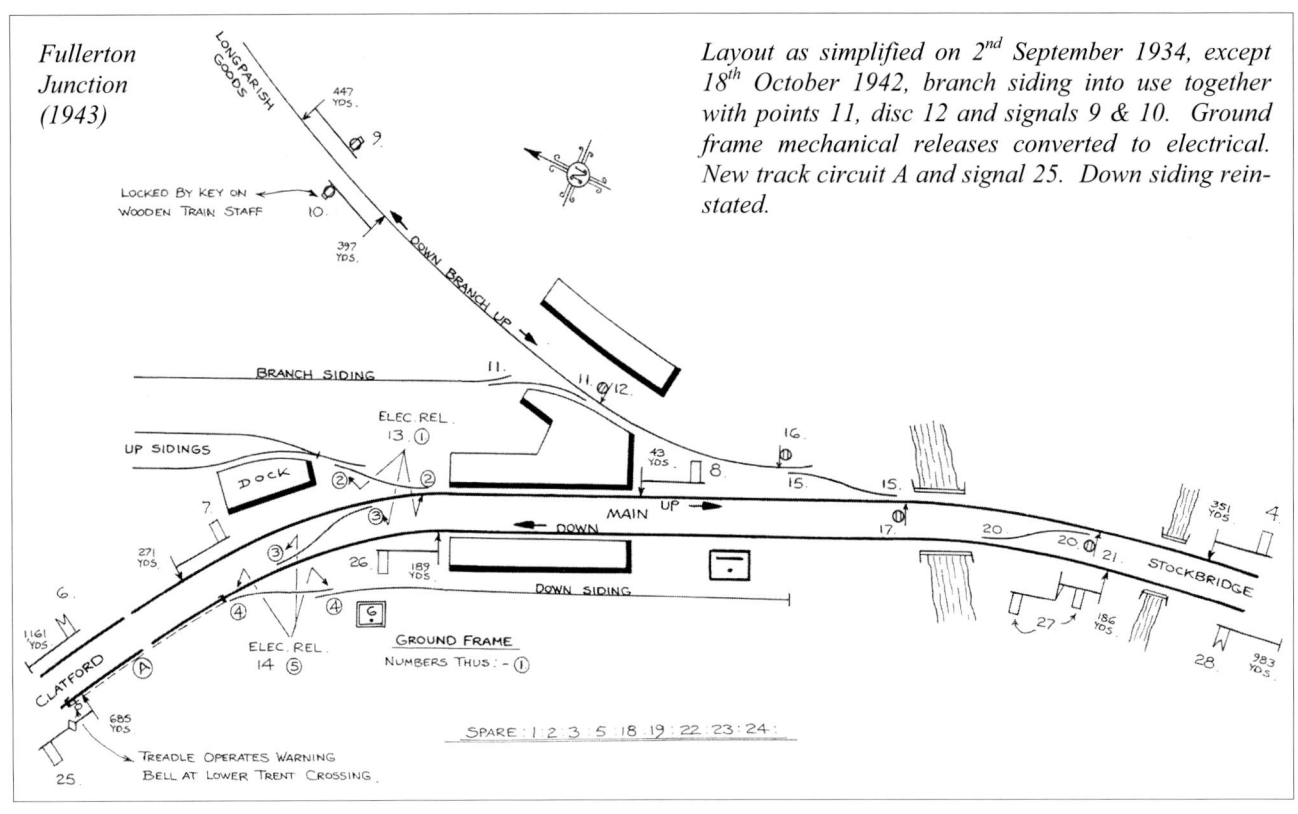

Fullerton Junction (1943)

Layout as simplified on 2nd September 1934, except 18th October 1942, branch siding into use together with points 11, disc 12 and signals 9 & 10. Ground frame mechanical releases converted to electrical. New track circuit A and signal 25. Down siding reinstated.

APPENDIX A

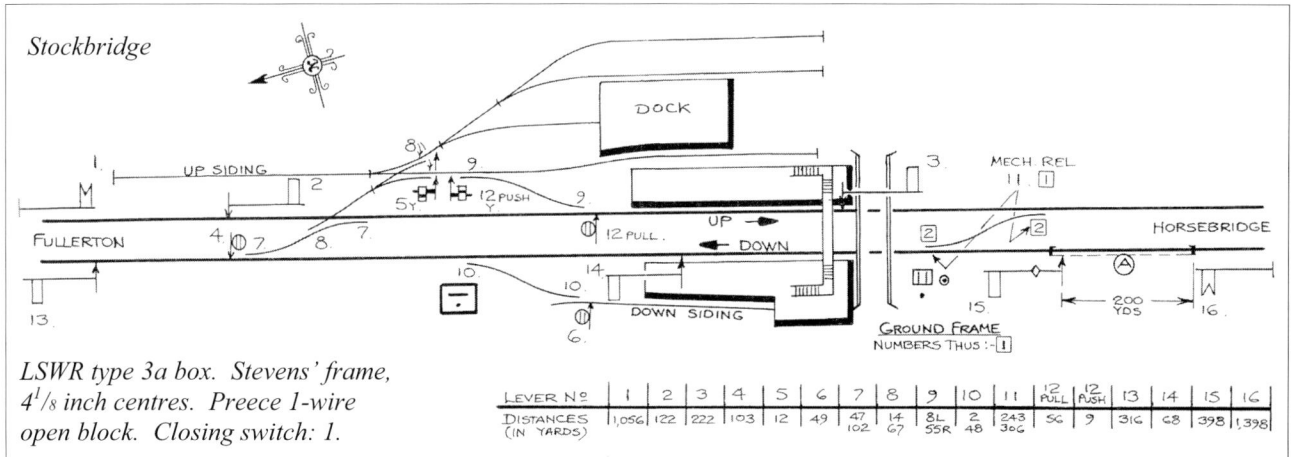

LSWR type 3a box. Stevens' frame, $4^{1}/_{8}$ inch centres. Preece 1-wire open block. Closing switch: 1.

Lever No.	1	2	3	4	5	6	7	8	9	10	11	12 PULL	12 PUSH	13	14	15	16
Distances (in yards)	1,056	122	222	103	12	49	47 / 102	14 / 67	8L / 55R	2 / 48	243 / 306	56	9	316	68	398	1,398

Stockbridge seen in August 1971, some three weeks before the station buildings were demolished. An article in the "Andover Advertiser" of 29th October 1897 observed that the LSWR was contemplating "...the erection of a footbridge at the station over the level crossing", but the structure pictured here was provided around 1905, at the same time as the footbridges at Milford-on-Sea, Swanwick and Chandler's Ford.   (Graham Sheppard)

APPENDIX A

Another view of the main station building at Stockbridge shortly before it was demolished in September 1971.
(Graham Sheppard)

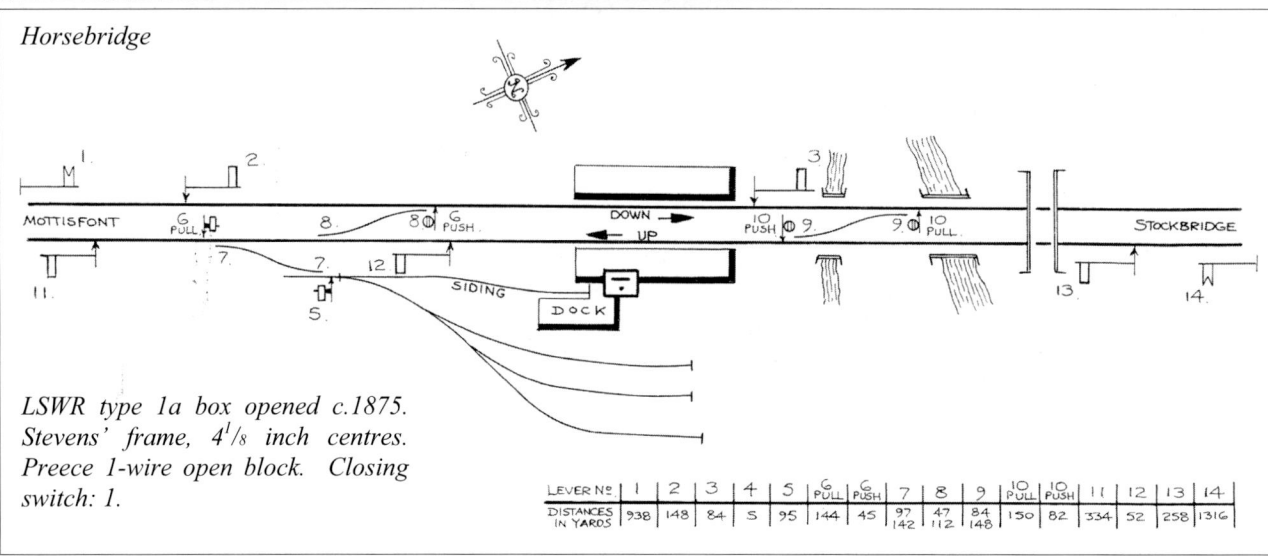

Horsebridge

LSWR type 1a box opened c.1875. Stevens' frame, $4^{1}/_{8}$ inch centres. Preece 1-wire open block. Closing switch: 1.

LEVER No.	1	2	3	4	5	6 PULL	6 PUSH	7	8	9	10 PULL	10 PUSH	11	12	13	14
DISTANCES IN YARDS	938	148	84	5	95	144	45	97 / 142	47 / 112	84 / 148	150	82	334	52	258	1316

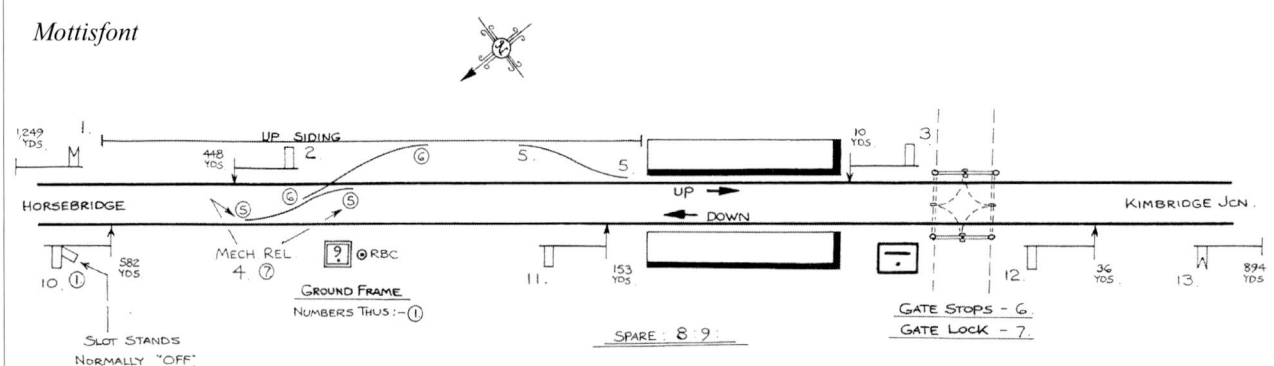

Mottisfont

LSWR type 1 box opened c.1875. Stevens' frame, $4^{1}/_{8}$ inch centres. Gates worked by wheel. Preece 1-wire open block. Closing switch: nil.

APPENDIX A

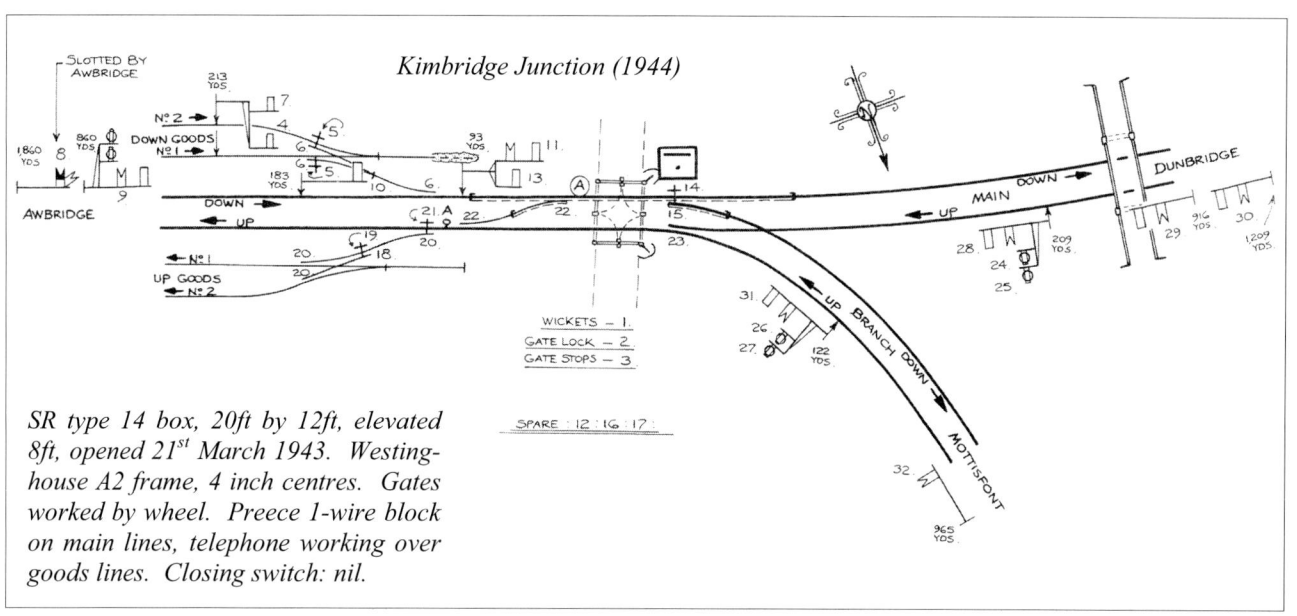

Kimbridge Junction (1944)

SR type 14 box, 20ft by 12ft, elevated 8ft, opened 21st March 1943. Westinghouse A2 frame, 4 inch centres. Gates worked by wheel. Preece 1-wire block on main lines, telephone working over goods lines. Closing switch: nil.

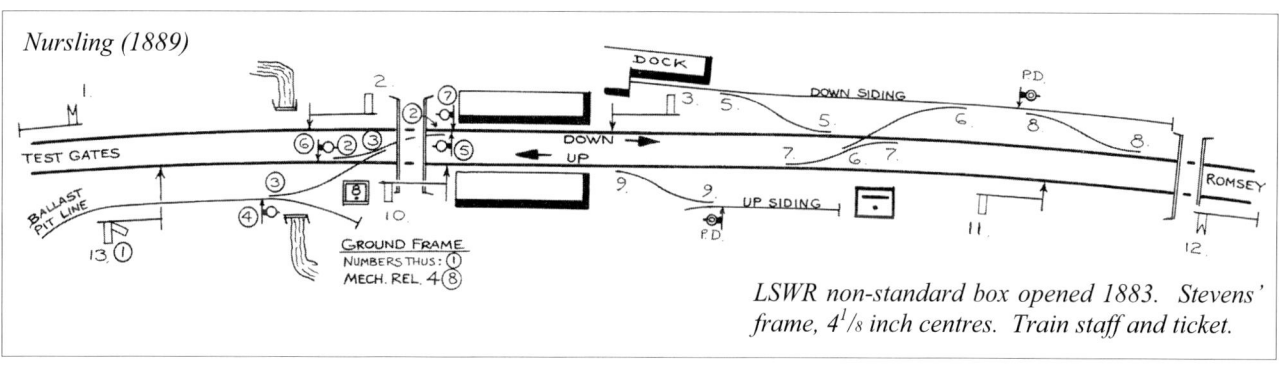

Nursling (1889)

LSWR non-standard box opened 1883. Stevens' frame, $4^{1}/_{8}$ inch centres. Train staff and ticket.

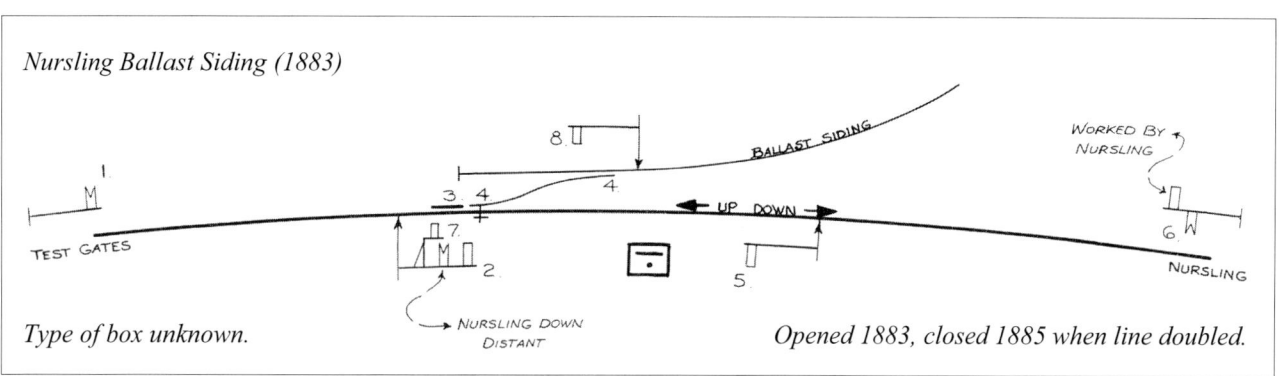

Nursling Ballast Siding (1883)

Type of box unknown.

Opened 1883, closed 1885 when line doubled.

GRADIENT AND CURVATURE PROFILES

Curvature given in chains

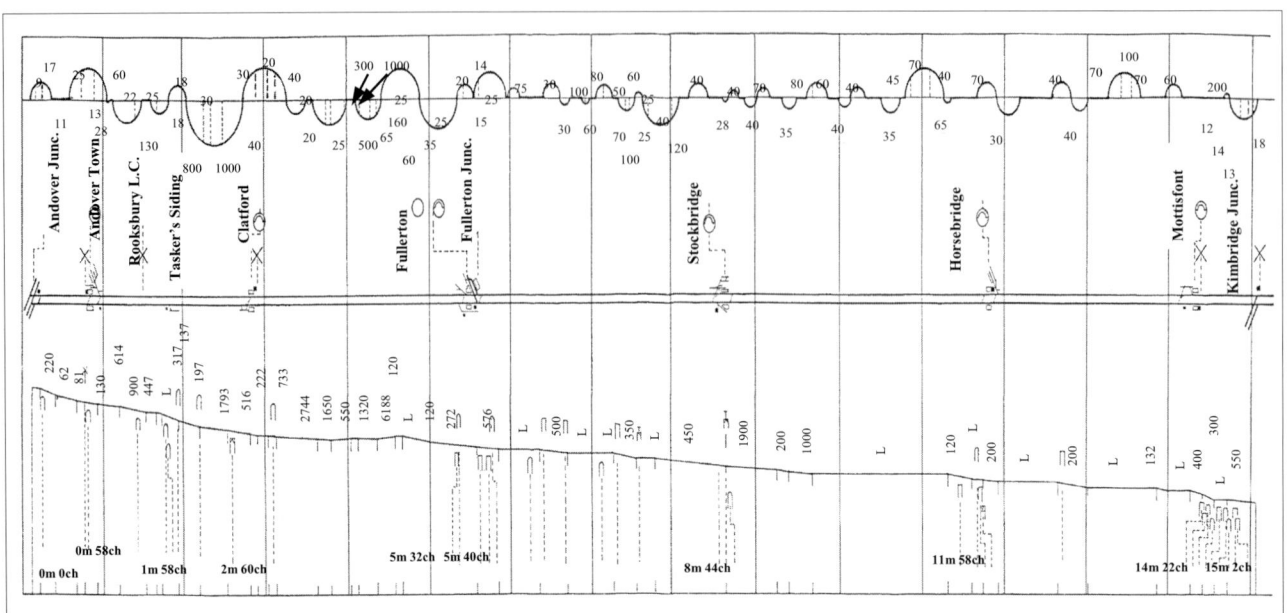

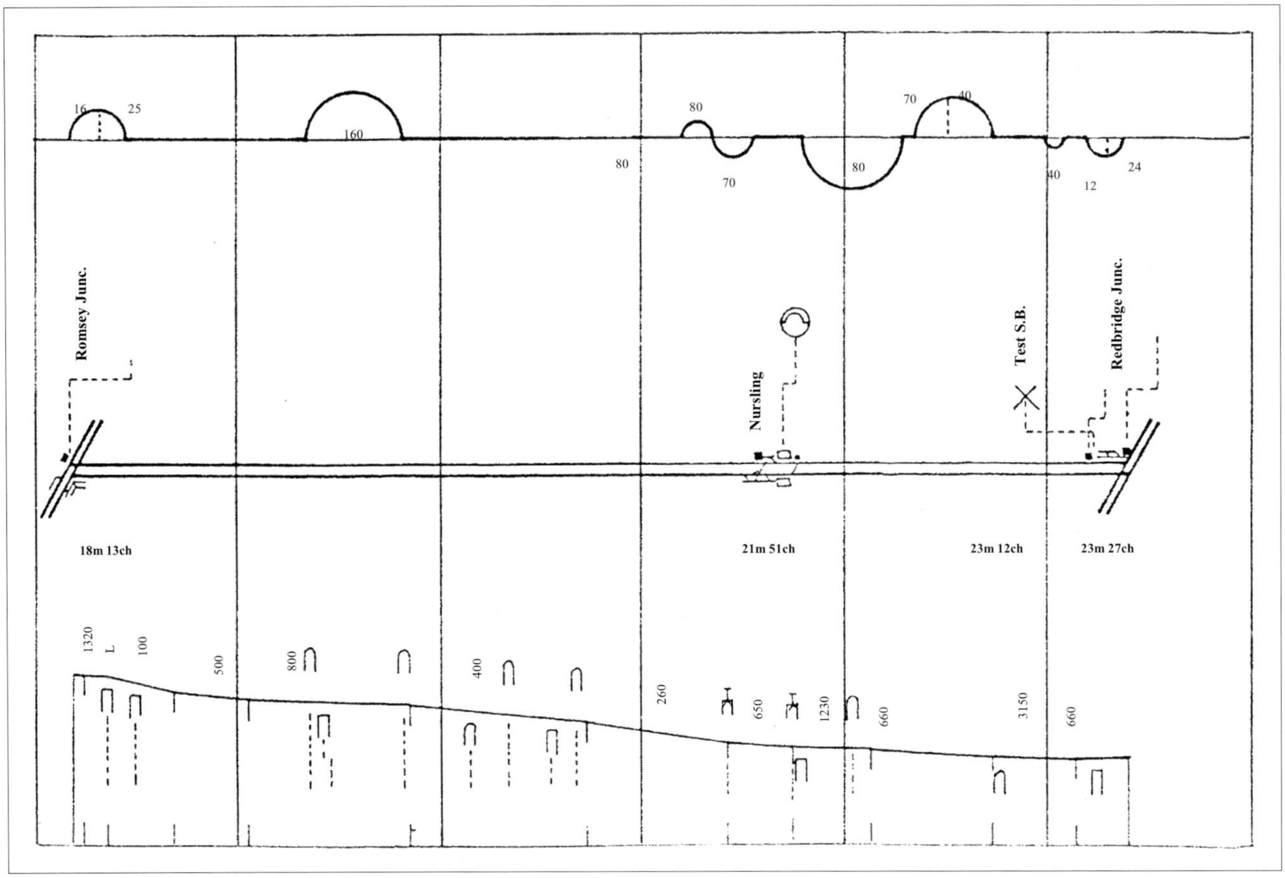

APPENDIX B

TRACK AND BUILDING PLANS

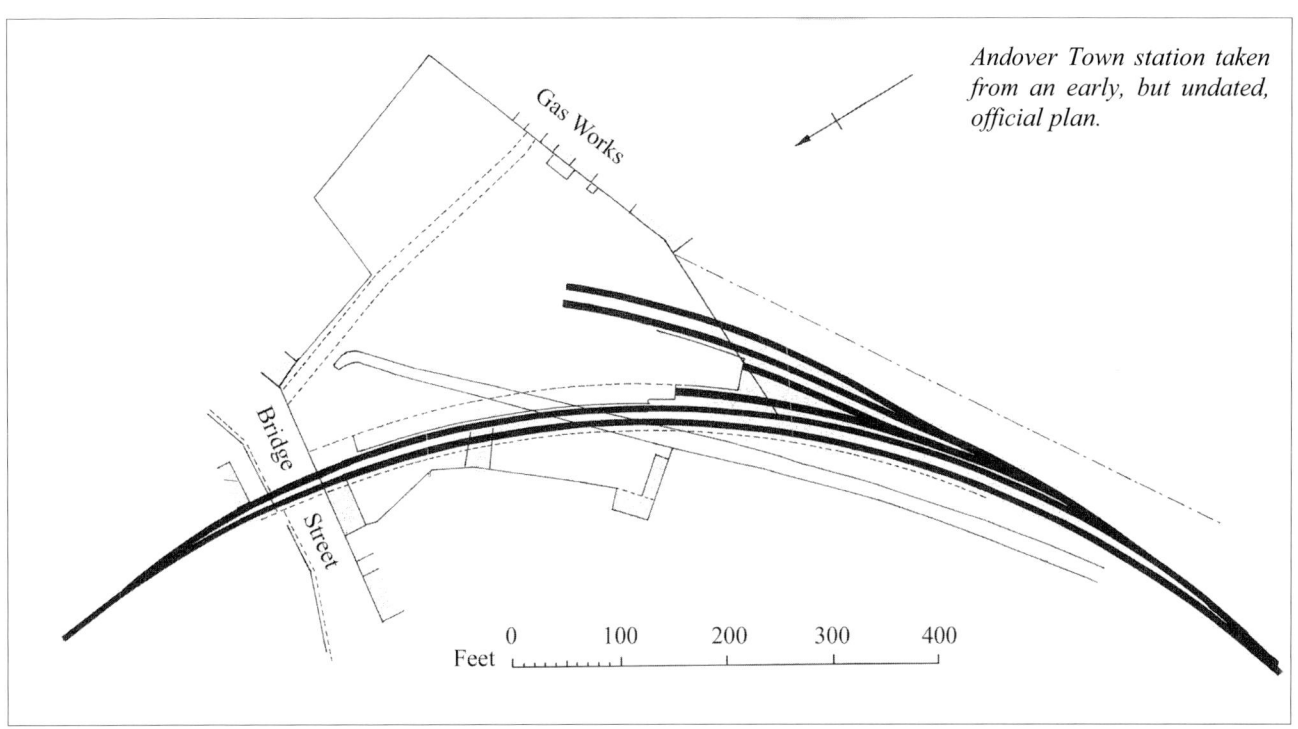

Andover Town station taken from an early, but undated, official plan.

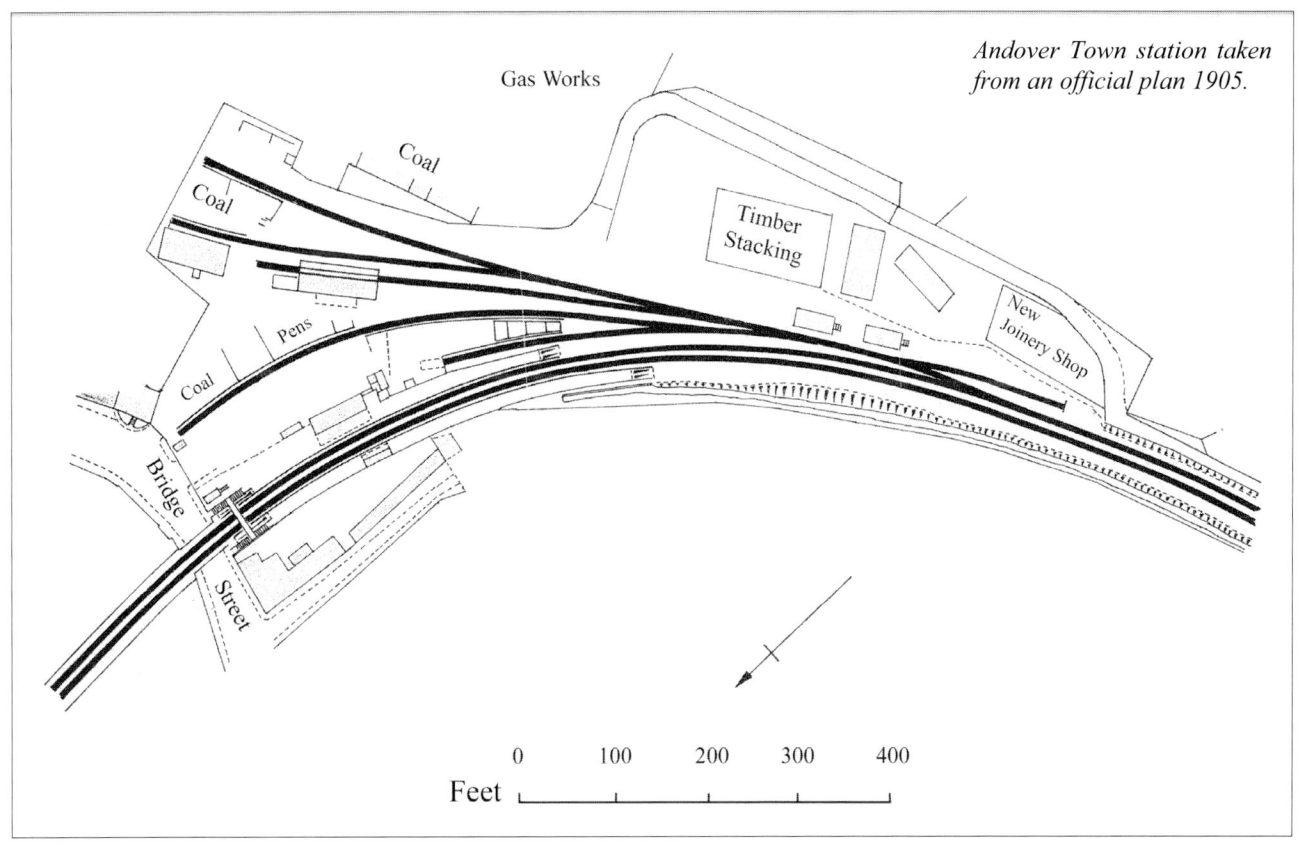

Andover Town station taken from an official plan 1905.

APPENDIX B

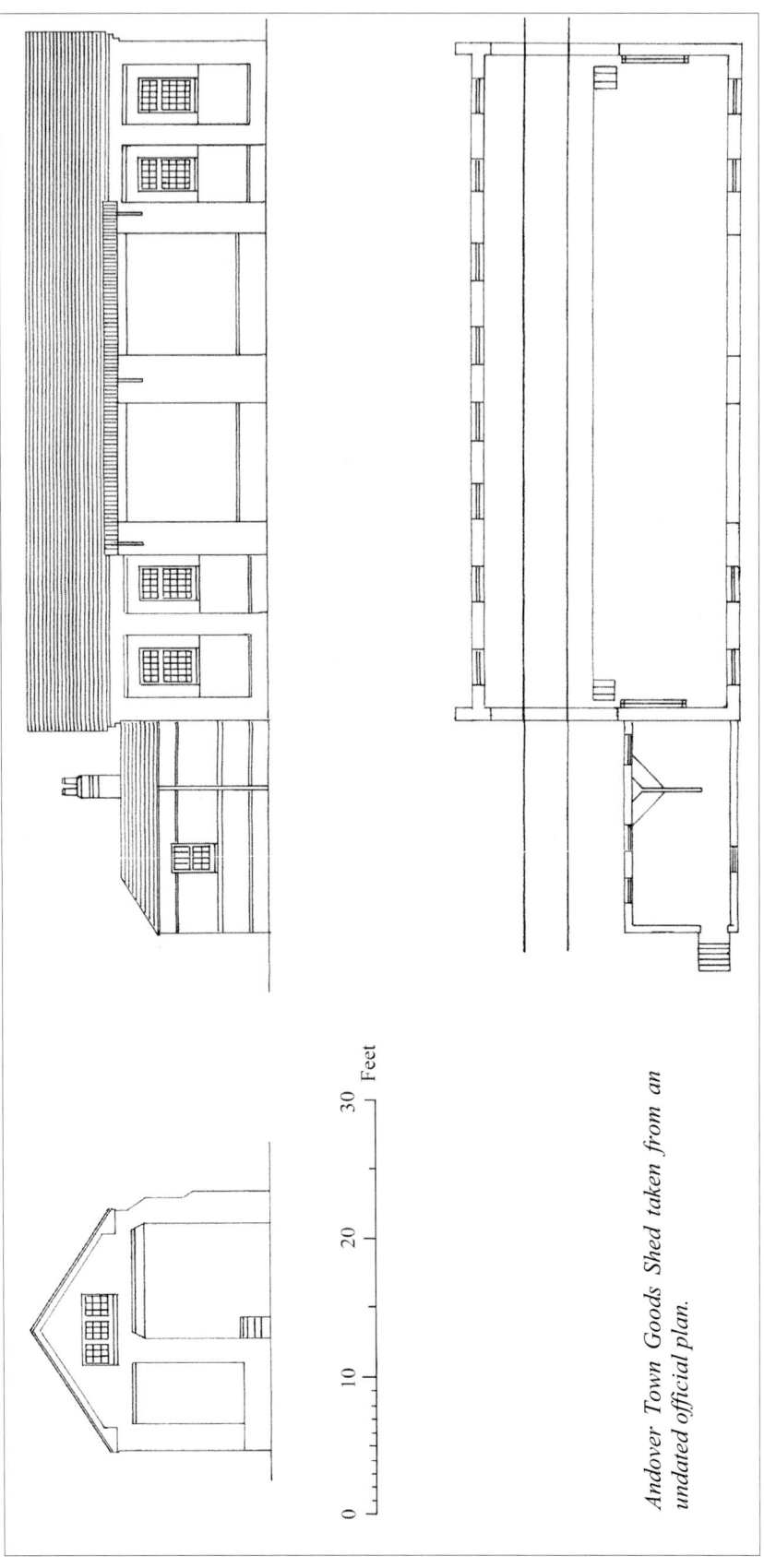

Andover Town Goods Shed taken from an undated official plan.

APPENDIX B

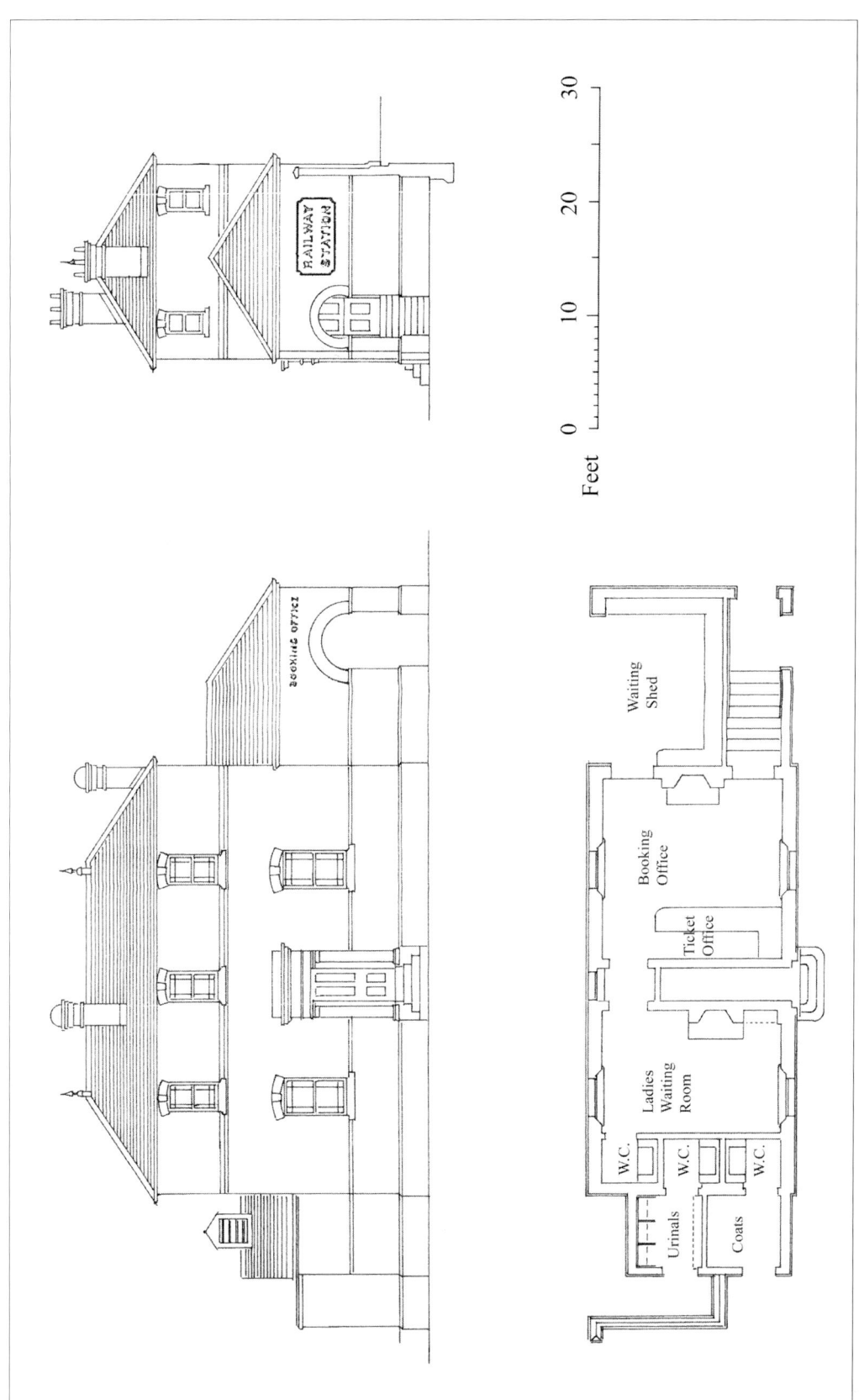

Clatford station buildings taken from an undated official plan.

APPENDIX B

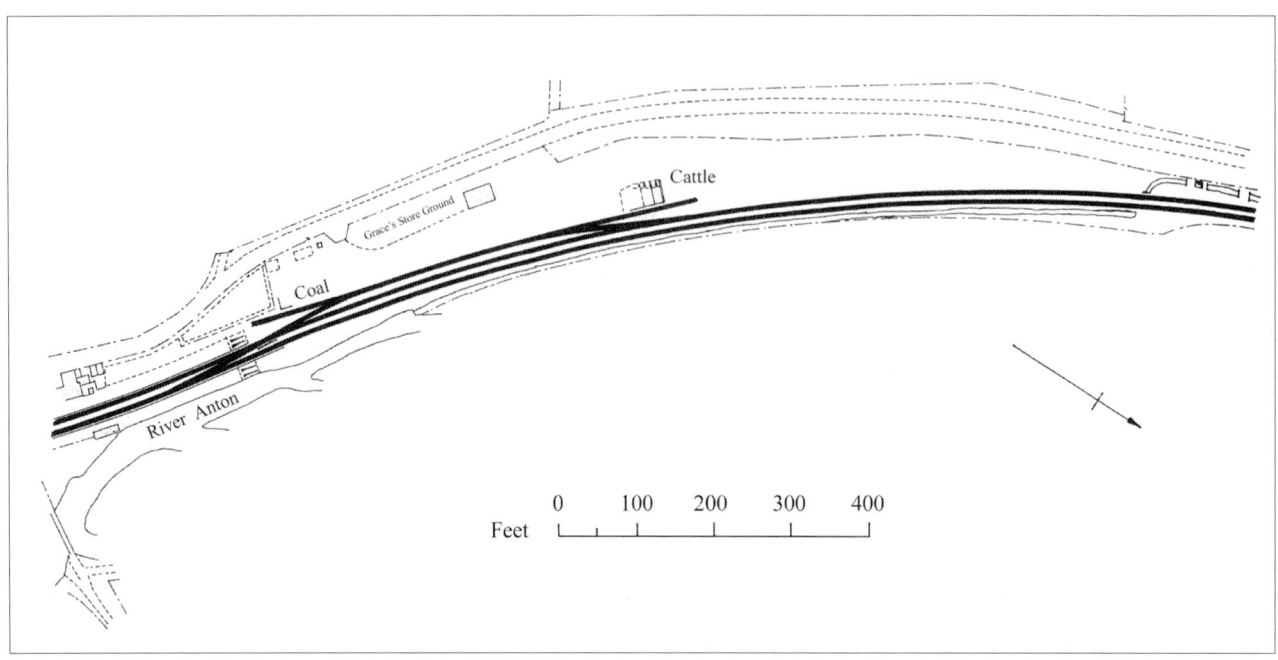

Clatford station taken from an official plan dated 20th November 1907.

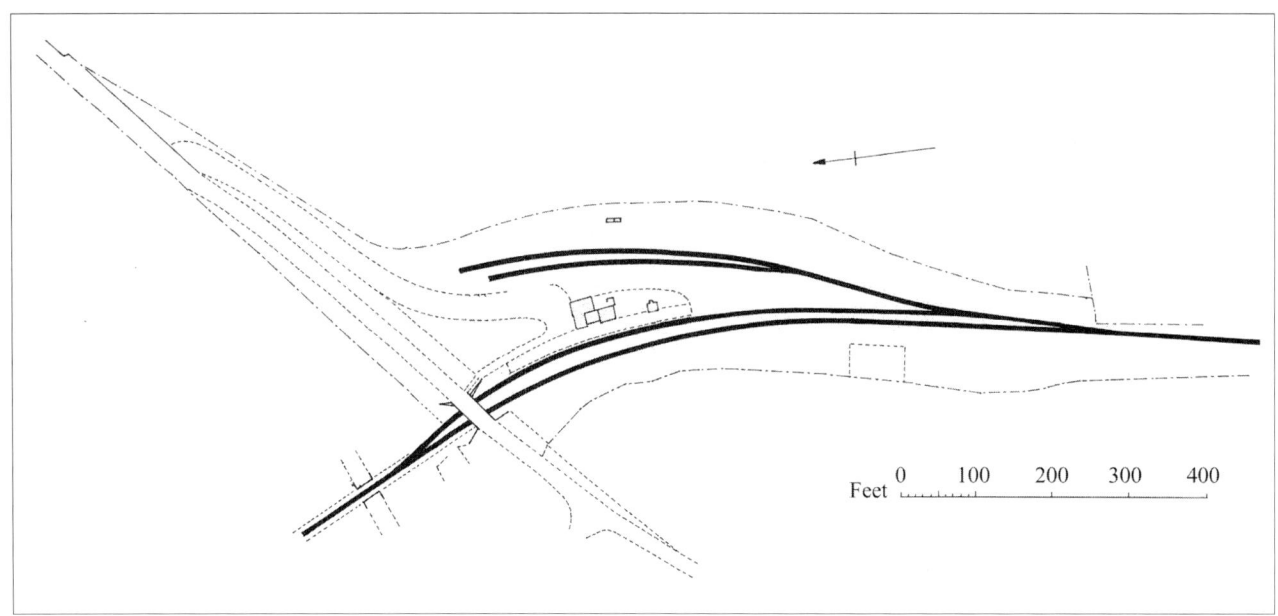

Fullerton station taken from an undated official plan.

APPENDIX B

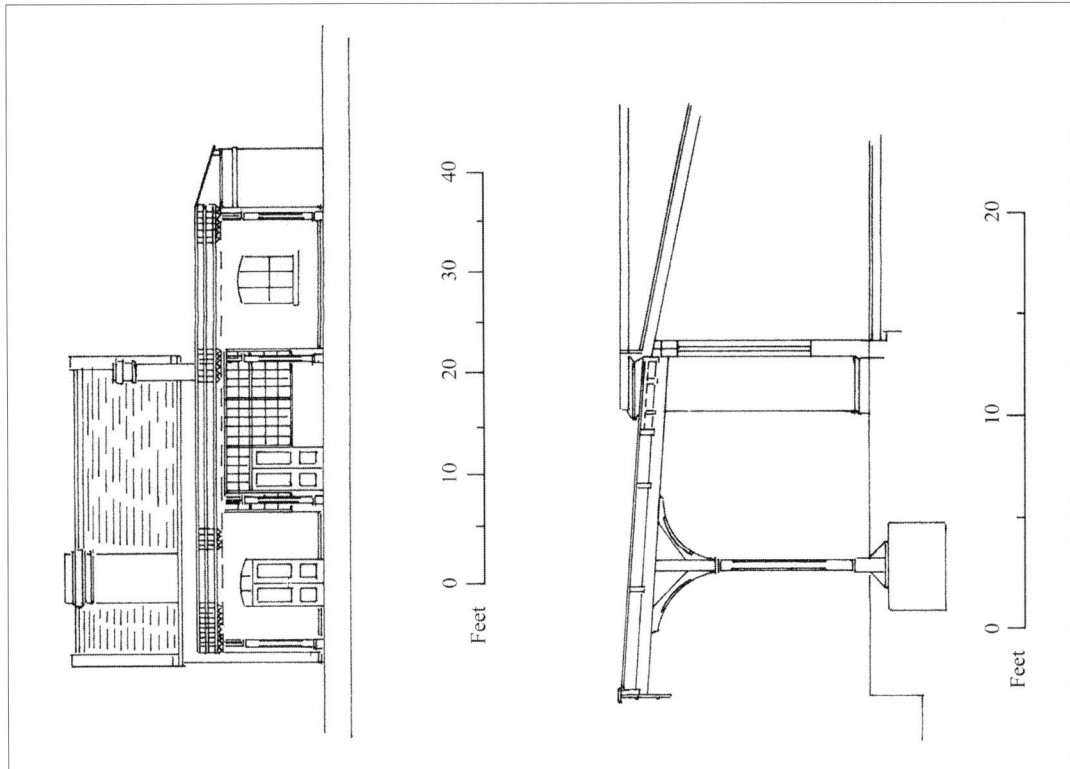

Horsebridge station building taken from an official plan dated 31st December 1895.

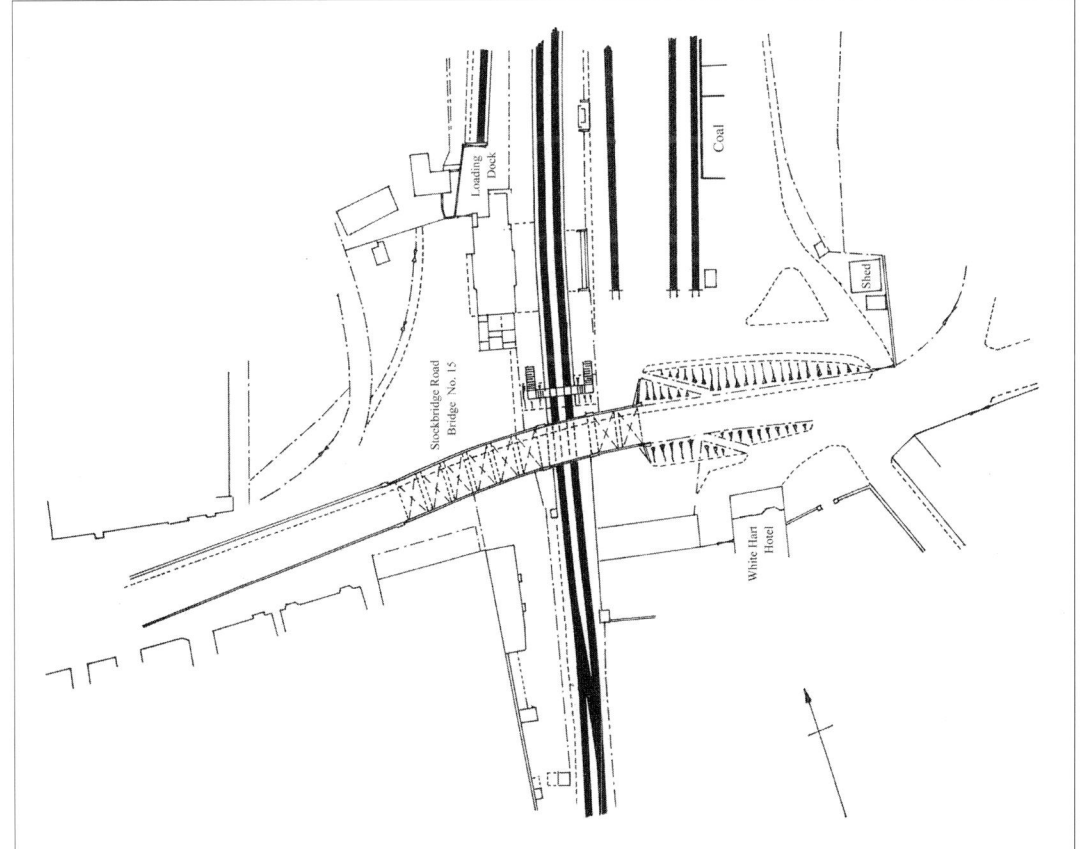

Stockbridge station taken from an official plan originally dated August 1897, but updated at some time by the Southern Railway.

APPENDIX B

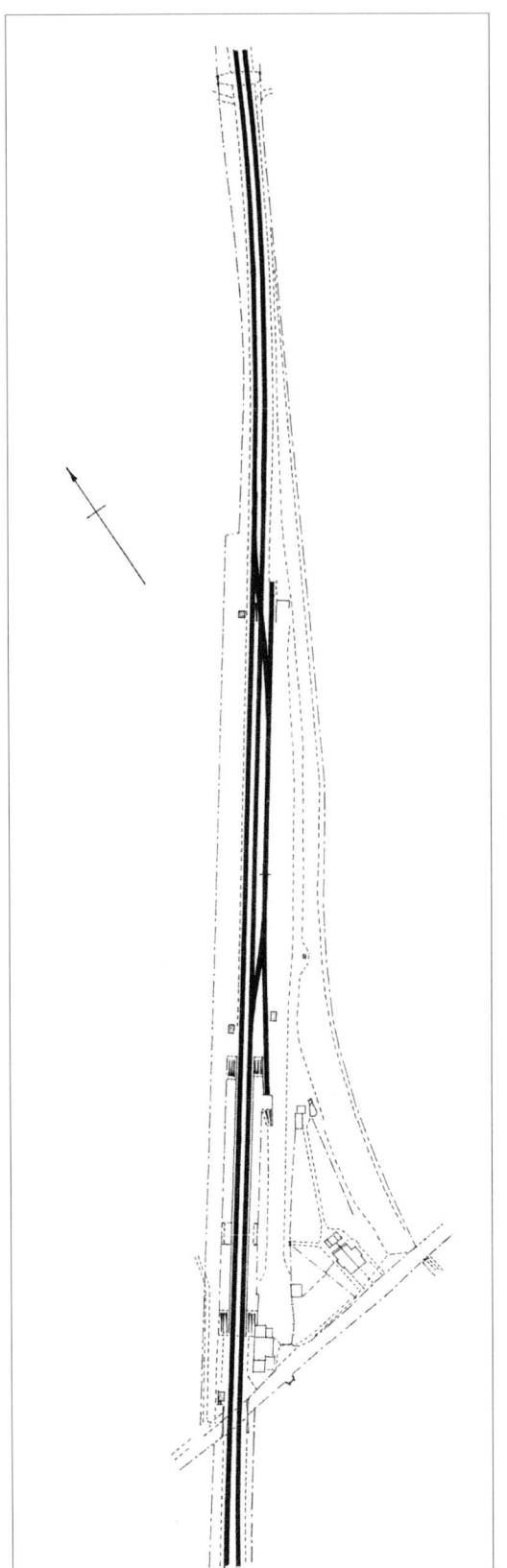

Mottisfont taken from an official plan dated 1905.

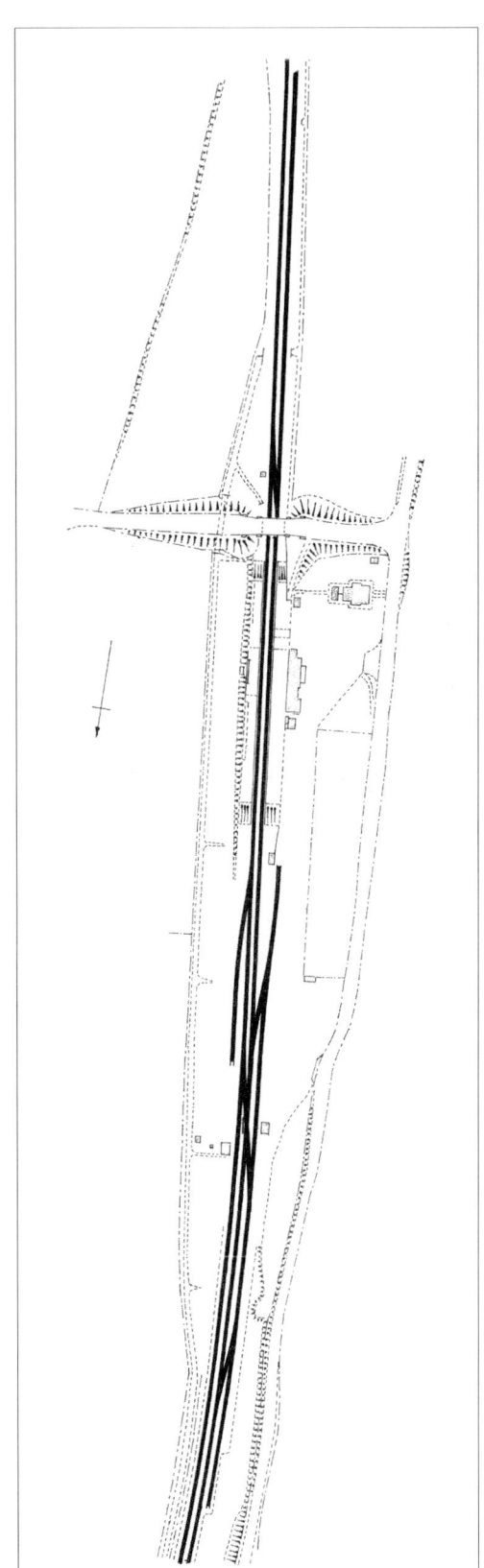

Nursling taken from an undated official plan.

APPENDIX B

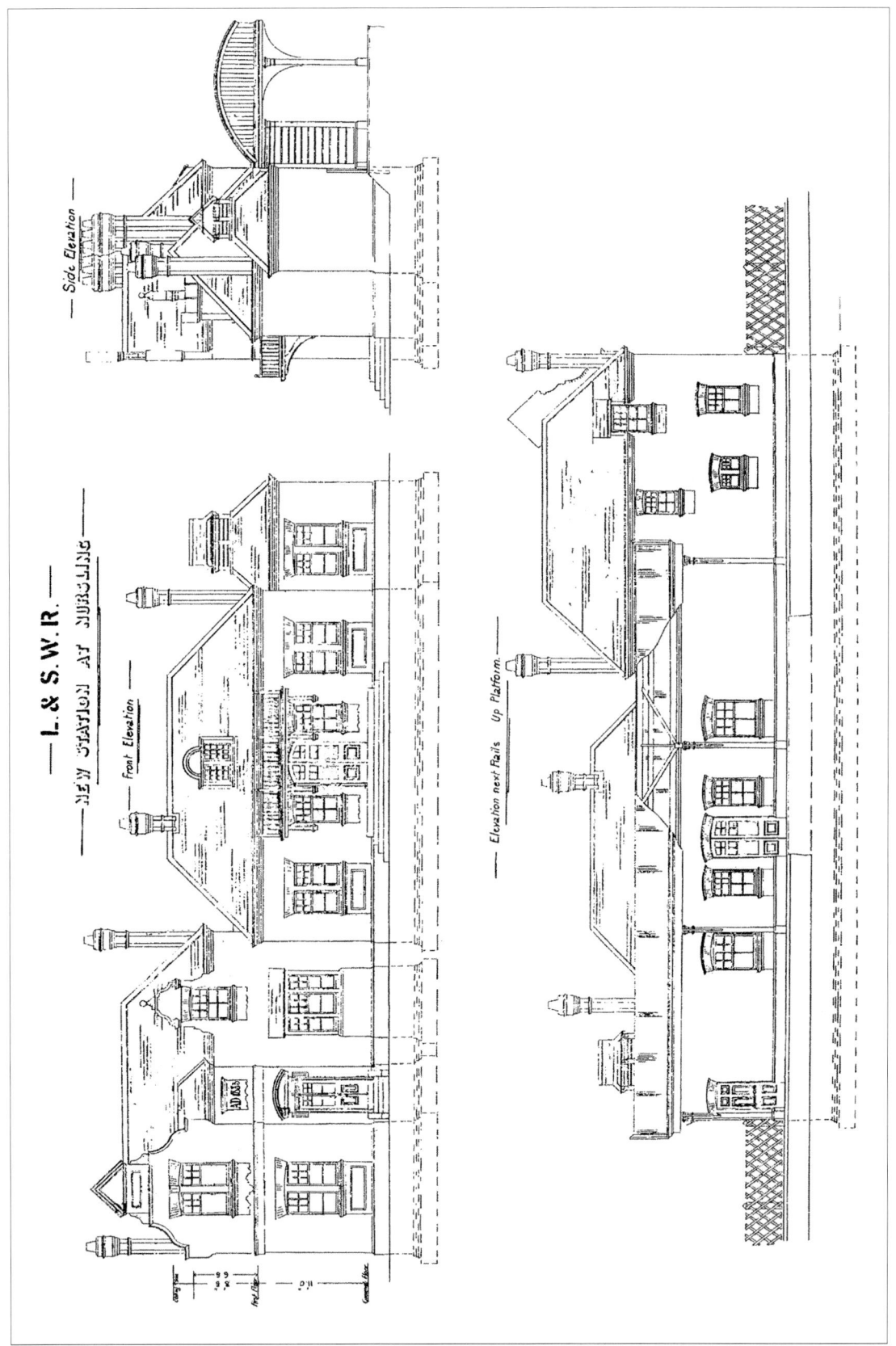

Nursling station buildings from a drawing dated 19th December 1882.

APPENDIX B

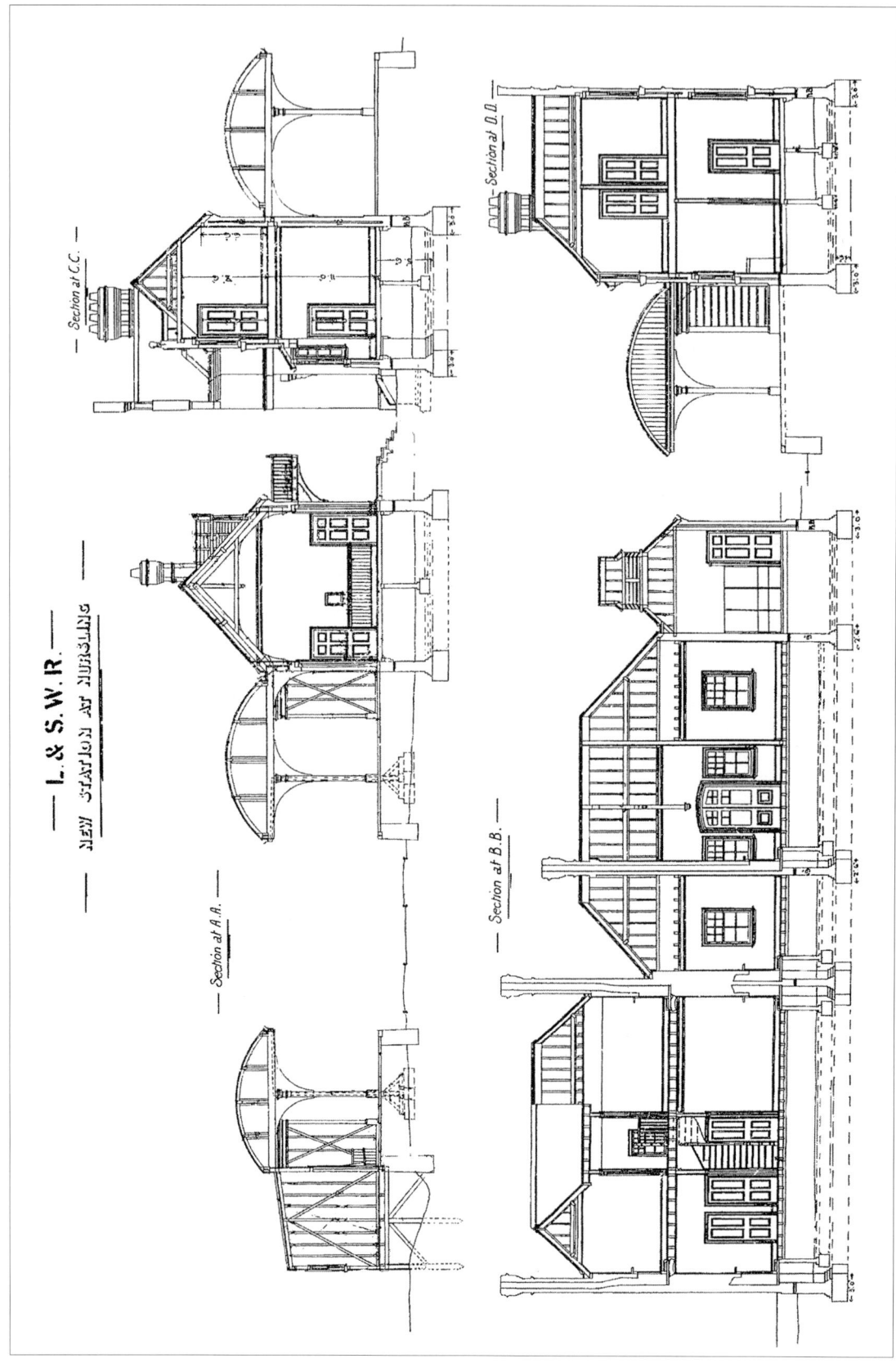

Nursling station buildings from a drawing dated 19th December 1882.

APPENDIX C

ANDOVER LINE TRAFFIC

Andover line traffic noted at Eastleigh by J.G. (George) Woodward 1926 - 1959

Key:

CAT W	Cattle wagon
CH	Non-corridor coach
COR	Corridor coach
E	Light engine
EXC	Excursion
G	Goods train
HB	Horse box
OCT	Open carriage truck
P	Passenger train
SG	Special goods train
SP	Special passenger train
V	Van train
*	Bank holiday
†	Excursions to Bournemouth from Tidworth for U.S. forces awaiting return to the U.S.A.

Date	Type	Loco	Train	Time at Eastleigh	Stock/Remarks
2/7/26	SP	GWR 1007	MSWJ – BOURNEMOUTH LINE	10.05 am	8 GWR CH, (Troops)
7/10/26	SP	E327 700	MSWJR – EASTLEIGH (FOR WINCHESTER)	-	8 CH, 6 HB, 2 VANS, (Troops)
15/11/26	P	E612 A12	EASTLEIGH – ANDOVER JUNCTION VIA SOUTHAMPTON WEST	12.22 pm	4 CH SET
17/11/26	P	E620 A12	EASTLEIGH – ANDOVER JUNCTION VIA SOUTHAMPTON WEST	12.22 pm	4 CH SET
17/11/26	P	E0464 0460	SOUTHAMPTON TERMINUS – EASTLEIGH – ANDOVER JUNCTION	3.11 pm	4 CH + VAN SET
16/4/27	P	E541 A12	EASTLEIGH – ANDOVER JUNCTION VIA SOUTHAMPTON WEST	12.25 pm	4 CH SET 81
16/4/27	P	ET1 T1	EASTLEIGH – ANDOVER JUNCTION (TRAIN EX-WEYMOUTH)	5.55 pm	5 CH, VAN
16/4/27	P	E0467 0460	ANDOVER JUNCTION – EASTLEIGH	7.54 pm	4 CH + VAN SET
18/4/27*	P	E0467 0460	ANDOVER JUNCTION – SOUTHAMPTON WEST – EASTLEIGH – ROMSEY – ANDOVER JUNCTION	9.10 am	4 CH SET
18/4/27*	P	E0467 0460	EASTLEIGH – SOUTHAMPTON WEST – ANDOVER JUNCTION	12.22 pm	3 CH SET 74
18/4/27*	P	E0467 0460	SOUTHAMPTON TERMINUS – EASTLEIGH – ANDOVER JUNCTION	3.00 pm	4 CH + VAN SET 297, 2 CH SET 16
18/5/27	P	E0468 0460	EASTLEIGH – SOUTHAMPTON WEST – ANDOVER JUNCTION	12.25 pm	4 CH SET
18/5/27	P	E0471 0460	SOUTHAMPTON TERMINUS – EASTLEIGH – ANDOVER JUNCTION	3.08 pm	4 CH SET
18/5/27	P	E0542 A12	EASTLEIGH – ANDOVER JUNCTION	5.19 pm	4 CH + VAN SET
4/6/27	P	E0477 0460	ANDOVER JUNCTION – SOUTHAMPTON WEST – EASTLEIGH – ROMSEY – ANDOVER JUNCTION	9.30 am	5 CH
4/6/27	P	E0464 0460	SOUTHAMPTON TERMINUS – ANDOVER JUNCTION	3.13 pm	3 CH SETS 69 & 84, 7 LMSR VANS
4/6/27	P	E662 X6	SOUTHAMPTON TERMINUS – ANDOVER JUNCTION	5.30 pm	4 CH SET 74
4/6/27	P	E0464 0460	ANDOVER JUNCTION – EASTLEIGH- SOUTHAMPTON TERMINUS	8.03 pm	3 CH SET
6/6/27*	P	E0474 0460	ANDOVER JUNCTION – EASTLEIGH – SOUTHAMPTON WEST - ANDOVER JUNCTION	12.32 pm	3 CH SET 61, COMPO 5374
6/6/27*	P	E0467 0460	SOUTHAMPTON TERMINUS – EASTLEIGH – ANDOVER JUNCTION	3.35 pm	3 CH SET 86, COMPO 0505
6/6/27*	P	E0467 0460	ANDOVER JUNCTION – SOUTHAMPTON WEST – EASTLEIGH	6.10 pm	3 CH SET 61
28/6/27	SP	GWR 1011	MSWJR – DOCKS	-	9 GWR CH (Troops)
17/7/27	SP	GWR 1128	MSWJR – BOURNEMOUTH	-	3 GWR CH, 3 GWR COR (EXC?)
1/8/27*	P	E657 X6	ANDOVER JUNCTION – SOUTHAMPTON WEST – EASTLEIGH	10.55 am	3 CH SET 71
1/8/27*	P	E391 K10	EASTLEIGH – ANDOVER JUNCTION	11.05 am	3 CH SET 71
1/8/27*	P	E0468 0460	ANDOVER JUNCTION – EASTLEIGH – SOUTHAMPTON TERMINUS	3.30 pm	2 CH SET 1 + 5 LOOSE
1/8/27*	P	E0467 0460	SOUTHAMPTON TERMINUS – EASTLEIGH – ANDOVER JUNCTION	3.30 pm	4 CH + VAN SET 299, 2 GWR HB
1/8/27	P	E0473 0460	ANDOVER JUNCTION – SOUTHAMPTON WEST – EASTLEIGH	6.22 pm	4 CH + VAN SET
13/8/27	P	E0467 0460	ANDOVER JUNCTION – SOUTHAMPTON WEST – EASTLEIGH – ANDOVER JUNCTION	9.25 am	5 CH, 5 VANS
13/8/27	P	E0473 0460	SOUTHAMPTON TERMINUS – EASTLEIGH – ANDOVER JUNCTION	3.15 pm	4 CH + VAN SET, 4 CH SET
5/4/28	P	E0470 0460	ANDOVER JUNCTION – SOUTHAMPTON WEST – EASTLEIGH – ANDOVER JUNCTION	9.27 am	4 CH + VAN SET
5/4/28	P	E0473 0460	EASTLEIGH – SOUTHAMPTON WEST – ANDOVER JUNCTION	12.26 pm	4 CH SET
5/4/28	P	E0473 0460	SOUTHAMPTON TERMINUS - EASTLEIGH – ANDOVER JUNCTION	3.07 pm	6CH
27/4/28	P	GWR 3284	EASTLEIGH – SOUTHAMPTON WEST - ANDOVER JUNCTION	12.15 pm	The previous working of these locos was:
7/5/28	P	GWR 3284	EASTLEIGH – SOUTHAMPTON WEST - ANDOVER JUNCTION	12.15 pm	
23/5/28	P	GWR 3284	EASTLEIGH – SOUTHAMPTON WEST - ANDOVER JUNCTION	12.15 pm	P CHELTENHAM - SOUTHAMPTON TERMINUS
14/6/28	P	GWR 1004	EASTLEIGH – SOUTHAMPTON WEST - ANDOVER JUNCTION	12.15 pm	
18/11/29	P	GWR 1009	EASTLEIGH – SOUTHAMPTON WEST - ANDOVER JUNCTION	12.15 pm	
16/1/30	P	GWR 1122	EASTLEIGH – SOUTHAMPTON WEST - ANDOVER JUNCTION	12.15 pm	LE to EASTLEIGH SHED
11/2/30	P	GWR 3268	EASTLEIGH – SOUTHAMPTON WEST - ANDOVER JUNCTION	12.15 pm	
26/2/30	P	GWR 3261	EASTLEIGH – SOUTHAMPTON WEST - ANDOVER JUNCTION	12.15 pm	Arrive about 11 am
17/10/30	P	GWR 3253	EASTLEIGH – SOUTHAMPTON WEST - ANDOVER JUNCTION	12.15 pm	

APPENDIX C

Date	Type	Loco	Train	Time at Eastleigh	Stock/Remarks
16/8/31	EXC	E627 A12	ANDOVER JUNCTION – EASTLEIGH – BOURNEMOUTH	-	10 CH SET 344
5/9/31	SP	E389 K10	ANDOVER JUNCTION – EASTLEIGH – FAREHAM LINE	-	5 GWR CH, 4 HB, 2 CATW (Troops)
14/3/32	P	E651 A12	ANDOVER JUNCTION – EASTLEIGH	6.05 pm	Duty 274
24/3/32	P	E121 T9	EASTLEIGH – ANDOVER JUNCTION	7.25 pm	Duty 274
26/3/32	P	E600 A12	EASTLEIGH – ANDOVER JUNCTION	7.25 pm	Duty 274
14/5/32	P	E293 C8	SOUTHAMPTON TERMINUS – EASTLEIGH – ANDOVER JUNCTION	9.02 am	3 CH SET 173, Duty 272
14/5/32	P	E381 K10	ANDOVER JUNCTION – EASTLEIGH – SOUTHAMPTON TERMINUS	1.14 pm	3 CH SET 173, Duty 273
14/5/32	P	E601 A12	EASTLEIGH – ANDOVER JUNCTION (TRAIN EX WEYMOUTH)	5.25 pm	3 COR SET 416, Duty 302
14/5/32	P	E291 C8	EASTLEIGH – ANDOVER JUNCTION	7.23 pm	4 CH SET 158, Duty 274
14/5/32	P	E293 C8	ANDOVER JUNCTION – EASTLEIGH	7.44 pm	Duty 272
23/7/32	SP	GWR 1122	MSWJR – SOUTHAMPTON TERMINUS	2.15 pm	4 GWR CH, 2 VANS
11/9/32	EXC	435 L11	ANDOVER JUNCTION – BRIGHTON		
9/5/33	P	590 X2	ANDOVER JUNCTION – EASTLEIGH – SOUTHAMPTON TERMINUS	1.05 pm	Duty 273
5/6/33	EXC	E587 X2	ANDOVER JUNCTION – PORTSMOUTH		9CH
14/7/33	SP	302 T9	SWINDON – PORTSMOUTH	8.34 am	10 CH SET 317 (GWR loco works holiday special)
14/7/33	SP	702 T9	SWINDON – PORTSMOUTH	9.20 am	10 CH SET 167 (GWR loco works holiday special)
19/7/33	G	GWR 6324	CHELTENHAM – SOUTHAMPTON DOCKS	8.35 am	
20/7/33	P	18 T1	EASTLEIGH – ANDOVER JUNCTION	7.54 am	Duty 318
20/7/33	G	GWR 4368	CHELTENHAM – SOUTHAMPTON DOCKS	8.39 am	22 WAGS, BV
20/7/33	P	E628 A12	ANDOVER JUNCTION – SOUTHAMPTON TERMINUS	1.03 pm	3 CH SET 69, Duty 279
20/7/33	P	E628 A12	EASTLEIGH – ANDOVER JUNCTION (TRAIN EX WEYMOUTH)	5.30 pm	3 CH SET 74, Duty 279
20/7/33	P	E598 A12	SOUTHAMPTON TERMINUS – ANDOVER JUNCTION	7.18 pm	3 CH SET 153, Duty 308
20/7/33	P	661 X6	ANDOVER JUNCTION – EASTLEIGH	7.51 pm	4 CH SET 139, Duty 309
26/7/33	G	GWR 6324	CHELTENHAM – SOUTHAMPTON DOCKS	8.35 am	These locos then work 10.10 am SOUTHAMPTON TERMINUS – SOUTHAMPTON WEST – CHELTENHAM
27/7/33	G	GWR 6379	CHELTENHAM – SOUTHAMPTON DOCKS	8.35 am	
1/8/33	G	GWR 4383	CHELTENHAM – SOUTHAMPTON DOCKS	8.35 am	
2/8/33	G	GWR 5394	CHELTENHAM – SOUTHAMPTON DOCKS	8.35 am	
3/8/33	G	GWR 6360	CHELTENHAM – SOUTHAMPTON DOCKS	8.35 am	
5/8/33	E	GWR 6360	SOUTHAMPTON TERMINUS – EASTLEIGH – MSWJR	1.00 pm	Failed at SOUTHAMPTON, 10.10 am to CHELTENHAM worked by SR loco
8/8/33	G	GWR 5394	CHELTENHAM – SOUTHAMPTON DOCKS	8.35 am	
17/8/33	G	GWR 5355	CHELTENHAM – SOUTHAMPTON DOCKS	8.35 am	
23/8/33	G	GWR 7300	CHELTENHAM – SOUTHAMPTON DOCKS	8.35 am	
31/8/33	G	GWR 7303	CHELTENHAM – SOUTHAMPTON DOCKS	8.35 am	
25/9/33	SP	GWR 4326	MSWJR – SOUTHAMPTON DOCKS		8 GWR COR, 4 OCT (Troops)
13/5/34	SP	713 T9	MSWJR - WORTHING		4 GWR COR, 4 GWR VANS (Troops)
13/5/34	V	121 T9	MSWJR - WORTHING		17 GW CAT W, 6 GWR HB, VAN
31/5/34	G	598 A12	ANDOVER JUNCTION – EASTLEIGH	6.15 pm	
20/6/34	SP	169 L11	ANDOVER TOWN – BOURNEMOUTH		11 COR (Children)
20/6/34	SP	150 K10	ANDOVER TOWN – BOURNEMOUTH		11 COR (Children)
30/6/34	SP	150 K10	ANDOVER JUNCTION – HAYLING ISLAND		10 CH (Ancient Order of Foresters 1834 – 1934)
30/6/34	SG	586 X2	AMESBURY – PORTSMOUTH		10 WELL WAGS, 15 OCT, 2 VANS, ARMY EQUIPMENT
6/7/34	G	640 A12	ANDOVER JUNCTION – EASTLEIGH		
11/7/34	G	GWR 4380	CHELTENHAM – SOUTHAMPTON DOCKS	9.00 am	
11/7/34	P	65 T1	ANDOVER JUNCTION – EASTLEIGH	9.35 pm	Duty 361
12/7/34	G	GWR 6379	CHELTENHAM – SOUTHAMPTON DOCKS	9.00 am	20 WAGS, BV
13/7/34	G	GWR 4300	CHELTENHAM – SOUTHAMPTON DOCKS	9.00 am	21 WAGS, BV
13/7/34	SP	GWR 6360	SWINDON – PORTSMOUTH		10 GWR COR (GWR loco works holiday special)
13/7/34	SP	GWR 6347	SWINDON – PORTSMOUTH		10 GWR COR

APPENDIX C

Date	Type	Loco	Train	Time at Eastleigh	Stock/Remarks
14/7/34	G	GWR 4300	CHELTENHAM – SOUTHAMPTON DOCKS	9.00 am	21 WAGS, BV
14/7/34	SP	724 T9	FAREHAM LINE – AMESBURY		6 COR, VAN (Troops)
16/7/34	G	603 A12	ANDOVER JUNCTION – EASTLEIGH	9.40 am	Duty 303
18/7/34	G	GWR 7303	CHELTENHAM – SOUTHAMPTON DOCKS	9.00 am	
20/7/34	SP	114 T9	BOURNEMOUTH/PORTSMOUTH – SWINDON		10 CH (return works holiday specials)
22/7/34	EXC	GWR 6371	CHELTENHAM – BOURNEMOUTH		9 GWR COR
26/7/34	EXC	GWR 6379	GLOUCESTER – PORTSMOUTH	1.20 pm	7 GWR COR, DINER
30/7/34	G	GWR 4388	CHELTENHAM – SOUTHAMPTON DOCKS	9.00 am	
2/8/34	SG	2441 C2'X	SINGLETON - STOCKBRIDGE		5 HB, GV
4/8/34	SP	2528 C2'X	CHICHESTER – TIDWORTH		8 CH (Tattoo special)
4/8/34	SP	705 T9	WEYMOUTH – TIDWORTH		8 CH (Tattoo special)
5/8/34	EXC	648 A12	ANDOVER JUNCTION – BRIGHTON		4 CH (Loco to EASTLEIGH only)
7/8/34	EXC	GWR 4383	CHELTENHAM – PORTSMOUTH		9 GWR COR
8/8/34	EXC	418 L12	BOURNEMOUTH – TIDWORTH		6 COR (For tattoo)
10/8/34	EXC	721 T9	WEYMOUTH – TIDWORTH		
11/8/34	EXC	2546 C2'X	BRIGHTON LINE – TIDWORTH		
11/8/34	EXC	412 L11	PORTSMOUTH – TIDWORTH		6 COR (For tattoo)
12/8/34	EXC	649 A12	ANDOVER JUNCTION – BOURNEMOUTH		4 CH (Loco to EASTLEIGH only)
14/8/34	G	GWR 6360	CHELTENHAM – SOUTHAMPTON DOCKS	9.00 am	
21/8/34	G	GWR 4352	CHELTENHAM – SOUTHAMPTON DOCKS	9.00 am	
26/8/34	EXC	GWR 4352	CHELTENHAM – PORTSMOUTH		10 GWR COR
29/8/34	G	GWR 4308	CHELTENHAM – SOUTHAMPTON DOCKS	9.10 am	
2/9/34	EXC	649 A12	ANDOVER JUNCTION – BRIGHTON		4 CH (Loco to EASTLEIGH only)
6/9/34	G	GWR 4383	CHELTENHAM – SOUTHAMPTON DOCKS	9.00 am	
16/9/34	SP	691 700	MSWJR – GOSPORT		BTK, 7 OCT, 4 HB, CAT W (Troops)
16/9/34	SP	696 700	MSWJR – GOSPORT		10 GWR COR (Troops)
17/9/34	G	GW 4308	CHELTENHAM – SOUTHAMPTON DOCKS	9.00 am	
22/9/34	G	GW 7311	CHELTENHAM – SOUTHAMPTON DOCKS	9.00 am	
12/12/34	G	611 A12	ANDOVER JUNCTION – EASTLEIGH	1.00 pm	
9/4/35	P	587 X2	ANDOVER JUNCTION – EASTLEIGH	12.15 pm	
22/4/35*	P	329 K10	ANDOVER JUNCTION – PORTSMOUTH	11.00 am	6 COR
1/6/35	SG	GW 2255	MSWJR – SOUTHAMPTON DOCKS		18 WAGS, Army equipment, BV
10/6/35*	P	590 X2	ANDOVER JUNCTION – PORTSMOUTH		10 CH (train returned by K10 144)
19/6/35	SP	302 T9	ANDOVER JUNCTION – BOGNOR REGIS		11 COR (Children)
19/6/35	SP	708 T9	ANDOVER JUNCTION – BOGNOR REGIS		11 COR (Children)
8/7/35	P	430 L12	EASTLEIGH – SOUTHAMPTON CNTL – ANDOVER JUNCTION	12.25 pm	
9/7/35	EXC	GWR 8386	CHELTENHAM – BOURNEMOUTH		8 GWR COR, DINER
9/7/35	EXC	GWR 7301	CHELTENHAM – BOURNEMOUTH		8 GWR COR, DINER
12/7/35	SP	GWR 4380	SWINDON - BOURNEMOUTH		GWR Railway Works holiday specials
12/7/35	SP	GWR 4339	SWINDON - PORTSMOUTH		
12/7/35	SP	GWR 4371	SWINDON - PORTSMOUTH		
14/7/35	EXC	285 T9	ANDOVER JUNCTION – BOURNEMOUTH		5 CH
21/7/35	EXC	GWR 4303	CHELTENHAM – PORTSMOUTH		8 GWR COR
21/7/35	SP	625 A12	BULFORD – EASTLEIGH (FOR WINCHESTER)		4 CH (Troops)
30/7/35	EXC	1633 U	BOURNEMOUTH – TIDWORTH		8 COR (Tattoo special)
3/8/35	EXC	313 T9	BRIGHTON – TIDWORTH		6 COR (Tattoo special)
5/8/35*	P	605 A12	ANDOVER JUNCTION – PORTSMOUTH		6 COR
5/8/35*	EXC	679 T6	ANDOVER JUNCTION – PORTSMOUTH		10 LMS COR (Returned by L11 439)
18/8/35	SP	405 L11	BOURNEMOUTH LINE – BULFORD		6 CH, 4 OCT, 4 HB, 2 VANS (Troops)
5/9/35	EXC	727 T9	BULFORD – BOURNEMOUTH		5 CH

APPENDIX C

Date	Type	Loco	Train	Time at Eastleigh	Stock/Remarks
20/9/35	SP	1796 U	WEYHILL – SOUTHAMPTON CNTL – ALTON – DOVER		8 CH SET 920 (Troops)
20/9/35	SP	1613 U	MSWJR – SOUTHAMPTON CNTL – ALTON – DOVER		7 CH SET 918 (Troops)
20/9/35	SP	434 L12	MSWJR – SOUTHAMPTON CNTL – ALTON – SHORNCLIFFE		9 CH SET? (Troops)
20/9/35	SP	1809 U	MSWJR – SOUTHAMPTON CNTL – ALTON – SHORNCLIFFE		9 CH SET? (Troops)
20/9/35	SP	403 S11	MSWJR – SOUTHAMPTON CNTL – ALTON – DOVER		8 CH, VAN (Troops)
20/9/35	SP	1806 U	MSWJR – SOUTHAMPTON CNTL – ALTON – DOVER		9 CH SET 899 (Troops)
24/9/35	SP	1623 U	ANDOVER JUNCTION – SOUTHAMPTON CNTL – ALTON LINE		6 COR, 5 VANS (Troops)
23/1/36	P	661 X6	EASTLEIGH – ANDOVER JUNCTION	7.15 pm	(Usually an A12 working)
25/1/36	P	GWR 5394	CHELTENHAM – SOUTHAMPTON TERMINUS	5.30 pm	Diversion, L11 156 derailed at Millbrook
25/1/36	G	GWR 5394	SOUTHAMPTON DOCKS – CHELTENHAM	7.30 pm	Diversion as above
5/4/36	SG	690 700	MSWJR – SOUTHAMPTON DOCKS		22 empty LMS Banana vans, BV
10/6/36	V	GWR 6379	MSWJR – EASTLEIGH (TO DOCKS, SR LOCO)	8.15 am	10 LMS VANS, BTK (Pigeons)
13/6/36	P	630 A12	EASTLEIGH – ANDOVER JUNCTION	8.00 am	
21/6/36	EXC	382 K10	BULFORD – PORTSMOUTH		5 CH
24/6/36	SP	305 T9	ANDOVER JUNCTION – WEYMOUTH		9 COR (Children)
24/6/36	SP	118 T9	ANDOVER JUNCTION – WEYMOUTH		8 COR (Children)
25/6/36	V	GWR 6379	MSWJR – SOUTHAMPTON DOCKS		8 VANS (Pigeons)
3/7/36	SP	305 T9	ANDOVER JUNCTION – HAYLING ISLAND		10 CH (Children)
12/7/36	EXC	GW 7305	CHELTENHAM – PORTSMOUTH		8 GWR COR
14/7/36	V	GW 7303	MSWJR – SOUTHAMPTON DOCKS		4 LMSR VANS (Pigeons)
17/7/36	G	GW 4339	CHELTENHAM – SOUTHAMPTON DOCKS		
17/7/36	EXC	302 T9	SWINDON – BOURNEMOUTH		10 CH
3/8/36	EXC	592 X2	ANDOVER JUNCTION – BOURNEMOUTH		10 LMSR COR
8/8/36	EXC	338 T9	BRIGHTON – TIDWORTH		7 CH (Tattoo)
1/10/36	SP	368 700	TIDWORTH – SOUTHAMPTON DOCKS		10 COR, VAN (Troops)
4/6/27	P	586 X2	ANDOVER JUNCTION – EASTLEIGH	7.40 pm	
22/6/37	P	51 M7	ANDOVER JUNCTION – EASTLEIGH	8.40 pm	
24/6/37	P	45 M7	ANDOVER JUNCTION – EASTLEIGH	8.40 pm	
25/6/37	P	45 M7	ANDOVER JUNCTION – EASTLEIGH	8.40 pm	
26/6/37	P	45 M7	ANDOVER JUNCTION – EASTLEIGH	8.40 pm	
2/8/37*	EXC	441 L11	MSWJR – PORTSMOUTH		10 LMSR COR
5/8/37	EXC	GW 7303	CHELTENHAM – PORTSMOUTH		6 GWR COR
5/9/37	EXC	437 L11	BULFORD – BOURNEMOUTH		4 CH (Loco to EASTLEIGH only)
3/12/37	P	666 X6	EASTLEIGH – ANDOVER JUNCTION	7.10 pm	
18/3/38	SP	530 Q	ANDOVER JUNCTION – DOCKS		9 COR (Troops)
6/6/38*	EXC	138 K10	ANDOVER JUNCTION – BOURNEMOUTH		10 CH (Loco to EASTLEIGH only, on by T9 725)
6/6/38*	EXC	148 L11	ANDOVER JUNCTION – PORTSMOUTH		11 CH (Loco to EASTLEIGH only, on by L11 172)
9/7/38	SP	630 A12	ANDOVER JUNCTION – HAYLING ISLAND		10 CH (Children)
15/7/38	SP	305 T9	BOURNEMOUTH – SWINDON		10 CH (Return works holiday special)
17/7/38	EXC	713 T9	ANDOVER JUNCTION – BRIGHTON		10 COR
2/8/38	EXC	GWR 6393	CHELTENHAM – PORTSMOUTH		6 GWR COR
16/8/38	P	627 A12	ANDOVER JUNCTION – SOUTHAMPTON TERMINUS	9.50 pm	
19/9/38	P	563 T3	EASTLEIGH – ANDOVER JUNCTION	7.15 pm	
29/5/39*	EXC	115 T9	ANDOVER JUNCTION – PORTSMOUTH		7 CH
21/6/39	Retn EXC	724 T9	BOURNEMOUTH – ANDOVER JUNCTION		9 COR (Children)
21/6/39	Retn EXC	531 Q	BOURNEMOUTH – ANDOVER JUNCTION		9 COR (Children)
5/7/39	SP	707 T9	ANDOVER JUNCTION – BOURNEMOUTH LINE		7 CH + 2 VAN SET (Children)
14/7/39	EXC	GWR 6343	MSWJR – PORTSMOUTH		7 GWR COR

APPENDIX C

Date	Type	Loco	Train	Time at Eastleigh	Stock/Remarks
22/7/39	P	598 A12	EASTLEIGH – SOUTHAMPTON CNTL – ANDOVER JUNCTION	12.25 pm	
6/8/39	P	329 K10	(SU) ANDOVER JUNCTION – EASTLEIGH	NOON	
7/8/39*	EXC	440 L11	ANDOVER JUNCTION – PORTSMOUTH		9 GWR COR (Loco to Eastleigh only)
During the period October 1939 to June 1940 there were numerous recordings of troop trains to the docks from "via Romsey". Which of these came from Andover and the MSWJR is not known so they are not included in this list.					
19/1/40	P	609 A12	EASTLEIGH – ANDOVER JUNCTION	7.55 am	5 CH (Pilot to Romsey X6 658)
20/1/40	P	642 A12	EASTLEIGH – ANDOVER JUNCTION	7.55 am	5 CH (Pilot to Romsey K10 394)
14/3/40	G	GWR 5394	SOUTHAMPTON DOCKS – MSWJR	4.23 pm	26 WAGS, BV
9/4/40	P	706 T9	EASTLEIGH - A NDOVER JUNCTION	852 am	3 CH SET
			ANDOVER JUNCTION - EASTLEIGH	12.10 pm	
9/4/40	P	408 L11	WEYMOUTH – ANDOVER JUNCTION	5.29 pm	5 CH, Duty 408
27/4/40	G	GWR 5396	CHELTENHAM – SOUTHAMPTON DOCKS		
12/6/40	SP	GWR 4326	MSWJR – SOUTHAMPTON DOCKS		10 GWR COR (Troops)
14/6/40	ECS	302 T9	ANDOVER JUNCTION – EASTLEIGH		7 CH + 2 VAN SET
16/6/40	ECS	GWR 6393	MSWJR – SOUTHAMPTON DOCKS		9 GWR COR
16/7/40	P	600 A12	SOUTHAMPTON TERMINUS - ANDOVER JUNCTION	8.53 am	5 CH, Duty 317
			ANDOVER JUNCTION – SOUTHAMPTON TERMINUS	1.35 pm	6 CH, Duty 317
16/7/40	P	366 T1	ANDOVER JUNCTION – SOUTHAMPTON TERMINUS	10.54 am	6 CH, 2 VANS, Duty 313
16/7/40	P	708 T9	WEYMOUTH - ANDOVER JUNCTION	5.33 pm	3 COR, 3 CH, Duty 298
			ANDOVER JUNCTION - EASTLEIGH	8.50 pm	3 COR, Duty 298
16/7/40	P	637 A12	FAWLEY – ANDOVER JUNCTION	6.16 pm	5 CH
16/7/40	P	150 K10	ANDOVER JUNCTION – EASTLEIGH	7.50 pm	3 CH
8/4/41	SG	404 S11	SOUTHAMPTON DOCKS – ANDOVER JUNCTION	7.15 pm	17 WAGS (Sheeted opens), BV
24/5/41	P	404 S11	WEYMOUTH – ANDOVER JUNCTION	5.25 pm	
12/11/41	P	313 T9	EASTLEIGH – ANDOVER JUNCTION (Ex Weymouth train)	5.30 pm	3 CH SET
15/11/41	P	641 A12	ANDOVER JUNCTION – SOUTHAMPTON TERMINUS	1.35 pm	
3/4/42*	P	337 T9	SOUTHAMPTON TERMINUS – ANDOVER JUNCTION	8.55 am	3 COR SET 401
7/4/42	SP	119 T9	EASTLEIGH – ANDOVER JUNCTION (Ex Fareham line)	4.15 pm	SALOON 291s, BCK 6591, 1st SLEEPER, LNER 1679
29/7/42	P	708 T9	SOUTHAMPTON TERMINUS – ANDOVER JUNCTION	8.53 am	3 CH SET 110
			ANDOVER JUNCTION - EASTLEIGH	12.24 pm	
29/7/42	P	642 A12	EASTLEIGH – ANDOVER JUNCTION (Ex Weymouth train)	5.30 pm	3 COR SET 419
			ANDOVER JUNCTION - EASTLEIGH	9.50 pm	
24/2/43	P	120 T9	EASTLEIGH – ANDOVER JUNCTION (Ex Weymouth train)	5.40 pm	5 CH
24/2/43	P	598 A12	FAWLEY – ANDOVER JUNCTION	6.21 pm	5 CH
12/6/43	P	313 T9	SOUTHAMPTON TERMINUS - ANDOVER JUNCTION	8.46 am	3 CH SET 166
			ANDOVER JUNCTION – EASTLEIGH	12.20 pm	
12/6/43	P	150 K10	EASTLEIGH – ANDOVER JUNCTION (Ex Weymouth train)	5.40 pm	3 CH SET 159
			ANDOVER JUNCTION - EASTLEIGH	9.50 pm	
20/11/43	G	390 K10 + 597 A12	ANDOVER JUNCTION – EASTLEIGH	5.00 pm	
21/3/44	P	120 T9	EASTLEIGH – ANDOVER JUNCTION	5.58 pm	5 CH
25/3/44	G	GWR 7813	CHELTENHAM – SOUTHAMPTON DOCKS		
19/4/44	SP	GWR 4507	ANDOVER JUNCTION – EASTLEIGH – SOUTHAMPTON CNTL – ANDOVER JUNCTION		GWR SALOON (Clearance tests)
14/6/44	G	GWR 7818	CHELTENHAM – SOUTHAMPTON DOCKS		
11/3/45	SP	GWR 5327	MSWJR – SOUTHAMPTON DOCKS		10 LMSR COR (Troops)
11/3/45	SP	GWR 6326	MSWJR – SOUTHAMPTON DOCKS		10 LMSR COR (Troops)
9/4/45	P	1743 D1	WEYMOUTH - ANDOVER JUNCTION	5.25 pm	
21/5/45	P	57 M7	WEYMOUTH - ANDOVER JUNCTION	5.25 pm	
28/5/45	P	719 T9	WEYMOUTH - ANDOVER JUNCTION	5.25 pm	
29/8/45	SP	1636 U	TIDWORTH – BOURNEMOUTH		10 COR (Troops) †
29/8/45	SP	1839 N	TIDWORTH – BOURNEMOUTH		10 COR (Troops) †

APPENDIX C

Date	Type	Loco	Train	Time at Eastleigh	Stock/Remarks
31/8/45	SP	311 T9	TIDWORTH – BOURNEMOUTH		10 COR (Troops) † (31AF37)
31/8/45	SP	548 Q	TIDWORTH – BOURNEMOUTH		7 COR (Troops) †
9/10/45	P	123 M7	ANDOVER JUNCTION – EASTLEIGH	10.30 am	3 CH SET (Loco ex-works 2/10/45)
9/10/45	P	28 M7	WEYMOUTH – ANDOVER JUNCTION	5.25 pm	
10/10/45	P	341 K10	EASTLEIGH – ANDOVER JUNCTION (Ex Weymouth train)	5.25 pm	
24/11/45	P	104 M7	WEYMOUTH – ANDOVER JUNCTION	5.25 pm	
6/4/46	P	597 A12	ANDOVER JUNCTION – EASTLEIGH	8.10 pm	
17/4/46	P	379 M7	WEYMOUTH – ANDOVER JUNCTION	5.25 pm	5 CH
10/5/46	E	GWR 6309	ANDOVER JUNCTION – SOUTHAMPTON TERMINUS	8.40 am	To work 10.10 am SOUTHAMPTON TERMINUS – CHELTENHAM
23/5/46	E	GWR 6384	ANDOVER JUNCTION – SOUTHAMPTON TERMINUS	8.35 am	
29/5/46	E	GWR 6322	ANDOVER JUNCTION – SOUTHAMPTON TERMINUS	8.40 am	
15/7/46	E	GWR 4381	ANDOVER JUNCTION – SOUTHAMPTON TERMINUS	8.35 am	
24/7/46	E	GWR 6360	ANDOVER JUNCTION – SOUTHAMPTON TERMINUS	8.45 am	
18/9/46	P	627 A12	ANDOVER JUNCTION – EASTLEIGH	8.05 am	
7/2/48	SP	420 L12	SWINDON – SOUTHAMPTON CNTL		8 CH (Football special)
8/7/48	P	711 T9	ANDOVER JUNCTION – EASTLEIGH	7.50 pm	
9/7/49	P	30302 T9	ANDOVER JUNCTION – EASTLEIGH	12.18 pm	
15/7/51	G	30316 700	ANDOVER JUNCTION – EASTLEIGH		12 WAGS, BV
21/7/51	G	30565 0395	EASTLEIGH - ANDOVER JUNCTION	7.15 am	
21/7/51	P	30426 L12	EASTLEIGH - ANDOVER JUNCTION	7.56 am	
22/7/51	P	30530 Q	EASTLEIGH - ANDOVER JUNCTION	11.05 am	(SU)
12/8/51	P	30287 T9	EASTLEIGH - ANDOVER JUNCTION	11.05 am	(SU)
14/12/51	P	31770 L	ANDOVER JUNCTION – EASTLEIGH	8.40 pm	
9/5/52	EXC	31634 U	ANDOVER JUNCTION – PORTSMOUTH		10 COR
19/6/52	EXC	4550 45XX	ANDOVER JUNCTION – EASTLEIGH (Train on to Bournemouth with SR loco)		7 COR
2/8/52	P	31776 L	BOURNEMOUTH – ANDOVER JUNCTION	6.10 pm	6 COR
2/8/52	P	41305 LM2	ANDOVER JUNCTION – EASTLEIGH	7.50 pm	3 COR
23/8/52	P	41293 LM2	ANDOVER JUNCTION – EASTLEIGH	7.50 pm	3 COR
23/8/52	P	31775 L	ANDOVER JUNCTION – EASTLEIGH	8.50 pm	3 CH SET
7/6/53	SG	6390 63XX	ANDOVER JUNCTION – EASTLEIGH		
8/11/53	P	30300 T9	EASTLEIGH – ANDOVER JUNCTION	11.05 pm	3 CH (SU)
21/3/54	SG	76027 BR4	ANDOVER JUNCTION – EASTLEIGH		11 WAGS, 2 BV (E.D. Train)
10/6/54	V	5394 53XX / 6360 63XX	MSWJ – SOUTHAMPTON DOCKS		Pigeon special
6/8/54	P	31619 U	ANDOVER JUNCTION – EASTLEIGH	8.35 pm	5 COR
8/8/54	SP	76029 BR4	LYMINGTON PIER – MSWJR		5 LMSR COR (Troops)
3/4/55	P	80031 BR4	ANDOVER JUNCTION-EASTLEIGH	8.30 pm	
18/1/56	P	4550 45XX	ANDOVER JUNCTION – EASTLEIGH	7.50 pm	(Due to failure of Eastleigh loco)
2/4/56	P	76026 BR4	ANDOVER JUNCTION – EASTLEIGH	8.35 pm	6 CH
18/5/56	P	30356 M7	ANDOVER JUNCTION – EASTLEIGH	8.40 pm	3 CH
21/7/56	P	76016 BR4	WEYMOUTH – ANDOVER JUNCTION	5.40 pm	3 CH
25/10/56	P	30707 T9	EASTLEIGH – ANDOVER JUNCTION	6.30 pm	3 CH
16/3/57	SG	6365 63XX	SOUTHAMPTON DOCKS – MSWJR		38 WAGS, BV
18/4/57	P	30284 T9	ANDOVER JUNCTION – EASTLEIGH	6.35 pm	3 CH
6/5/58	P	30125 M7	EASTLEIGH – ANDOVER JUNCTION	3.40 pm	2 CH, P.P. SET
10/5/58	P	30481 M7	EASTLEIGH – ANDOVER JUNCTION	3.40 pm	2 CH, P.P. SET
10/6/58	P	30379 M7	EASTLEIGH – ANDOVER JUNCTION	1.40 pm	2 CH, P.P. SET
12/6/58	P	30301 T9	ANDOVER JUNCTION – SOUTHAMPTON TERMINUS	8.40 pm	2 COR SET 384
5/9/58	P	30125 M7	EASTLEIGH – ANDOVER JUNCTION	7.40 pm	
5/9/58	P	30378 M7	EASTLEIGH - ANDOVER JUNCTION	5.40 pm	

APPENDIX C

There are no more records of Andover line trains at Eastleigh after September 1958. J.G. Woodward did not normally record DeMUs. The Andover line trains recorded below were seen at places other than Eastleigh by J.G. Woodward and Bryan Barber.

Date	Type	Loco	Seen at	Train
13/12/44	G	150 K10	Romsey	Goods to Andover Junction
12/3/45	G	155 L11	Romsey	Goods to Andover Junction
5/6/45	G	150 K10	Romsey	Goods to Andover Junction
13/6/45	SP	549 Q	Millbrook	New Docks – MSWJR, Ambulance train 69
15/4/48	-	336 T9	Andover Shed	OFF train from Southampton
15/4/48	P	302 T9	Andover Junction	Train to Eastleigh
2/7/49	P	30432 L12	Fratton	7.45 pm Portsmouth and Southsea – Andover Junction
6/1/53	P	30300 T9	Andover Junction	Passenger, ex-Eastleigh
6/1/53	P	30130 M7	Andover Junction	Swindon line train (SR loco as line beyond Swindon closed for engineering works)
5/8/57	P	31802 U	St Denys	7.45 pm Portsmouth and Southsea – Andover Junction
30/3/59	P	82014 BR3	St Denys	6.40 pm Andover Junction – Southampton Terminus

Andover line traffic noted at Netley by Tony Sedgwick 1950 – 1957

All trains are the 7:45 Portsmouth and Southsea – Andover Junction, except those marked as follows:
* 11.08 am Portsmouth and Southsea – Andover Junction
† Excursion from Cheltenham to Portsmouth Harbour

Date	Loco	Date	Loco	Date	Loco	Date	Loco
24/6/50	30120	30/6/51	30289	22/7/52	30300	11/7/53	30729
7/7/50	165	7/7/51	30725	9/8/52	30283	18/7/53	41304 *
26/8/50	30313	11/8/51	30426	16/8/52	31777	18/7/53	31786
7/10/50	30300	23/8/51	30288	27/9/52	30282	7/8/53	31786
14/10/50	433	8/9/51	30530	17/1/53	31787	26/9/53	31789
21/10/50	S282	23/2/52	30283	14/3/53	30288	3/4/54	30117
21/4/51	30426	8/3/52	31778	4/4/53	30729	12/6/54	31621
24/4/51	S282	15/4/52	31773	18/4/53	30287	26/6/54	31788
5/5/51	30422	17/5/52	31775	2/5/53	31787	3/7/54	30288
15/5/51	30117	24/5/52	31775	5/5/53	31787	10/7/54	30284
19/5/51	30283	21/6/52	31776	16/5/53	31789	10/6/56	GWR 6320 †
16/6/51	30423	1/7/52	31774	13/6/53	30285		GWR 6384 †
23/6/51	30426	19/7/52	31775	20/6/53	30728	5/8/57	31802

APPENDIX C

Andover Shed Duty Numbers, 15 September 1952 to May 1953, Weekdays

The following is extracted from *Engine Workings, London West and Southern Districts, Weekdays 15th September 1952 and Until Further Notice*.

DUTY 266, T9 CLASS
OFF SHED 5AM
9.37AM GOODS, ANDOVER JUNCTION – FULLERTON – LONGPARISH, ARR 11.05AM
11.45AM GOODS, LONGPARISH – FULLERTON, ARR NOON
12.14PM GOODS, FULLERTON – ROMSEY, ARR 2.16PM, SHUNTING AS REQUIRED
SX
2.35PM GOODS, ROMSEY – NURSLING, ARR 2.55 PM
3.14PM GOODS, NURSLING – ROMSEY, ARR 3.24PM, SHUNTING AS REQUIRED
6.05PM GOODS, ROMSEY – EASTLEIGH ARR 6.39, LOCO TO SHED
SO
3.30PM L/E, ROMSEY – EASTLEIGH SHED, ARR 3.48PM
4.40PM L/E, EASTLEIGH SHED – SOUTHAMPTON TERMINUS
5.25PM PASS, SOUTHAMPTON TERMINUS – PORTSMOUTH, ARR 6.37PM
7.45PM PASS, PORTSMOUTH – SOUTHAMPTON CENTRAL – ANDOVER JUNCTION, ARR 10.04PM

DUTY 267, LM 2 CLASS
TIDWORTH PASS AND GOODS AM
SX
4.12PM PASS, ANDOVER JUNCTION – ROMSEY, ARR 4.50PM
5.03PM PASS ROMSEY – SOUTHAMPTON TERMINUS, ARR 5.35PM, SHUNTING AS REQUIRED
6.58PM PASS, SOUTHAMPTON TERMINUS – ALTON, ARR 8.18PM
8.38PM PASS, ALTON – EASTLEIGH ARR 9.34PM, TO EASTLEIGH SHED
SO
6.40PM PASS ANDOVER JUNCTION – EASTLEIGH ARR 7.50PM, TO EASTLEIGH SHED

DUTY 268, T9 CLASS
OFF SHED 6.20AM
6.45AM PASS, ANDOVER JUNCTION – SOUTHAMPTON CENTRAL – SOUTHAMPTON TERMINUS, ARR 7.58AM
8.33AM PASS, SOUTHAMPTON TERMINUS – EASTLEIGH – ANDOVER JUNCTION, ARR 9.52AM
TO ANDOVER JUNCTION SHED, OFF SHED 11AM
SX
11.25AM PASS, ANDOVER JUNCTION – EASTLEIGH, ARR 12.18PM
1.05 PASS, EASTLEIGH – PORTSMOUTH, ARR 1.49PM
TO FRATTON SHED AND RETURN
3.45PM PASS, PORTSMOUTH – EASTLEIGH – ROMSEY, ARR 4.49PM
5.50PM PASS, ROMSEY – EASTLEIGH, ARR 6.06PM
TO EASTLEIGH SHED AND RETURN
7.22PM PASS, EASTLEIGH – PORTSMOUTH, ARR 8.10PM
9.49PM PASS, PORTSMOUTH – EASTLEIGH, ARR 10.33PM
TO EASTLEIGH SHED
SO
11.25AM PASS, ANDOVER JUNCTION – EASTLEIGH, ARR 12.18PM
1.05PM PASS, EASTLEIGH – PORTSMOUTH, ARR 1.49PM
TO FRATTON SHED
3.05PM L/E, FRATTON SHED – COSHAM, ARR 3.14PM
SHUNT AS REQUIRED 3.15PM – 4.40PM
4.40PM L/E, COSHAM – FRATTON SHED
6.15PM L/E, FRATTON SHED – PORTSMOUTH AND SOUTHSEA, ARR 6.25PM
6.45PM PASS, PORTSMOUTH – SOUTHAMPTON CENTRAL, ARR 7.52PM
8.03PM L/E, SOUTHAMPTON CENTRAL – EASTLEIGH SHED

DUTY 269, 43XX CLASS
7.30AM PASS, ANDOVER JUNCTION – ROMSEY, ARR 8.07AM
8.32AM PASS, ROMSEY – EASTLEIGH, ARR 8.47AM
9.02AM PASS, EASTLEIGH – SOUTHAMPTON TERMINUS, ARR 9.22 AM
10.10AM PASS, SOUTHAMPTON TERMINUS – CHELTENHAM, ARR 1.30PM
3.20PM GOODS, CHELTENHAM – ANDOVER JUNCTION, ARR 7.42PM
TO ANDOVER JUNCTION SHED

DUTY 270, 43XX CLASS
7.45AM PASS, ANDOVER JUNCTION – CHELTENHAM, ARR 10.35AM
2.03PM PASS, CHELTENHAM – SOUTHAMPTON TERMINUS, ARR 5.50PM
6.30PM L/E, SOUTHAMPTON TERMINUS – SOUTHAMPTON OLD DOCKS, ARR 6.33PM
7.04PM GOODS, SOUTHAMPTON OLD DOCKS – ANDOVER JUNCTION, ARR 8.41PM
TO SHED

APPENDIX C

Andover line workings from other S.R. sheds

EASTLEIGH DUTY 295, L1 CLASS (SX), Q CLASS (SO)
SX
6.40AM GOODS, EASTLEIGH – ANDOVER JUNCTION, ARR 10.45AM
TO ANDOVER JUNCTION SHED
3.16PM L/E, ANDOVER JUNCTION SHED – ANDOVER TOWN, SHUNTING UNTIL 4.55PM
5.00PM GOODS, ANDOVER TOWN – ANDOVER JUNCTION, ARR 5.05PM
6.40PM PASS, ANDOVER JUNCTION – EASTLEIGH, ARR 7.50
SO
6.40AM GOODS, EASTLEIGH – ANDOVER JUNCTION, ARR 10.45AM
TO ANDOVER JUNCTION SHED
5.30PM SHUNTING AT ANDOVER JUNCTION UNTIL 8.00PM
8.50PM GOODS, ANDOVER JUNCTION – EASTLEIGH, ARR 10.25PM
TO EASTLEIGH SHED

EASTLEIGH DUTY 298, M7 CLASS
6.57AM PASS, SOUTHAMPTON TERMINUS – ANDOVER JUNCTION, ARR 8.54AM
9.30AM PASS, ANDOVER JUNCTION – EASTLEIGH, ARR 10.24AM

EASTLEIGH DUTY 306, LM 2 CLASS
SX
11.19AM PASS, PORTSMOUTH – SOUTHAMPTON CENTRAL – ANDOVER JUNCTION, ARR 1.27PM
SHUNTING UNTIL 2.00PM, TO SHED, THEN SHUNTING 3.30PM – 8.00PM
TO SHED, STABLE FOR ANDOVER JUNCTION DUTY 267
SO
11.19AM PASS, PORTSMOUTH – SOUTHAMPTON CENTRAL – ANDOVER JUNCTION, ARR 1.27PM
TO ANDOVER JUNCTION SHED AND STABLE FOR ANDOVER JUNCTION DUTY 267 MONDAY

BOURNEMOUTH DUTY 403, T9 CLASS
SX
7.45PM PASS, PORTSMOUTH – SOUTHAMPTON CENTRAL – ANDOVER JUNCTION, ARR 10.04PM
STABLE FOR DUTY 268

EASTLEIGH DUTY 290, T9 CLASS
6.30PM PASS, EASTLEIGH – ANDOVER JUNCTION
STABLE FOR DUTY 266

EASTLEIGH DUTY 292, T9 CLASS
3.56PM PASS, BOURNEMOUTH CENTRAL – ANDOVER JUNCTION, ARR 6.45PM
7.35PM PASS, ANDOVER JUNCTION – EASTLEIGH, ARR 8.36PM

SWINDON DUTY 74, 45XX CLASS
12 NOON GOODS, ANDOVER JUNCTION – ROMSEY, ARR 1.23PM
2.12PM GOODS, ROMSEY – ANDOVER JUNCTION 3.05PM

CHELTENHAM DUTY 21, 43XX CLASS
8.04AM GOODS, ANDOVER JUNCTION – SOUTHAMPTON DOCKS, ARR 10.10AM
11.00AM L/E, SOUTHAMPTON DOCKS – BEVOIS PARK, ARR 11.08AM
11.30AM GOODS, BEVOIS PARK – ANDOVER JUNCTION, ARR 1.12PM

CHELTENHAM DUTY 22, 78XX CLASS
10.10AM PASS, CHELTENHAM SPA – SOUTHAMPTON TERMINUS, ARR 2.06PM
4.36PM PASS, SOUTHAMPTON TERMINUS – CHELTENHAM SPA, ARR 8.06PM

BIBLIOGRAPHY

N. Barnes-Evans and L.A. Mack, *The Hants and Sussex DeMUs,* article in *Railway South East, the Album,* Capital Transport Publishing, 1994.
P. Berrow, B. Burbridge and P. Genge, *The Story of Romsey,* Lower Test Valley Archaeological Society, 1988.
D.L. Bradley, *LSWR Locomotives – the Drummond Classes*, Wild Swan.
D.L. Bradley, *L.S.W.R. Locomotives, Vol.1*, Wild Swan.
J.R. Fairman, *Making Tracks* (story of Redbridge track assembly depot), Kingfisher Railway Productions, 1988.
G. Freeman Allen, *The Southern Region since 1948*, Ian Allan.
E. Goodridge, *The Early History of the Railway in the Andover Area,* 1986.
P.A. Harding, *The Longparish Branch Line,* 1992.
John Spedan Lewis, 1885-1963, John Lewis Partnership, 1985.
C.G. Maggs, *The Midland & South Western Junction Railway,* David & Charles, revised 1980.
B. Moody, *Southampton's Railways,* Waterfront Publications, 1993.
G.A. Pryer, *A Pictorial Record of Southern Signals,* OPC, 1977.
G.A. Pryer, *Signal Box Diagrams of the Great Western & Southern Railways, Vols. 7 & 9.*
G.A. Pryer, *Signal Boxes of the London & South Western Railway,* Oakwood Press, 2000.
L.T.C. Rolt, *Waterloo Ironworks: The Taskers of Anna Valley*, David & Charles.
J.H. Russell, *A Pictorial Record of Southern Locomotives,* Haynes Publishing, 1991.
T.B. Sands, *The Midland & South Western Junction Railway,* Oakwood Press, revised 1990.
H.P. White, *A Regional History of the Railways of Great Britain, Vol. 2, Southern England,* David & Charles, revised 1982.

Andover Advertiser.
Bennett's *Business Directory of Hants, Wilts & Dorset,* 1907.
John Lewis Partnership Archives, Leckford Abbas.
Railway Clearing House Gazetteer of Stations, 1956.
Railway Magazine.
Railway Observer.
Southern Evening Echo.
Steam Days.
Stockbridge Parish Council website.
Trains Illustrated.

A final look at Andover Town station as T9 class 4-4-0 No 30726 prepares to take its train down the line towards Clatford. *(Rod Hoyle)*